Grow Up!

Also by Dr. Frank Pittman

Man Enough: Fathers, Sons, and the Search for Masculinity

Private Lies: Infidelity and the Betrayal of Intimacy

Turning Points: Treating Families in Transition and Crisis

Grow Up!

how taking responsibility can make you a happy adult

DR. FRANK PITTMAN

Golden Books
NEW YORK

Golden Books®
888 Seventh Avenue
New York, NY 10106

Designed by Molly Leach

Manufactured in the United States of America

10   9   8   7   6   5   4   3   2   1

Library of Congress Cataloging-in-Publication Data

Pittman, Frank S.
    Grow up! : how taking responsibility can make you a happy adult /
Frank Pittman.
        p.   cm.
    Includes bibliographical references (p.   ).
    ISBN 0-307-44064-8 (alk. paper)
    1. Maturation (Psychology).   2. Responsibility.   3. Adulthood—
Psychological aspects.   I. Title.
BF710.P58   1998
155.2'5—dc21   97-52576
                                                       CIP

TO OUR GRANDCHILDREN

Justin Wesley Wagers
January 23, 1995

Frank Smith Pittman V
June 7, 1997

Christopher Jensen Wagers
October 9, 1997

and those yet to come

Acknowledgments

My wife, Betsy, is my partner in life, in happiness, in responsibility, in adulthood, and often in my regressions back into childhood. This book, like everything else I do, is done with her and maybe even because of her. Her reactions and observations about me and my reactions keep me grounded and sane. She's been the safety check on my reality testing throughout my struggles toward adulthood.

Our children and their mates, Tina and Ken, Frank and Gaybie, Ginger and Dale, continue to fascinate me, bolster me, connect me, and educate me, as they have done from the beginning. And now their children, Justin, Frank V, and Christopher, inspire me and project me into the future.

Most of this book arises not just from my personal experiences but from the search for the secrets of adult happiness that I share with my patients, who have granted me the enormous honor of opening up their lives to me.

In writing this book, and especially in the audacity of writing a chapter entitled "How to Be a Grown Woman," I needed help with the part of life I have not directly experienced. Of course, Betsy has opened herself totally to me for all these years, but in addition I have called most frantically and humbly upon the other women in my family.

My psychologist daughter, Tina Pittman Wagers, who has been my writing partner on projects before, has been my strong right arm in this frightening chapter. She is not totally satisfied with the end result, but it does not drive her quite to the distraction that the first few drafts did.

My sociologist/writer niece, Virginia Rutter, has been an especially insightful editor, supervisor, and critic, as has her psychologist husband, Neil Jacobson. There are few issues about life that I do not debate regularly with Virginia and Neil.

Our daughter, Ginger Pittman Pistilli; our daughter-in-law, Gaybie Pittman; my sister, Joanna Pittman Fox; my sister-in-law, Julie Brawner; and our nieces, Anne Brawner Namnoum, Jennifer

Brawner Semple, Aubrey Brawner, Ann Hoag, Catherine Rutter, and Shannon Valentine, are an impressive bunch of women. I've used them all for impromptu consultation about this chapter and about many other aspects of life. More than they know, they make me aware of the lives of women today.

People who have come to my workshops on character building, responsibility, and happiness have brought me wisdom. After a workshop I did in St. Louis, Doug Clark came up and offered to share news clippings he had collected about the effect of divorce on kids. Others refer me to movies and books that inspired them and might inspire me and you. Susan Ginsberg's collection, *Family Wisdom,* has been invaluable.

My editors stand by, trying to protect me from confounding my readers and/or making an absolute fool of myself. Rich Simon, who has edited my movie review column in the *Family Therapy Networker* for the past fourteen years, has been conjointly my buddy, social conscience, and cheerleader. Rich has taught me to write.

Hara Marano, who edits my "Dear Dr. Frank" advice column in *Psychology Today,* inspires me to do something that is rarely done: bring common sense into mental health. The chapters "How to Be a Grown-up Even Around Your Own Parents" and "The Magic of Raising Children" came to life under her sparkling eye on the pages of *Psychology Today.* Hara gives me confidence about my message and the way I deliver it. (She's been known to send me a fan letter over my choice of a single word.)

My agent, the stalwart Audrey Adler Wolf, pushed me to write this book. Laura Yorke, who had shaped *Man Enough* out of my autobiographical ramblings and my conflicts about life as a man, jumped at the idea. Laura is both an enormously respectful reader and an absolutely no-nonsense editor. With a minimum of strokes, she can do with writing what Michelangelo did with marble: see the figure behind the superfluous gravel and chisel it out.

More than anything I have done in my life, except of course raising my children, writing this book has helped me forgive my parents for not being just the parents I, in my immature narcissism, thought I deserved. That is the most difficult, most necessary step toward becoming a grown-up. I hope reading this book will have some of the effect on you that writing it had on me.

Contents

Introduction | My Life as a Grown-up   1

1 | The Pursuit of Happiness and Unhappiness   9

2 | The Twilight of Patriarchy, the Death of James Dean, and the Decline of the House of Windsor   40

3 | How to Be a Grown Man   70

4 | How to Be a Grown Woman   98

5 | How to Be a Grown-up Even Around Your Own Parents   137

6 | How to Have a Grown-up Marriage   158

7 | Love, Lies, and Divorce   197

8 | The Magic of Raising Children   231

9 | The Secrets of Happiness   253

Bibliography   280

About the Author   291

INTRODUCTION

My Life as a Grown-up

"AS I'VE LIVED MY LIFE AS A MAN, I'VE LEARNED THE SECRETS of happiness. I pass them on to my kids and I pass them on to you: forgive your parents, join the team, find some work and some play to do, get a partner to do it with, keep it equal, and raise children, wherever you find them." Those words, which ended my last book, *Man Enough,* have been haunting me since, begging for further elaboration. This book is that elaboration.

I grew up in a family that was just as dysfunctional as anybody else's, and while I could see how much love I was getting, I didn't realize until later how much wisdom I was getting as well. My parents and grandparents are dead now, and I miss them; I am surrounded by things they valued, though, and I carry them inside me. In that long ago world, we weren't given very attractive alternatives to just going ahead and doing the work and playing the roles of grown-ups. By the time I was twenty-five, I was a doctor, a husband, and a father, proudly living an adult life and gradually coming to feel I belonged there.

I've been married to Betsy for thirty-seven years, and my marriage is a source of inestimable comfort and stability and joy. We've worked together for twenty-five years and played together a lot longer. Like anyone else who is totally, permanently married, we bicker and, if we are lucky, run through the full range of human emotions toward one another on a daily basis. Ours is more than a happy marriage; it is a total marriage.

We have three children; all are wonderful adults, all are

1

married to wonderful adults, and all are starting to raise their own children. We now have three grandchildren and hope for more. We've also had a hand in raising our seven nieces and nephews who have become wonderful grown-ups, fully partnered husbands and wives, and most of them eager parents as well.

And for the last four years we have been taking care of Betsy's father, a wise and mellow retired psychiatrist who came to live with us and, alternately, with his son and daughter-in-law after he had buried his second wife.

The first few years he was with us he could go with us to dinner and the movies, and could talk about his long life and what he had learned in it. Toward the end, when he was fully alert at ninety-three but could no longer walk or talk, he settled for watching the Atlanta Braves play baseball on television. Since he did not always agree with the constantly yakking sportscasters and couldn't talk back, he cut off the sound and accompanied the game with the lively music of Rossini operas. He knew how to be happy with his life, whatever his options.

A few months ago he spent his last week with all his children, grandchildren, and great-grandchildren, and then he died quietly. Totally content with the life he had lived, as his body gave out but before his mind did, he was ready to go. On the day he died, I started writing this book.

This courtly and eminently diplomatic man was quite a different model for me than my brilliant, flamboyant mother or my determinedly outspoken warrior father, and I have yet to master the virtues he modeled for me. He taught me much more than I am ready to learn about the satisfactions of selflessness and the virtues of patience. More important, he allowed me to give something of my life to him by letting me tend him in his last years, something I did not get to do for my parents.

I hope to live and die as contentedly as my father-in-law

did. Meanwhile, my life has been and continues to be a happy one. I work at it, trying to exercise every muscle and every emotion every day.

What I See and Hear Around Me

I spend my days in a little room facing people who have come to tell me that they have not been granted the happiness they deserve. Some would like to learn to be happy grown-ups; others would prefer to magnify their misery and find someone to blame it on. Some tell me that their parents didn't adore them uncritically enough. Others tell me that their husbands or wives haven't found the formula for eliciting the love they know they would feel if they were married to the right mate. Still others tell me that their children have not yet done what it would take to turn them into good parents. And then there are those who tell me that their bosses have not helped them achieve the glory for which they were destined.

I spend many of my nights at the movies, pursuing my lifelong hobby of film criticism. The movies represent the ideal cultural artifact for tracking the changes in society. Over the last half-century we have seen on the screen drastic changes in how society views matters of family, of relationships, of character, and of adulthood. I see the same trends in films that I see in my office: people fearful of maturing and entering the adult generation and taking on the responsibilities of a real life.

The people I see in my office and on the screen are no different from those I see in the world ("It's not my fault that I did a lousy job. I only work here."), in the news ("It's not my fault I stole and lied. My lawyer gave me bad advice."), and in the tabloids ("It's not my fault that I wasn't faithful to her. My daddy made me marry her."). These people are clearly not living their real life: They have defined themselves as victims of imperfect love or imperfect luck somewhere along the road to adulthood, and so they have not yet become grown-ups—and, they are quick to assure you, it is not their fault.

Some of them are striving to learn how to be grown-ups even though they have never really known one. They know they are missing something, and they want to learn it. Not having been raised by healthy, functioning adults, all they can do is guess at what is normal.

Some of them are adult children, people who have had some pain or disappointment in their lives and are now waiting for someone else to come along to kiss it and make it better. Adult children give nothing back since they believe they weren't given enough in the first place. They owe no loyalty to others, but they expect others to take care of them and are angry when they don't.

Some of them are stuck in perpetual adolescence, seeing themselves as powerless in a world filled with powerful adults, lacking the self-confidence to strive for the rewards their bloated self-esteem craves, seeing everyone else less as fellow human beings than as barriers to the great nipple of life they want to suck. And even as they exhaust us with their interminable self-absorption, they are furious when anyone expects them to follow the same rules as everyone else.

But of course I also get to see people at their best; people who are learning to deal with imperfect mates, forebears, and offspring; people who are coping with the daunting realities of life, finding strength, developing wisdom, and teaching me the secrets of both survival and happiness as they share with me the tragedies and comedies of their crisis-filled lives.

The Collapse of Patriarchy

We are cursed or blessed to be living in interesting times. These are times of rapid, drastic, and increasingly confusing social change. At the heart of the crisis, the world has simply ceased to pose enough natural dangers to require the traditional patriarchal model of male sacrifice and female subservience. A generation of boys decided that they didn't want to sacrifice their lives in wars and careers as their fathers had done, so they refused to grow up and recoiled from the sacrifices men had been expected to make in life. When the time came for them to be men, they ran away from home instead, usually in the company of women they hadn't hurt yet and with whom they still had hopes of achieving heroism without risk or effort. Women at first responded by increasing their levels of self-sacrificial nurturance, but that didn't entice the men or the children into adulthood. It merely made the men see mothering as a source of guilt, and they ran away even faster from women who would trap them into adulthood. Soon women were running away from men and family as well, often declaring it a blow for woman's rights. Simply, in the 1960s and 1970s, a generation rebelled against the rigid gender roles and the expectation that men would die for their masculinity and women would subordinate their lives to men. Great, but what did they intend to do instead?

In the space of two generations, rather than fixing what was wrong, our society effectively destroyed family life and declared it beyond repair. We made the home a place no one wanted to be and raised a generation of men and women who are often unfit for family life. The problem now is not just that we find ourselves burdened by a generation of petulant geriatric adolescents who demand everything and give little back in return, but that each generation that runs from adulthood, from marriage, and from parenting means another generation being raised without adult parents.

The collapse of patriarchy, though far from complete, is now giving men and women enormous freedom they never had before but with no clear instruction books on how to function in this murky new world. People no longer know how to be grown-ups, and there aren't enough grown-ups around to tell them how to do it. The old rules no longer apply. All I learned about gender when I was growing up is illegal today.

Feminism, which responded to the change and encouraged it but is not the force driving it, has tried to offer women new models for a postpatriarchal world, and some of them have worked. Male models for the new world have been less evident as the few men who have noticed the change have overlooked the advantages to them and instead have banded together in pitiful efforts to bring back patriarchal privilege, albeit without the patriarchal sacrifices and self-restraint.

The Pursuit of Happiness in a Narcissistic World

The fall of patriarchy has not only resulted in tremendous gender confusion but has allowed ours to become a culture of narcissism in which all manner of cultural and economic forces implore us to consume more and pamper ourselves more and more desperately. In effect, we see ourselves as the culmination of civilization and far too important to be concerned with either the past or the future. Popular culture accepts and encourages this escape from adulthood. In fact, our world seems largely created for alienated hyperactive teenage boys, reinforcing cultural myths and amplifying rhythms that either soothe or stimulate them. But self-indulgence certainly does not make people happy.

The enormous mental health industry—therapists, writers of self-help books, whimper groups, and daytime talk shows—has turned itself upside down and no longer tries to empower people and help them mature and develop into adults. Instead, it encourages them to define themselves as victims, identify their persecutors, and refuse to change or grow up. Thus it abets the narcissistic culture. In some mental health circles, concern for others is considered "codependency," while rudeness is considered "self-expression" and selfishness is considered "self-actualization." Therapy increasingly feeds the inner child and starves the inner adult. The victim position is valued. If you think you had a happy childhood and have been loved, then you have clearly forgotten the abuse, which proves how terrible it really was. The mental health industry is not empowering people to make themselves happy.

Grow Up!

The rest of us—those less caught up in blame, victimhood, or narcissism—are trying to do the right thing, trying to live a life at a time of great confusion, trying to be a man or a woman when maleness and femaleness are no longer what we were led to expect them to be, trying to know what to pass on to our children, trying to know if it is safe to have children, trying to make marriage work when little about it resembles the marriages of our parents. And we end up confused, seeking guidance and instruction that looks to the future rather than longs for a return to the past.

Grow Up! How Taking Responsibility Can Make You a Happy Adult is distilled from my sixty-two years of life, my thirty-seven years as a psychiatrist and family therapist, my sixty-two years as a moviegoer and fourteen years as a movie critic, and my six years as an advice columnist, first for *New Woman* magazine and then for *Psychology Today*. I want to pass on what I have learned about our changing society and what it is doing to people—and let them know they can become happy and responsible grown-ups even in a screwed-up world.

This book is not just for those who would like to become

better adults but didn't have good enough models of adulthood to have learned it automatically. It is for those who don't quite understand the concept of adulthood and are a bit wary about its benefit to them. It is also for those who are trying to treat people, supervise people, and even "raise" people who have reached the age of majority without taking on the attitudes, activities, and trappings of adulthood. And finally it is for those who are married to people who are finding adulthood strange, foreign, unknown, and even potentially damaging to their health.

Our times are enamored with youth; we seek to escape the confusion of social change by lustily celebrating the freedom of adolescence while dreading the still, calm contentment of maturity and age. People mired in adolescence have no way of knowing that the best is yet to come; it is just past the point where you take responsibility for yourself and your relationships, and leave your self-pity behind. Adulthood has been vastly underrated. I have lived as an adult, and I have watched others doing so with even more patience and finesse.

I have found the secret of happiness in adulthood. It is responsibility—responsibility for yourself, your life, your choices, your world, and especially your loved ones.

1

The Pursuit of Happiness and Unhappiness

> *Why is happiness such a precious thing? What have we done with our lives so that everywhere we turn, no matter how hard we try not to, we cause other people sorrow?*
>
> —William Styron, *Lie Down in Darkness*

AS A PSYCHIATRIST AND FAMILY THERAPIST FOR THE LAST thirty-seven years, I've spent most of my waking hours around people who are not as happy as they would like to be. They don't think they are asking for too much. Wanting to be happy, they make themselves and anyone else who cares about them miserable because they aren't happy enough.

Some of these people are desperately depressed and just don't have the juices in their brain to permit happiness, but a far larger number go through life vaguely unhappy because they don't understand happiness well enough to figure out how to get it. Maybe it is a bad question to ask. As John Stuart Mill said in his autobiography, "Ask yourself whether you are happy, and you cease to be so." It is depressing to think about your relative lack of happiness if you are waiting passively for it to come to you.

Some of the miserable multitudes refuse to be happy until everything in their life is just right; they might even require that everything in their past be just right as well and that an ideal future be assured.

Some people are unhappy because they want to be happy all the time, with no pit stops in between, somewhat like a seesaw that only goes up.

Some of them are unhappy because they want to be happy without any effort on their part, as if it should fall out of the sky and hit them on the head and knock them happy.

An even larger number are unhappy because they want others to make them happy, even to bring them happiness—without expecting to give anything in return, even appreciation. (And of course there are a few who can't imagine being happy unless someone else is miserable.)

Some even think they may be able to coerce happiness from the universe by seduction or intimidation or just by whining or moaning or griping.

Unhappiness is not foreign to even the happiest of us (I've certainly had my moments), but most of us soon get our fill of it and do something that will get us out of it. For others, unhappiness becomes a way of life or even an alternative to living. For them unhappiness feels like a refuge, a place of familiar sanctuary from the unpredictable ups and downs and ins and outs of real life.

It's strange how the revolutionary right of free people to use their life and liberty to *pursue* happiness got perverted into an *entitlement,* as if it were up to the government or some social agency to guarantee happiness to every citizen. Or it might be up to one's mother, one's wife or child, or even the guy one went out with who didn't call back to provide happiness.

Some of the people cursing the gods or berating their loved ones for not making them happy actually put a lot of energy into their unhappiness, as if happiness were the consolation prize granted by the universe or the family for a surfeit of suffering.

Some people were simply not taught the skills necessary for happiness. Their parents didn't know how to be happy and didn't teach it to the children. Happiness is learned behavior. It has to do with activity, interaction, exploration, and openness to sensations and experiences, but it also has to do with honor, integrity, responsibility, and concern with your power to make others feel good or feel bad. Happy parents demonstrate happiness to their children.

Happiness is not something we passively receive, but something we actively do. The greatest barrier to happiness is our failure to understand what it is and how to do it.

What Is Happiness?

Webster gives several definitions of happiness, one of which fits the sort of relationship to life I'm talking about: "a state of well-being characterized by relative permanence, by dominantly agreeable emotion ranging in value from mere content to positive felicity, and by a natural desire for its continuation." It is that anticipation of pleasant and satisfying experiences that makes people happy.

Happiness to me is the willingness, even eagerness, to go on and see what lies ahead, what comes next, rather than the sense that we are not up to the next step, that we must drastically change our life or even end it rather than go on.

Happy people learn that happiness, like sweat, is a byproduct of activity. You can only achieve happiness if you are too busy living your life to notice whether you are happy or not. Benjamin Disraeli said it well: "Action may not always bring happiness, but there is no happiness without action." Actually, happiness may simply be what happens when you get a lot of exercise or do a lot of work, congratulate yourself on your efforts, and go home to somebody you like to love.

Happiness for adults is different from happiness for children. Children can be happy in moments of abandon, when they are free from the restraints of adult concerns and from the grown-ups who keep them from doing what they like to do when they like to do it. Grown-ups, on the other hand, can never ignore the connections between the past, the present, and the future; in fact, grown-ups get much of their joy from making those connections.

Children, like adults, are happy when they feel they belong, but after a certain age, kids want to belong to their generation, while grown-ups want to belong to their family in all its generations. Children, so overwhelmed by the power of the adult world, seem to think the ideal world would be filled with people of their own age.

Children are happy when they can abandon purposeful activity and just kill time. Happy grown-ups don't have time to waste. Children require more intense stimulation than grown-ups do, but both feel happy when they are in motion—although grown-ups prefer purposeful motion, while children want their motion to be free and spontaneous.

It is a pity that grown-ups sometimes forget what children know about happiness. But what the grown-ups learn about happiness is far more important.

Both children and grown-ups feel happiness at moments of wonder, but grown-ups feel even greater happiness from sharing those moments of wonder. When our first grandson, Justin, was two, we took him to the aquarium in New Orleans. As Justin walked into the glass tunnel and was surrounded by fish and turtles, he squealed, jumped up and down, and practically levitated with pleasure, as did we at the sight of his joy. Surely the greatest happiness comes from feeling and internally amplifying the happiness of those you love. That is a grown-up thing. (As I write this, I am baby-sitting my seven-month-old grandson, Frank V, who is jumping up and down with joy at the festive sounds of Wagner's "March of the Meistersingers" and now, every time I hear that music, I can associate it with my grandson's bouncy joy.)

Happiness is not so fleeting and shallow as pleasure, though I certainly think pleasure is a good thing and recommend that people partake of it often if it is not too much trouble. The simplest pleasures are the best, though. Any pleasure that causes you to go to a lot of bother is bound to be a disappointment. As Thoreau put it in his *Journal*, "That man is the richest whose pleasures are the cheapest." But even if the pleasures are nice and simple, happiness cannot be achieved by intensification of pleasure and certainly not by the sacrifice of other things in life for pleasure. Happiness is deeper than pleasure.

To me happiness is not good fortune. A reliance on good luck or fortune seems to dominate the hopes of many people who want desperately to be happy but who fear the pain, struggle, surprises, and losses of real life. Many stargazers long to be elevated to the realms of special people who are so beautiful, so rich and powerful, so loved and celebrated that they are on the cover of *People* or *Time* or *Fortune* and are excused from living the way the rest of us live. Those who need to be protected from life's sorrows are, of course, the least likely to achieve the real happiness that comes from embracing life and striving toward connectedness and usefulness.

Happiness is not a prize you get for winning enough contests. It is nice to win, but losing is a necessary part of a happy life, too. Rudyard Kipling told us, "If you can meet with Triumph and Disaster and treat those two impostors just the same," then you may become a happy human being. Hildegard Knef, the post–World War II German actress, said it even better, in *The Gift Horse:* "In my life I have experienced great success and great failure. Both are highly over-rated, but failure gives you more to talk about."

Failure is something all humans have experienced, and it can pull us together. It is a necessary experience. Those who haven't tasted enough failure are not only ill-prepared for life but hard to like. All humans, at least all those you'd want to have anything to do with, share familiarity with the humiliation of defeat and the pain of loss.

It is the shared experience of life's "necessary losses," to use Judith Viorst's intriguing term, that gets us over the shame of being only human and makes it unnecessary for us to achieve greatness, glory, glamour, eternal youth, and buns of steel all in the same lifetime.

John W. Gardner said in *Self-Renewal: The Individual and the Innovative Society* that "storybook happiness involves every form of pleasant thumb-twiddling: true happiness involves the full use of one's powers and talents." Happiness is not the province of those who have just won the lottery but of those who know they are doing the right thing, however it is turning out, and who can face with courage what lies ahead. Happy people aren't happy all the time, but it doesn't make them unhappy to feel all the other feelings that normal people feel.

Happiness and Honor

Aristotle tried to make sense out of happiness in his *Nicomachean Ethics*. He acknowledged that "most men, and men of the most vulgar type, seem (not without some ground) to identify the good, or happiness, with pleasure, which is the reason why they love the life of enjoyment." On the other hand, "People of superior refinement and of active disposition identify happiness with honor." Aristotle goes on to define honor: "With regard to honor and dishonor the mean is proper pride, the excess is known as a sort of empty vanity, and the deficiency undue humility."

In other words, it is vulgar and shortsighted to think of happiness as an abundance of pleasure or, for that matter, an abundance of stuff or the wherewithal to get an abundance of stuff. Instead, happiness is a full measure of honor—not enough honor to create a separation from our erring fellow creatures but enough to keep us from feeling humiliated in their company. We are a communal animal, and we need enough honor to make us honorable among our fellows.

Adult happiness seems more dependent on a sense of one's honor and integrity than it is on a high level of pleasurable experiences. People who feel good about themselves and what they have done and will continue to do can continue to feel good even after the music wanes and the dancing stops. They can like life even when they are not excited by anything special.

Simply, happiness is an outgrowth of character, not of victory or of luck or of perfection or even of pleasure.

Unhappy people tend to suffer from shame all the time, just as truly depressed people seem positively paralyzed by it. Shame is the antithesis of honor, a sense of unworthiness and deficiency to your very core, a belief that you are not good enough, that you would not be loved or taken care of if people knew the real you.

Shame is quite different from guilt, which is the awareness that you have done something wrong which hurts other people. Shame is the sense that something is wrong with what you are, with your *essence*, rather than there being something wrong with what you have done, with your *behavior*. Behavior is easy enough to change; one's essence is not.

Guilt is the inescapable bedrock of civilization. Guilt is good for people if, as Robert Beavers said in *Successful Marriage*, "it lasts no longer than five minutes and leads to a change in behavior." People who can't let themselves feel guilty, people who shoot you a bird if you honk or flash your lights to let them know they are driving the wrong way on a one-way street, and people who lash out when you call errors to their attention are people who can't change and can't learn from their experiences. They will most likely continue to do the wrong thing, make more and more mistakes, and get madder each time. People who are very much at the mercy of their shame may have trouble feeling true guilt, are not aware of their importance to others, and don't realize the effect their actions have on them.

Freud talked of turning abject misery into normal human unhappiness. One way of doing that would be to empower shame-based people sufficiently to feel guilt and take responsibility for their actions, helping them see that they have the power to do good things as well as bad, which leads directly into taking control of their lives.

Happiness, Shame, and Psychotherapy

The formula for happiness or unhappiness in Freudian psychology—perhaps the most important concept in this book—lies in the discrepancy between the self concept and the ego ideal, the distance between what we think we are and what we think we should be. If we are unhappy, the problem may be in our self-esteem, our sense of what we are worth as human beings. Or our problem may be in our ideals, our incorporation of our parents' or society's expectations of us. Either way, the result is the same: People who think too little of themselves are just as unhappy as people who expect too much of themselves.

Or the problem may be that we really are inferior or not very nice. We may have many things to feel guilty about, many habits we should change. Our depression may be an appropriate effort to slow down our lives and take stock of who we are and where we are going.

Some of what makes us happy or unhappy, like what makes us depressed or manic, is hardwired into us and is the equipment with which we operate, but there are other factors, too. For the most part we have the power to make ourselves happy and to make ourselves miserable.

Therapists were supposed to help people change. Increasingly, though, therapists and patients have been so overwhelmed by the magnitude of the changes around them that they settle just for identifying a persecutor, declaring patients to be victims, and trying to protect them from having to change even as the world changes around them.

There is an enormous growth industry in self-help, pop psychology, and feel-good psychotherapy which makes little or no effort to change people and instead tries merely to help them escape shame and guilt by convincing them that their lives are not their fault and that they are not responsible for their own happiness, their own relationships, and their own share of nurturing the universe.

Though Cassius may assure his coconspirator that "the fault, dear Brutus, is not in our stars, but in ourselves, that we are underlings," a pop astrologist could surely assert that Brutus's stars were to blame. Pop psychiatrists specialize in assuring people that their problems come from their brain chemicals, which are faulty because their genes are no good. They assure people that what they do is not their fault but was caused by their imperfect parents. (Mothers were the culprits for decades, always loving children too much or too little or in the wrong way, but we're having a run on father culprits lately, all of whom either touched the children in the wrong place, with the wrong attitude, or not at all.) And pop social workers can surely find some way in which anything anyone does is the fault of the rest of society or even the rest of the world.

In their well-meaning efforts to reduce toxic levels of shame, therapists have conspired to erase normal levels of appropriate guilt and have created monsters of guiltless narcissism with unbounded self-esteem and no conscience or even any sense that a conscience would be helpful. In Elaine May's 1972 movie *The Heartbreak Kid*, Charles Grodin is a newlywed whose bride is back in the hotel room while he is asking a new woman's parents for their daughter's hand in marriage. He explains his "messy" situation: "I married my wife because it was the decent thing to do. I've found that decency doesn't always pay off." Consciences aren't always comfortable, and doing the right thing isn't always fun, but without guilt family relationships and even civilization would be impossible. The rules of appropriate ways to act and to treat other people aren't very different from culture to culture, century to century, or even millennium to millennium.

Happiness and Religion

Surveys generally show that religious people are happier or perhaps that happy people are more religious. I certainly notice the same thing. Religious people have a sense of belonging and a sense of purpose, important components to happiness, and they have a set of rules that enables them to figure out how to do the right thing. Perhaps even more important, they are encouraged to see themselves as redeemable through some effort of their own. Perhaps religion is therapeutic because it offers acceptance of human essence and thus erases shame, while it offers a code of behavior that encourages guilt when people don't do the right thing.

As theologian-psychologist William James pointed out in *The Varieties of Religious Experience*, "When all is said and done, we are in the end absolutely dependent on the universe." We all know that, and happiness is only possible for those who have found a way of coming to grips with that dependency; this may take the form of creating, in their minds and in their lives, a special personal connection with the divine.

Acceptance of nature and humankind's infinite and eternal connection to nature—made, as we are, of the dust, ashes, grass, and dinosaur piss of the ages, to which we will inevitably return—can take the place of religion. If we know we will pass and leave behind only our seed, memories of us, and the impact of our works, that, too, will affect our sense of purpose and the choices we make in life.

I grew up Episcopalian. In my teens, as the church organist in a small town, I got to substitute for vacationing organists at other churches. Since then I have worked with people from every known religion, including witches and snake handlers, and have concluded that all religions seem to work about as well as long as you don't believe that your religion is right and the others are wrong and that you are supposed to do something about it.

Maybe religion works best for people who aren't too sure about it and therefore approach it with humility and respect for those who doubt it. Religion is powerful and can do more harm than good in the hands of righteous zealots who think they are speaking for God. Undoubtedly, the greatest function of religion is to remind ourselves that we are not God.

I often think that the function of religion is to give people grounding in the universe, a sense of both belonging and purpose, and a belief that our basic human nature is indeed what it is supposed to be and that we must then make the best of our lives despite our flawed nature.

The Chemistry of Happiness

*Some people are survivors and others are
annihilated by life's tragedies. That is just one
of the cruelties of living.*

—Woody Allen, *September*

19

Adverse life experiences affect different people differently, which may be a result of differences in brain chemistry or differences in basic psychological security. Certain people—such as those who have been physically abused, those who did not get much love early on, those whose parents have separated or divorced, and those whose academic aptitude made them frustrating to the school system—may have grown up without the basic trust necessary to live in comfort with the world. They may have to work harder to learn happiness and to overcome bad fortune.

Interestingly, abuse that must be kept secret is far more damaging than war, pestilence, famine, or plague; parental divorce is more traumatic than the death of a parent; and attention deficit disorders, which don't show on the outside, mess up a kid's security even more than an obvious crippling disability. The things that cause us confusion and shame are the ones that do us in.

In contrast, some children, notably those who get a lot of loving, interactive attention in early childhood, breeze right through later disasters. The disasters affect their behavior and their worldview but not their mood.

The tendency toward happiness or unhappiness may be in part a genetic trait. We may well be born either little optimists or little pessimists, tending to see the glass half full or half empty. Certainly, the tendency toward either mania or depression is, at least in part, genetic. Depression is a chemical state, not a defect in character, not a deficiency of love or money, and not even really a failure to understand and achieve happiness. Depression is caused by a relative shortage of certain neurochemicals in the brain cells, among them norepinephrine and serotonin, and it amounts to an actual chemical inability to look into the future and foresee a favorable outcome. Depression can be triggered by a profound loss that undercuts one's security and connection to life. It can be instituted by chronic pain or by chronic use of sedatives, tranquilizers, narcotics, or alcohol. But it can also come out of nowhere to attack someone with a charmed life and defective brain chemistry.

Recent serotonin studies, described by Peter Kramer in *Listening to Prozac,* explain much about unhappiness and its opposites: Charisma, leadership, confidence, security, and courage are all associated with high levels of serotonin, which enables the brain to think out problems and see solutions clearly and optimistically. People without much serotonin look at life's problems and react with either anger or anxiety because the problems seem insoluble, unfair, or dangerous.

Consequently, antidepressants that increase serotonin (Prozac and its cousins, all selective serotonin reuptake inhibitors, or SSRIs) can be lifesaving for the depressed person. But antidepressants are not enough. Antidepressants make depression treatable and happiness possible, but they won't work unless the sufferer avoids alcohol, gets regular exercise, does enjoyable things, and has the attitude needed to be happy.

While some especially fortunate people are so optimistic they can actually be happy at rest, most of us need activity. Unhappy people can become happy people if they get a daily dose of exercise, sex, joy, and triumph. It works better if the exercise is free of angry competitiveness or the fear of losing; the sex is free of guilt and selfishness; the joy is free of anxiety or destructiveness; and the triumph is honorable and free of cruelty. Anger, anxiety, jealousy, envy, and guilt produce a quite different set of neurochemicals; still, they must be pleasurable emotions for some people, because many go to a great deal of trouble to experience them. But they do not seem to lead to happiness, whereas clean and celebratory exercise, sex, joy, and triumph seem to be a regular part of the lives of the happy.

Whatever its roots, most human unhappiness can be resolved by activity and human contact, by resolving shame and helplessness, by making a stronger connection to the human condition and the life cycle, and by stopping habits that depress the brain chemistry, such as sloth, wrath, envy, avarice, gluttony, or the regular use of alcohol or tranquilizers. (I'm not against all of the seven deadly sins. Pride, Saint Thomas Aquinas aside, is necessary for happiness, and lust is good for you—but only if you know you don't have to act on it.)

Like all therapists, I'm a mechanic rather than a wise man or a magician. We therapists see people whose brains are misfiring and people with dead batteries and empty tanks; sometimes something is broken and someone has to fix it. But most of the people we see are going through life with serviceable equipment, the best of intentions, and a faulty instruction book on life. They are trying to get around on an outdated map. Most of them are not truly depressed; they are what we call *dysthymic*, which means simply "bad mood," or as the ill-tempered Shirley MacLaine insisted in *Steel Magnolias,* "I am not crazy. I've just been in a bad mood for forty years."

Dysthymic people may not know how to be happy. Perhaps they have been misinformed by parents and teachers who had the very best of intentions but whose models were already out of date then and are certainly out of date now. So these misinformed people get increasingly frantic as they try to apply the solutions they learned in the past to the problems they face in the present. Doing the wrong thing harder or louder or more often will work no better.

The Troubles I've Seen

People come to my office who are in pain. Sometimes they are poor, weak, plain, and unloved, and their unhappiness would seem to come directly from their failure to find success and popularity or even friendship, much less love. Some of them have been actively trained since birth for unhappiness.

But people also come to my office who have been on the cover of *Time, People, Fortune, Vogue,* or *Sports Illustrated;* people who have been honored by the world with awards and love, with fame and fortune; people who are millionaires and billionaires, who are big and beautiful and strong and wise and universally adored. But all the successes that others envy make no contribution to their happiness, only to their isolation from those who are less favored by the world.

The rich and famous are no better at being happy than the poor and overlooked, and the energy that has driven them to achieve their successes may actually derive from the difficulty they have in finding happiness in a more ordinary life. And it may be my job to keep them from going crazy over their isolation and lack of fulfillment. I try to teach them how to be happy.

Fortunately, some people who come to my office already know something about happiness and are able to teach me. Over the past thirty-seven years I've learned a lot about human suffering and a lot about societal change. But the most important things I've learned are about happiness. And I've learned it from those who have had the courage to be happy when all was not well in their world.

Thirty-plus years ago when I was just a beginner, a young man named Andy was assigned to me. Andy had lost his leg to bone cancer and was dying from metastatic cancer of the lungs. His family came by and cried and prayed over him and pretended he would recover, though they knew he knew better. I was called in to relieve Andy's pain through hypnosis. That worked fine, but he was left lying in bed out of breath, bored, angry, and resentful because his life was being cut short. He demanded to know why God was punishing him in this way. The Book of Job, offered by his family, was no help to him because it told about God going out of his way to torment innocent people.

He would have no opportunity to achieve heroism in life, he would not produce a family with children to succeed him, and he would not get his chance to conquer the world. Achieving greatness could not be his goal, and he was unhappy. My idea that he might be able to achieve some modicum of happiness under these horrifying circumstances seemed like a cruel joke. But I had recently seen *The Diary of Anne Frank,* and I believed in the power of the human spirit to triumph over anything.

As we talked about how he could use the last few weeks of his life to give him some feeling of having lived, we came up with the idea of reading a great novel about life. Andy had been an athlete with little patience for school, and he had never read a book. He chose Leo Tolstoy's *War and Peace,* the longest novel we could find, and dedicated himself to reading it, determined that he would live until he had finished it. He was a slow reader, and he lived weeks longer than anyone thought possible. He refused all pain medication that might cloud his brain, and each day we discussed what he had read and learned about life.

Andy's favorite scene was the one in which the young Russian count Nicholas is unhorsed and knocked out on the battlefield. He comes to and notices the cloud formations and then the cloud of dust on the horizon. As he realizes that the dust is being kicked up by a Napoleonic French soldier on horseback coming to kill him, Nicholas wonders, "Why would anyone want to kill me, me whom everyone has always so loved?" The wonderful absurdity of that level of sunny self-satisfaction connected Andy to all the rest of us who are doomed to die. Whether we deserve it or not, whether we embrace the world or shrink from it, whether we burst with self-esteem or shrivel with self-loathing, we're all going to die. The implications of the thought made Andy laugh long after he had lost his ability to breathe on his own.

Andy died peacefully the night he finished the book, probably still chuckling over the randomness and impersonality of the human comedy that is life. He no longer felt singled out for death by a cruel or capricious god. Instead, he felt he was sharing the human condition—a part of the human condition that was different from what he had expected to experience at this age but nonetheless part of what is universal for humankind.

I learned much about happiness from Andy. I also learned much from Brenda, a fifteen-year-old girl who was sent to me for a custody evaluation. She had been trapped since early childhood in a seemingly endless custody dispute between her divorced parents. Brenda's father was a philandering divorce attorney who delighted in showing his daughter his collection of nude photographs of himself and his various female clients, one or the other of whom was usually in residence with him. Brenda's mother was a beaten down and usually unemployed lesbian. She always collapsed upon people who seemed more powerful than she and now lived with her female divorce lawyer, who devoted her profession to sniffing out homophobia and child sexual abuse and going into battle against them. The two women had to move a lot because of their unending sense of persecution. Each of the parents thought the other unfit and disapproved of their former partner's choice of bedmates. In addition, both of the lawyers seemed willing to turn this case into their primary employment and could keep any judge's head swimming.

As a result, Brenda had been ordered repeatedly by various judges to move back and forth between the two households. She had learned to get along with each of her absurd parents and their equally absurd partners, which was easy once she stopped caring about them and centered her life on her friends.

Brenda had never spent an entire year at the same school, so there was no continuity in her friendships. She assured me that it was no longer a problem for her since she had discovered the secret of popularity. She explained that she would sit back silently and invisibly for the first day at each new school so she could identify the popular group and what they were wearing. Then she would show up dressed as they were, act as if she were one of them, and treat them as if they liked her. Since they really didn't care one way or the other, they always found it easier to assume they did and promptly, without any conflict over the matter, accepted her. Once she'd been accepted by the popular group, everyone else wanted to be her friend, and she could make friends with anyone she chose. Her approach worked so well, she felt able to handle any disruption in her life, and since she had determined that both parents were stark raving mad, it really didn't matter which of them she was with. She had developed enough confidence to carry her security with her wherever the judge sent her.

Recently, I saw the most inspiring couple of all. Cy was a young man, barely out of his teens, who had fallen into industrial machinery at work, an encounter that cost him both legs and one of his arms. The rehabilitation center wanted me to see Cy because he was not depressed.

When Cy and his wife, Cloe, came by to thank me for my willingness to see them, they assured me that they were getting along quite nicely. Cy said he had felt depressed when he first woke up and found that so much of him was gone, but within a few days he realized that even the simplest of activities was a challenge and he was daily given opportunities to use his ingenuity and develop new skills. He realized he was lucky that he had been left with one arm so he could do things for himself and one knee so he had hopes of getting around on artificial legs. When he went to shopping centers, everyone was nice to him, and he had lot of things to talk about. And he admitted that it was a relief to be out of the economic rat race. He had been granted a free pass through life. He no longer had to fear that he would fail to achieve success. All it had cost him was an arm and legs.

Cloe was shy and disliked working but disliked being home alone even more. Now Cy was with her all the time, they didn't have to go to work, and they practically owned the company that had sliced off so much of Cy. Cloe confided that sex had gotten much better, too, because Cy had been a restless, hyperactive person before the accident and "now, with fewer body parts, he can focus better."

Cy and Cloe are being offered more help than they can fit into their busy schedule. They are enjoying the challenges of a drastically changed life and don't think they need therapy. While I'd like to be part of their lives, I think they have already done for themselves the most important thing therapy could do for them: convert life's tragedies into just another part of the human comedy. Maybe the challenge for Cy and Cloe will wear thin and then they may need me, but now they know something that most of my patients don't know: Resilient people such as Cy, Cloe, Brenda, and Andy may have special genes for resiliency, but they teach all of us that real tragedies are easier to survive than imagined or anticipated tragedies; real loss is far easier to bear than imagined loss; and visible, obvious, even devastating loss is far easier to live with than the shame that people feel when they know they are not whole inside and yet must pretend to be. If only the shamed people knew that we are all in it, that we are all feeling the same inadequacy and confusion.

Cy and Cloe wheeled past Daphne in my waiting room. Daphne was an impossibly lean and bosomy monument to the wonders of plastic surgery; she had flown in from another state to unload on me her unhappiness over the unforgivable thing her latest husband had done to her. He was building a four-million-dollar beach house for her, but he had gotten his feelings hurt when she had an affair with the builder; in retaliation, he refused to let her expand the dining room by four feet (at a cost of fifty thousand dollars) to accommodate a new dining room table she had found that would seat sixty-four people. She wailed that without the larger dining room, she couldn't make a graceful entrance down the spiral staircase in a hoop skirt. Her dreams had been shattered and her life ruined because of her cheap husband's pettiness. She used up an entire box of tissues and never wasted a tear on anyone other than herself. Daphne took no notice of the laughing one-limbed man in the wheelchair and his glowing bride who spoke to her when she came in. In her shame over whatever deficiency she found in herself, she was cognizant only of the imperfections that might show on the outside of her body and the stage setting she was erecting to her glory.

It is perhaps even crueler when people, eaten alive by shame, require perfection not from themselves but from others. Elmer and his wife, Edna, had been referred by another therapist who saw only individuals. They came so I could help him explain to her that he could be happy only if he left her. Elmer had discovered in his previous therapy that he had married the wrong woman. As he explained, Edna was clearly too short for him; they looked ridiculous together, so he could never hope to be happy with her. It would be hard to leave her since they had four small children who would be hurt by his leaving, and there was also the practical consideration that Edna supported him while he stayed at home memorizing self-help books. Nevertheless, he had learned from his recent therapy that he had been devoting too much of his life to worrying about other people, and it was time for him to pursue his own happiness. To my mind, what Elmer needed was not a taller wife but an older therapist.

The frantic search for true love and the happiness it is supposed to bring can lead people to look in strange places.

Decades ago I saw Floyd, an exceedingly effeminate little round man, a professional poodle groomer who self-consciously worked at fulfilling every gay stereotype. He swished, lisped, walked like Mae West, smoked like Bette Davis, and dressed like something between Liberace and Dolly Parton. He must have practiced for years in front of a mirror. He broadcast gayness, yet he had not come out at work. I've rarely known anyone who was both so self-conscious and so lonely. He scared off everyone without letting anyone know he was in pain.

Once a week for fifty minutes Floyd complained to me about his inability to find true love. He let no one in his real life know that he was desperately seeking a partner, but several nights a week, in search of love, he would leave a tuna casserole in the oven while he went cruising the bushes of a local park famous as a haven for closet gays hoping to find furtive moments of anonymous sex. Floyd would creep through the shrubbery and invite unseen men in the bushes to come home with him for dinner. Most remained silent, some declined, and a few accepted his hospitality. But no true love developed, and Floyd pondered whether the men were turned off by his body or his cooking.

As Floyd's therapist, I told him that true love would be hard for him to find in the bushes, whatever the state of his body or his tuna casserole. Martha Stewart or Arnold Schwarzenegger would have the same trouble as he. But Floyd refused to let me normalize his problem. He wanted his life to be a dramatically unique tragedy. Ashamed of his homosexuality largely because he had never known anyone who was gay and normal at the same time, he turned it into his entire identity while keeping it a secret so no one could accept it and connect with it.

Floyd had discovered the secrets of unhappiness: a high level of shame, isolation from the human condition, self-defeating personal habits, and dramatizing the awfulness of the problem while taking actions guaranteed not to work.

I watched his suffering with deadpan sympathy until he went too far in absurdity: He found the one goal for himself he could never achieve and declared his life's happiness depended on it. During one session Floyd leaped up and pounded the wall, wailing, "The tragedy of my life is I've always wanted to be an interior decorator, and I'm colorblind." I did not feel disrespectful when I laughed and declared, "Floyd, you have just been chosen Queen for a Day!" Floyd finally saw his own absurdity and was able to laugh at himself and start the process of changing.

The Fear of Unhappiness

It is the very pursuit of happiness that thwarts happiness.

—Viktor E. Frankl, *The Unconscious God*

There are those who dread unhappiness, who fear that if they venture into the quicksand of unhappiness, they will be stuck there and pulled under. Norman Bradburn, in his book *In Pursuit of Happiness,* said that "it is the lack of joy in Mudville, rather than the presence of sorrow, that makes the difference" between the happy and the unhappy. Some who pursue happiness too desperately believe they can achieve it by avoiding sorrow, and by so doing they avoid life. I even have friends who avoid movies that would make them sad—they call them "downers"—for fear that that much connection with reality would make them unhappy.

People who avoid total immersion in life because they fear unhappiness are rather like athletes who fear losing. Those who fear loss are far more vulnerable and less likely to achieve their goals than athletes who hunger for victory.

Those who fear losing are always looking out of the corner of their eye for some justification for their loss so they can declare, "See, it is not my fault." Likewise, those who fear unhappiness more than they crave happiness can whine that they are victims of something and their victimhood keeps them from reaching happiness or even trying for it.

Some try to avoid unhappiness by running from sad emotions. I love movies that make me cry, from *Bambi* through *Schindler's List* to *The English Patient.* I am likely to revisit them over and over, and as I cry, I feel many things but not unhappiness. In fact, crying and sharing emotional pain may be as big a contributor to happiness as physical pain after a good workout, or knowing on the way down from climbing a mountain (and often for days afterward) that I have earned my aches.

When I cry, I open myself up to feelings and awarenesses that enter me. When Vivien Leigh and I return to Tara and find the house and the family gone with the wind, we know that they're not going to lick us, that we're willing to "lie, steal, cheat, or kill" so we and our folk will never be hungry again. When John Wayne, after a lifetime of searching, brings his niece Natalie Wood back home from her life of captivity with the Apaches and can't seem to enter the house with the rest of the family, he and I know that the lives we have chosen make other lives outside our limits. When Mel Gibson runs his heart out and still can't get there in time to stop his buddy from doing his duty by charging the hopeless position at Gallipoli, he and I know that it is not always enough to do our best, but it is still necessary. There can be profound loss without guilt, shame, a sense of failure, or even regret.

Clint Eastwood and I have stood many times in the Iowa rain with tears rolling down our cheeks as we watched Meryl Streep drive off in an old truck with her husband. Meryl and I have sat in that truck with our hand on the handle of the door, wanting to open it and jump out but knowing that we can't. Meryl, Clint, and I know we are doing the right thing. My sadness does not make me unhappy; it makes me more connected to a man and a woman who know that a love so much bigger than life must be cut off before it decays, turns gangrenous, and destroys those who feel compelled to sacrifice their lives for it.

Leigh, Wayne, Gibson, Eastwood, Streep, or I may be in tears at these moments of loss, disappointment, and pain, but we feel good about ourselves and know we are not alone in the world and can go on. The pain of the moment makes us more, not less, connected with life and with the others who live it. Sharing that pain makes us happy in a way that suffering it in lonely silence could not.

The Culture of Blame: The Disgruntled

There are people who fail to identify themselves as unhappy but live in a state of disgruntlement over their less than utopian lives. To use a phrase coined by John Watzlawick, John Weakland, and Richard Fisch in *Change,* such people demand that their lives be "utopian—a constant state of ecstatic wonder and they will settle for nothing less." They may drink or do drugs in an effort to achieve that constant state of ecstatic wonder. They may jump from relationship to relationship or from job to job trying to catch, cage, and maybe cook and eat the elusive bluebird of happiness. They don't see the problem as their mood, their attitude, their habits, their manners, or their neurotransmitters; they believe the problem is that their life is not the way it should be. They are mad as hell about it. Obviously a villain must be found.

Such people may blame some historical event that changed their world. Many in Yugoslavia have decided that their unhappiness must be due to something their neighbors did to their ancestors four hundred years before. In my youth in Alabama, I grew up among poor white people who blamed their current state of disgruntlement on the Civil War almost a century before; because their ancestors lost that war, they didn't inherit slaves who would serve them, protect them from having to work, and supply them with whatever their hearts desired. I knew people who would dress up in bed-sheets and burn crosses in the yards of black people who were not volunteering for slavery. Meanwhile, many African-American people who are descendants of slaves are still blaming their lives on their great-great-grandmother's slavery. Such a stance is certainly a great deal more sympathetic and may even be somewhat more rational, but it is not one bit more helpful. That was then; this is now.

Other people whose lives are not what they had hoped they would be may blame economics, politics, or even organized athletics for their failure to find a place in the world. I've heard an underemployed woman blame her lowly economic state on the patriarchal attitudes of medical schools back in her youth, which kept her from becoming a doctor. White men who get passed over for a promotion may blame either affirmative action or working women who "should be home tending children while men get the jobs that would support their families." Repulsive men who can't pick up the women they're hitting on blame "women's lib." Fat women who can't find the husband of their dreams may blame a recent societal ideal of female beauty that favors the anorexic over the previously more desirable zaftig. A few decades ago, people who couldn't find the happiness they wanted often blamed Communists. Communists as bugaboos are outdated now, and the stylish enemy du jour bounces from corporate raiders to the Internal Revenue Service to Arab terrorists. But I've seen more than one patient who blamed his or her unhappiness on homosexuals who want to get married and increase everybody else's insurance premiums. For those who want to justify their unhappiness, logic or even sanity is no barrier.

But the disgruntled who rail at the world are not nearly so dangerous to themselves and others as those unhappy people who have decided that it is some specific person in their life who is the culprit. They may therefore sue the obstetrician who delivered them, the plastic surgeon who was supposed to make them look the way they wanted to look, the psychiatrist who was supposed to make them feel the way they wanted to feel, the illusive dreamboat who was supposed to give them the love they thought they needed, or the boss who was supposed to give them the money that would solve all their problems. They may find lawyers who will affirm their idea that their life is not their fault and a villain must be found to blame it on.

More frequently there are disgruntled people who have determined that their loved ones are the source of their dissatisfaction. They blame their parents, their spouse, or even their children for giving them a life that is not what they ordered. This is presumably based on the notion that one's family exists to provide and even guarantee happiness; if you are not happy, then your loved ones have failed you and should be dismissed or punished. Such unhappy people may even find therapists who assure them they are too delicate to tolerate imperfect relationships, so they must divorce their spouse, disown their parents, and put their children up for adoption.

Gender Roles and Unhappiness

Increasingly, therapists are culture brokers and gender brokers. They explain the changes, the culture, and what is happening to people as the world turns ever faster; they explain to people who are confused by the changing world that they are indeed misinformed but are in good company. It is happening to everyone else. It is happening to me, too.

Most of the confusion lately has had to do with gender. Most shame is gender-based—but not necessarily sex-based. Sex is biological and absolute (one is biologically either male or female or a real mess), and sex determines one's function in reproduction. But one's function in society or even in the family is determined by the artificial cultural concept of gender. Gender is very much a matter of trend and custom. (Pictorial designations on restrooms show women with long hair and skirts, and men with short hair and pants, even though young men wear their hair as long as women do now, and women wear slacks almost as often as men. I assume such restroom signs are found even in Scotland, where men wear skirts, as they did in ancient Greece and Rome.) Even if gender is purely a matter of style, it is still compelling.

While we are growing up, our parents and peers and the whole world seem to join forces to shame us into the gender mode in style at the time, asking us in effect to sever the half of our emotions and activities that have been assigned to the other gender and mold ourselves to a cultural stereotype that affects everything we do, say, wear, or even feel. It even affects how we walk, sit, cross our legs, or scratch our ass. And if we fail to conform to the gender ideal, we risk the punishment of crippling shame.

But for decades we have been undergoing a period of revolution in our definitions of gender and the degree to which our destiny is controlled by our biology. While for some this relieves shame and increases freedom, for almost everyone it brings confusion. Most of the shame that makes it hard for us to learn to be happy comes from this gender confusion because we don't know what to do with ourselves or with one another. What we were taught by our well-meaning families about our gender and what we have been shamed into accepting is outdated long before we reach the point where we can put it into practice, and yet we feel shame when we try to free ourselves from it.

It is hard to be happy, that is, to get your self-concept close to your ego ideal; if your ego ideal is strongly gendered and outdated, it is absurd, crippling, socially unacceptable, and maybe even illegal. The world is changing, and not only do we have to change with it, but we have to change our image of what we should be. We can't do that unless we are paying attention.

As the world changes we have to understand that these changes are happening to everyone, not just us. We see men working with a diminished patrimony, unable to find for themselves the heroism they assumed was their destiny, and they are ashamed. In their shame they look for places to hide and justifications for running away. We see women faced with more choices than they ever dreamed possible; but they have few models for fulfilling these new roles, and there is little precedent to guide them in fitting the new roles in with the old ones they aren't ready to discard yet.

I am convinced that the largest contributor to current unhappiness in our society is confusion about what we are supposed to do with our gender in a world changing so fast that we cannot automatically accept our parents' models of gender the way we tend to accept, without thinking, their language, accent, religion, and worldview. We have to start thinking about it long before we are old enough to feel securely grounded in it, and thus adulthood becomes more disorienting than it ever was before.

Happiness and the Life Cycle

No one is, or could be, informed about what is going to happen next, and the past is no longer a reliable predictor of the future. People are having a hard enough time just surviving. On top of that, they want to be happy. Sometimes they even demand to be happy. But they can't find happiness if they base it on separating themselves from the inescapable human life cycle.

We are born, if someone permits it. We survive if someone is willing to go to the enormous trouble of loving and nurturing us. We learn from the people around us how to be part of the human race and the human community—it does not come naturally. We go through the disorientation of adolescence when our bodies and our worlds change almost overnight, and we make decisions, assumptions, and choices about our gender and how to use it. We try to find ways to make ourselves useful so the world will let us survive further, and that takes up most of our time. We try to find a partner and then adapt to each other, which is likely to be as frustrating as it is exciting. We reproduce and find our lives centered on our children rather than ourselves. We grow old, and it is not a pretty sight. And we die. We can try to fight against these inevitabilities, but we do so at our own peril. There is no surer way of achieving unhappiness than the effort to escape the life cycle.

In the 1940 film of John Steinbeck's Depression-era classic *The Grapes of Wrath,* earth mother Ma Joad gets tougher from adversity and seems to enjoy it. The survivors of the Joad family have left the dust bowl of Oklahoma, and after a series of disasters and unending indignity, they are in their beat-up truck driving through California looking for work:

PA JOAD (Russell Simpson): You're the one that keeps us going, Ma. I ain't no good no more. Seems like I spend all my time these days thinking about how it used to be, thinking of home. I ain't never gonna see it no more.

MA JOAD (Jane Darwell): Well, Pa, a woman can change better than a man. A man lives sort of—

well—in jerks. A baby's born and that's a jerk; he gets a farm or loses it and that's a jerk. But for a woman it's all in one flow like a stream—eddies and waterfalls, but the river goes right on. A woman looks at it that way.

PA JOAD: Maybe, but we sure have taken a beating.

MA JOAD (laughing): That's what makes us tough.

Pa Joad, like so many men who have been raised to see life as a competition for things or glory or even survival, saw each of life's jerks as a defeat, an indication that he wasn't good enough, that he had failed in some way—and each disaster increased his sense of shame. But Ma Joad was connected to the human life cycle and did not expect life's ups and downs to be any different in kind for her and her family than they were for anyone else. She had no illusions of winning or losing at life, no sense that life's tragedies and inconveniences lessened her in any way. She merely saw bumps in the road as opportunities for her to get tough and overcome any tendencies to see life as a win-or-lose contest. Ma Joad, despite it all, was happy.

Happiness is a simple thing. A Buddhist friend tells me that happiness is the "freedom from desire," the satisfaction and contentment that enables us to live the life we have, anticipating and savoring its mysteries without feeling the compulsion to escape it. Such rootedness to the world, in which we experience each of life's seasons in turn and join the flow of the life cycle, is mundane, but it works. It connects each of us with everyone else.

You would never be able to convince adolescents of this, but adults are happier and grow happier every year. Adults are not as desperate for love and have largely stopped concerning themselves with acceptance. The more they have lived and known other people, the lower their levels of shame and anxiety. Their pleasures are simpler. They know they won't miss much if they skip the party. They don't require perfection, even if they know how they want things to be and what they have to do to get things that way. Grown-ups don't have to get their way all the time. They can wait their turn. They can even slow down and actually feel the pulse of life and connect with its flow rather than paddle furiously against it.

One of the most important secrets of happiness is this: If you would be happy, accept the human condition, act your age, do your job, and grow up.

But that's pretty hard to do unless you have a fairly good idea of what a grown-up is. The world has been changing entirely too fast for that to be very clear, so your best bet is to understand what in the world is going on.

2

The Twilight of Patriarchy, the Death of James Dean, and the Decline of the House of Windsor

"What's Going to Happen to the Children When There Are No More Grown-ups?"

—Song title by Noel Coward

ADULTHOOD IS SCARY.

When we try to pass ourselves off as grown-ups, other people may not know we are just adult impersonators; they may expect us to know all sorts of things, do all sorts of things, and take responsibility for all sorts of things. They may expect us to consider their compelling state of mind more urgent to us than our own. As grown-ups we may even be expected to "keep our heads when all about us are losing theirs and blaming it on us."

After all, adulthood means never getting to say "it's not my fault."

If we're having a good time just as we are; if we haven't succeeded at childhood yet and want to try, try again; if we

40

never really knew a grown-up up close or didn't know one we wanted to be like; if we are adult children of imperfect parents who haven't yet made us feel fully secure about ourselves, and we're not ready to forgive them yet and move on; if we tried it once and it didn't work for us; if we don't know how much adulthood would be enough and assume we would be capable of only the junior size; if adulthood just doesn't look stylish or glamorous enough for the life we had in mind for ourselves—for any or all of these reasons, we may be tempted to pull back from such a daunting endeavor as adulthood.

It might be tempting to fall back into perpetual adolescence—like those millionaire geriatric rock stars who tour through town in torn jeans between visits to their plastic surgeon, their tattooist, and Betty Ford.

It might be tempting to abandon concern for anyone else and devote ourselves to self-indulgence or self-improvement. Magazine sellers have discovered that they sell fewer magazines with articles promising "Ten Ways to a More Sterling Character" than those with articles offering "Ten Steps to Tighter Buns." Ours is a world in which our biggest worry is how sexy we will look as we walk away from our loved ones.

And, worst of all, it might be tempting to opt out of adulthood by declaring ourselves victims of an imperfect world or imperfect parents.

In our panicky crush to avoid stepping off the cusp of adolescence into adulthood, we may not have considered that there are reasons grown-ups, even imperfect grown-ups, are the happiest people alive (especially married, employed middle-aged men like myself). There are often overlooked advantages to being a grown-up:

1. Others are less likely to tell you what you ought to do and more likely to ask you what *they* ought to do.

2. You don't have to decide whether to obey the rules or defy the rules, because when you are a grown-up, they're your rules even if some of them were made by a previous generation.

3. You don't have to worry about making a fool of yourself since you have already survived doing so over and over again.

4. You don't have to worry about looking your best since you've already looked better than you'll ever look again.

5. You can wear comfortable old clothes instead of the latest trend.

6. You don't have to listen to bad music even if it's popular.

7. You may get children and grandchildren to share the play and adventure of every stage of life, only this time you get to go through it without the insecurity and self-consciousness.

8. You get to go to bed before your bedtime because nothing that happens after the eleven o'clock news could possibly be worth staying awake for.

9. You are no longer the only thing you're concerned with. Everything in the world affects you, and you know it, and it is all of interest to you. You are now part of the past and the future and the world and everyone in it. You no longer fear boredom if you are not being adored and stimulated every moment. If you can get outside yourself and stop being concerned only with how things are going for you, you may become so fully alive you will never be bored again.

10. And the best thing of all about adulthood is that, like recovery from alcohol or drugs, recovery from childhood is never complete. Adults are perpetually in recovery from adolescence, narcissism, or victimhood, and are in constant danger of slipping back. We would-be adults can pride ourselves on striving for adulthood even though we know we'll never quite reach it. We might not even want to do it all the time, but we would be well advised to overcome our fear of it and put it in our repertoire.

We never know when we'll need a grown-up, and if one is not around, we may have to be it.

The Nature of Maturity

Erik Erikson charted human maturation across the life span, seeing psychosocial development arising from a lifetime of struggles between competing emotions and impulses as the would-be adult either masters or is mastered by each task along the way. Erikson (to summarize his landmark work) determined that human maturation involves the development of *hope* from the conflict in infancy between basic trust and basic distrust. *Will* develops in early childhood from the contention between autonomy and shame or doubt. *Purpose* comes later on from the opposition between initiative and guilt. *Competence* develops at school age out of the competing demands of industry and inferiority. People with good genes and good luck may also grow up with parents who love them and each other, who don't beat them or molest them, who don't go crazy or get divorced, and who don't chase each other around with sticks and stones. And they may seem fairly well intact by the time they hit puberty. But then they must face the toughest struggle of all: finding out who they are and identifying themselves.

Identity is the struggle that keeps us in turmoil from the stroke of puberty until we die, still trying to figure out who we are and who we want to be. We can't create an identity alone. It takes models. Erikson says *fidelity* arises out of the adolescent struggles between identity and identity confusion. Fidelity, which he defines as "the ability to sustain loyalties freely pledged in spite of the inevitable contradictions of value systems," is the crucial strength of family life. But as we all know, our struggle to create a firm identity is never over, and every time we face an identity crisis, our fidelity and all our commitments are in jeopardy.

Those rare Adult Children of Normal Parents presumably embrace life with absolutely ideal quantities of hope, will, purpose, and competence, and a firm identity—at least until school, coaches, peers, and the people who reject their invitation to the prom get their chance to cut them back to size. The rest of us limp through life risking each day despite our basic distrust of the world, trying to function despite our personal shame, trying to set goals despite our deep sense of guilt, trying to achieve competence despite nagging feelings of inferiority, and trying to maintain a clear identity even if we've never had a map or a model to follow. Some of us, understandably, collapse back into childlike narcissism.

Ready or not, as young adults we either take the risk of intimacy and develop our capacity for love, or we live with the pain of isolation. And as adults we take on the often overwhelming commitments and responsibilities of *care* as we make our choices between generativity and stagnation. We can't wait until we get perfect. We either live, love, care, and generate, or we miss our lives.

We can only hope in old age to achieve *wisdom* as we sort through our life and choose between integrity and despair, a choice that, like so much about maturity, involves respect for life itself rather than just our tiny personal part in it. Wisdom is possible only if we get past the notion that we ourselves are the center of the universe.

Erikson seems to be expecting a lot of us, but it boils down to the same things that Freud was talking about: You grow up with startling rapidity in order to spend a lifetime loving and working, caring for others, and generating whatever the products of your life will be—your children, your work, your good deeds, your good examples. You do this in the hope of earning love and achieving comfort and security, of course, but most of all an adult lives his or her life in the hope of achieving wisdom and integrity at the end of a life well lived and a job well done.

Grown-ups are doing well enough at maturity when they can take care of themselves and give back more than they take. The usual, but not the only, expression of human maturity is the sustenance of oneself and the maintenance of a commitment to another person at least long enough to raise, nurture, and train children cooperatively. Marrying and raising children is not the only way to do this, but for most people, it is the most natural.

Certainly people may be mature grown-ups and find a different way of connecting to society and to others and of creating and nurturing something for the future. Marriages don't have to be heterosexual or even sexual at all, and they certainly don't have to follow any specific legal or religious format. Children don't have to be your own children; they don't even have to be children but can be someone or something outside yourself that needs to be tended and nurtured. Mother Teresa and George Washington are impressive examples of people who managed to be successful and productive grown-ups without raising their own children.

People of either gender trying to do a good job of being an adult today must be able to both love and work, and to find a balance between caring and generativity—or, in

Freudian terms, *lieben und arbeiten* (love and work). Grown men and women must balance both family and career, with the sometimes conflicting demands of marriage, children, creative ambitions, and financial obligations. And whatever balance they achieve is never ideal. And it doesn't even stop there. True maturity requires that the concern shown to your family extend even beyond the family into the world.

Robert Bly insists in *The Sibling Society* that adult caring must extend vertically to the past and the future. He tells us: "It is an adult perception to understand that the world belongs primarily to the dead, and we only rent it from them for a little while. They created it, they wrote its literature and its songs, and they are deeply invested in how children are treated, because the children are the ones who will keep it going. The idea that each of us has the right to change everything is a deep insult to them."

To be a grown-up you first have to enter the parental generation and give of yourself to others around you while joining yourself to the succession of generations and thus connecting the past and the future. When this merging finally happens, everything that has gone before suddenly makes sense.

The Waning of Patriarchy

None of this is easy, but it has seemed even more confusing in recent generations, as the world started shifting under our feet. We are living in interesting times of rapid social change in which the long-standing system of male dominance over females, in society, and in family matters grinds to a halt. As it does, each generation is that much more confused about the meaning of their gender.

Patriarchy was a social arrangement between men and women that established both a male-dominated hierarchy and an assignment of rules and roles based solely on gender. According to Gerda Lerner in *The Creation of Patriarchy* and Riane Eisler in *The Chalice and the Blade,* men and women made the patriarchal agreement a few thousand years ago. It seems outrageous in retrospect, but it probably seemed like a pretty good deal at the time. In the hunter-gatherer society, men would go out and hunt and maybe they'd return with meat, or maybe they wouldn't. Hunting had its dangers, required physical strength, and brought a certain prestige. Women, who had a seemingly magical ability to bring forth life from their bodies, stayed home with the children, maintained a society and a stable base camp, and gathered whatever food and supplies they could. They had to learn to get along without either men or meat. The women never knew when the men would return or what they would be dragging behind them.

About seven thousand years ago, women, tired of gathering food far from the necessarily immobile base camp, invented agriculture and began to bring forth life from the earth as well as from their bodies. They started breeding animals, too, and quickly discovered the function of the rooster in the henhouse and the contribution of the father to the miracle of birth.

With the discovery of paternity, men for the first time knew they, too, had some small part in the creation of life. Men had worshiped their mothers and sisters since they could create life when men could not; they knew now that they could be fathers instead of just uncles. In time, men began to put their names on things, such as wives, children, businesses, books, and towns. And after they had named everything they could, they started taking things away from one another. They invented war, not just to get more stuff to name but to scare women—so they'd feel in danger and ask the men to be their heroes. After millennia of uterus envy, men were just trying to feel important.

After paternity was discovered, men surely invested even more of themselves in their children. Under patriarchy, fathers saw themselves as indispensable to family life and practiced their profession, plowed their fields, and minded their store at home. As civilization developed, their status and respect in the community depended on how well they functioned as paterfamilias. How they performed as husbands and fathers was the most significant measure of their worth as men, which usually kept them off the streets.

The patriarchal protection racket seemed like a good deal as long as the world was really scary, but a couple of hundred years ago the world got safer and the whole thing started to collapse.

With the industrial revolution, men were expected to go forth into the world to work and send money home while women demonstrated what they had known during hunter-gatherer times: They could manage fairly well on their own.

During the last couple of centuries, as patriarchy has been winding down, both men and women have had some degree of liberation from the stifling restrictions and inefficient limitations of patriarchal gender rigidity. Men don't have to die for their masculinity (though many still do), and women don't have to pretend to be incompetent in order to keep from scaring men (though many still do that, too). Women are presented with all manner of choices and have been assured they don't need men; they can "have it all" if they are willing to "do it all." (And some seem to do it all even if there is a man around.) Consequently, men have seemed both less necessary and less important, and have been less evident in family life.

The human family does not require patriarchy, and everyone will be better off without it once the dust settles and the instruction books are rewritten, studied, and digested. Meanwhile, however, there is much confusion about roles, rules, and identity. We know what women are supposed to do now—whatever they like. The problem has to do with men's and women's confusion about what men are supposed to do now.

Even if families could get along without men (and studies show that many unmarried women are happier than their married sisters and a lot happier than the ones who are divorced), men don't seem to do very well without families. Men without families moan depressively. They seem to grunt, stomp, and, in their competition with one another, turn themselves into either street fighters or tycoons who make the world unfit for decent people to live in. Even if Daddy can't be the boss anymore, we have to find something for him to do to keep him out of trouble.

For two hundred years each generation of men has come into a diminished patrimony, inheriting less of the power and prestige that his father wielded. Men have been raised to believe they are supposed to have power they don't find in themselves anymore; women have been raised to think men still have this power, and it is their job to seduce, bully, or trick them into giving it up. Men feel increasing shame over their lack of power and increasing bewilderment over the anger coming from the women, so they run away.

Patriarchy is fading at such a rapid rate that everything little boys and little girls learn about their gender is severely outdated and probably illegal by the time they are old enough to put it into operation. Because of men's recent habit of running away from family life and child raising, little girls learn about gender from their mothers. That information may be only one generation outdated. Little boys also get the bulk of their information from their mothers, but it is based on vague familiarity with their fathers and fantasies or frustrations about their husbands. Boys often have no firsthand and little secondhand information about what it feels like to be a man.

While patriarchy may be against the law and socially unacceptable in some parts of our society, it still lurks in the hearts and glands of men. Patriarchy is still much loved and mourned by millions of men and women, many of whom don't listen to Rush Limbaugh, vote for Pat Buchanan, or think the last word on gender relations was written by Saint Paul or John Gray. They would breathe it back to life if given half a chance. In some parts of the world, such as Africa and the Middle East, patriarchy is in militant ascendancy, and ultraconservative militants such as Iran's Ayatollah Khomeini can lead the patriarchal revival by pointing with alarm to domestic disorder in the West.

Whether we think we have come far enough toward gender equality or not, we won't make sense out of the world today unless we recognize that the postpatriarchal world we live in is far different from either male dreams of glory or feminist nightmares. The world is changing even as we speak, and while the waning of patriarchy and the ascendancy of feminism are good things, they are creating most of the confusion and disorientation about what men and women are supposed to do with themselves and with one another.

We don't need to stop the change—we can all welcome it—but we do need to understand its implications. Most disorienting, people now don't know what is expected of them as postpatriarchal grown-ups, or they fear it or dread it, so they shrink back into adolescence and refuse to grow up.

The Death of James Dean and the Worship of Adolescence

Adolescence was invented in the years after World War II. Prior to that, children did what they were told and learned what they were taught; then, after undergoing whatever puberty rituals were in vogue, they were elevated to adult status and took upon themselves all manner of adult responsibility. We needed them in the adult world and were not about to offer them the alternative of choosing to be nonproductive, complaining, disruptive consumers.

Against all logic, after we had lost so many of our youth in World War II, we began to pamper children and offered them a brief waiting period before stepping up to adulthood. At first it was the few years between puberty and the draft age or college age of eighteen. Adolescence was gradually extended through the twenties and well into the thirties, from puberty until self-sustaining parenthood. Originally it was a stage everyone had to pass through, but increasingly it became a life goal in itself, an identity, a separate culture, even a separate species, and the natural enemy of adults.

Adolescence was invented on September 30, 1955, when a shuffling, mumbling little puppy of a boy finished the third of his starring movies and, at the age of twenty-four, celebrated his success by crashing and dying in his new Porsche. James Dean, with the face of a mischievous Renaissance cherub, had grown up in Indiana; his doting mother died when he was nine, and his father turned him over to an aunt to raise. No one could ever love him enough, and he was dead before he had time to know how famous he would become. He has been mourned and imitated ever since by scruffy teenagers of every age, eternally pouting because they are not sufficiently loved.

In his three films, *East of Eden, Rebel Without a Cause,* and *Giant,* James Dean invented the misunderstood adolescent resented or rejected by father figures but protected by strong women. In *East of Eden* he tries to win his father's favor and collapses crying on his shoulder when the old man rejects his gifts. In *Rebel Without a Cause* he asks his aproned father how to become a man, and when his father dithers, he runs away and risks his life for his masculinity in a drag race. In *Giant* he tries to get Rock Hudson to adopt him and accept him, and finally settles for turning Hudson's sister, wife, and daughter against him while he pathetically cries in his beer.

And then he died, leaving him forever in adolescence, where we can't find out how a miserable, misunderstood kid can ever metamorphose into a happy grown-up. Forty-odd years later, Dean remains our model of tortured adolescence. The idea seems to be to make a big splash, a big display of alienation from parental expectations, as a way to keep from growing up.

Dean, along with compatriots Montgomery Clift (with the pained look of a soulful Romantic poet), Marlon Brando (with the face and body of a lusty, greedy Roman satyr), and Paul Newman (with the cockiness of a miniature Greek god), defined the alienated young postpatriarchal man rebelling against the family and against society's demand that he subdue his natural passions for the sake of the social order.

In the aftermath of World War II, conquering heroes—growlingly macho stalwarts such as Clark Gable and John Wayne, steady family loyalists such as Jimmy Stewart and Spencer Tracy, romantic lovers such as Cary Grant and Gregory Peck—were always ready to give their all for those they would love or defend. Heroes in those days were men who had been raised to die; they felt no pain of their own, had no needs of their own. They merely did their duty.

Clift, Brando, Dean, and Newman offered something new—good men who preferred not to die but instead retreated into their own emotional pain or selfish appetites. For generations men had been raised to risk their lives for love or duty without giving it a second thought. Suddenly we were presented with a quartet of celluloid rebels who did something subversive, something John Wayne would never do: They thought about it. They chose not to die, which sounds like a wise choice, but then they chose not to live, either—not to make commitments, not to develop character, not to fulfill obligations, not to join the succession of the generations, not to preserve or improve civilization and make the world a better place. Dean and Clift self-destructed early on. Newman and Brando survive; one cooks, the other eats. Newman, the only one of the quartet to grow up in an intact family, got all the way into a marriage himself, and grew up; Brando, whose appetites in every area were bigger than life, has turned into a floating island in the Pacific.

The worship of adolescence leads to narcissism—the belief that the world exists to serve or adore you rather than you existing for your value to others.

The Society of Narcissism

For a few decades now a certain degree of narcissism has been considered normal. The culture has sent messages that it could be dangerous to one's mental health to care about something outside one's self. Polonius's advice to Laertes in *Hamlet*—"This above all: to thine own self be true, and it must follow, as the night the day, thou canst not then be false to any man"—has been taken literally rather than seen as the pompous posturings of a self-satisfied windbag.

Under patriarchy, whatever its cruelties, men and women had a set of jobs and responsibilities through which each earned his or her emotional and economic keep. In the post-patriarchal world, people don't seem to believe they should have to do anything for anyone else in order to receive love.

Narcissism is defined by the fourth edition of the American Psychiatric Association's *Diagnostic and Statistical Manual of Mental Disorders* as "a pervasive pattern of grandiosity (in fantasy and behavior), need for admiration, and lack of empathy, beginning by early adulthood and present in a variety of contexts." People with a narcissistic personality disorder "react to criticism with feelings of rage, stress, or humiliation." They are "interpersonally exploitative, taking advantage of others to achieve their own ends." They have a "grandiose sense of self-importance." They "believe their problems are unique and understood only by other special people." They are "preoccupied by fantasies of unlimited success, power, brilliance, beauty, or ideal love." They "have a sense of entitlement and unreasonable expectations of especially favorable treatment" and "require constant attention and admiration." They are "unable to recognize and experience how others feel" and may be "preoccupied with feelings of envy." Much of that definition applies to any of us.

Narcissists see no problem with their narcissism. They consider their lack of empathy, their grandiose needs and expectations, their engulfing sense of themselves to be desirable. And the world assures them that whatever they want, whatever they think, whatever they feel is right.

It is hard to consider narcissism an individual pathology since it seems to arise directly from the culture. Narcissists do tend to feel part of the culture, close to whatever is in style, even if they don't feel connected to the society and the people who may need something from them. Narcissists don't see relationships with other people as valuable, so they don't make commitments to family, community, or history.

Christopher Lasch, in *The Culture of Narcissism,* notes that many people in our society seem concerned with little outside themselves.

> To live for the moment is the prevailing passion—to live for yourself, not for your predecessors or posterity. We are fast losing the sense of historical continuity, the sense of belonging to a succession of generations originating in the past and stretching into the future. . . . People today hunger not for personal salvation, let alone for the restoration of an earlier golden age, but for the feeling, the momentary illu-

sion, of personal well-being, health and psychic security.

We now have a world full of narcissists, of all ages and genders, and none of us has escaped exposure to the forces that balloon our egos out of proportion to our wisdom. We have met the narcissists, and they are us. The baby boomer generation, born between 1946 (the year after the end of World War II) and 1963 (the escalation of U.S. involvement in Vietnam, the assassination of President Kennedy, and the loss of our national optimism) has, in particular, experienced a world very different from the one experienced by those of us who came before or after those years. Their sense of family and of gender was fixed between the sexual revolution and the gender revolution, after women got the pill and men got *Playboy,* but before women got their voices (angry) and everyone who let it all hang out got AIDS.

There were so many baby boomers, they dominated consumerism and production, popular arts and entertainment, and the focus of the culture. The world, wanting to sell them things, catered to them, soothed and pampered them, and assured them that they owed it to themselves to purchase, experience, consume, or discard whatever their hearts desired. They and their loved ones have suffered most.

In "The 'Me' Decade," written in 1976, Tom Wolfe considered advertising a major contributor to our self-centered world. He cites such commercials as "If I've only one life, let me live it as a blonde" and the Schlitz commercial: "You only go around once in life, so you have to grab all the gusto you can." In *Bonfire of the Vanities,* Wolfe went on to satirize the ridiculous lives of the self-indulgent and narcissistic yuppies in the '80s, the "Masters of the Universe."

Some slowing down of the economy, as the Reagan boom ate itself up, left us with large numbers of people who expected lives of total personal excess but now found they couldn't afford it. Those who don't get all they want are almost as frustrated as those who get it all and discover it didn't (and doesn't) make them happy.

Psychotherapy in a "you owe it to yourself" market has also made a major contribution to personal narcissism. While narcissism is considered mental illness in the textbooks, it is actually encouraged not only by the culture and the economy but by the self-help industry as well. Self-help slogans urge people to "get all the love you deserve," to "have it all," to "be your own best friend," and to "fly as high as Jonathan Livingston Seagull." In the past decade or so, pop psychology became a method of "pampering your inner child." If the well-acculturated citizen of the age of narcissism gave thought to anyone outside him- or herself, it was as the audience for efforts to boost his or her ego by "knocking 'em dead" and making them "eat their hearts out."

As Robert Bly describes in *The Sibling Society,* the goal of human development ceased to be the achievement of character, goodness, and relationships but the achievement of popularity and fame. People no longer cared whether they loved their loved ones effectively or were loved by them in return as long as they were loved by strangers.

I have heard trendy mental health professionals assure parents that they "should not stay married for the children's sakes" and should not have any dealings with their parents if their parents make them feel bad. They tell people who find themselves depressed after a decade or two of marriage that they are officially incompatible with their mate, that they married for "the wrong reasons," and that they will surely be miserable if they stay married when they are no longer crazily in love. People who have had a lot of therapy—even *good* therapy—have been known to walk away from criticism or the anger of people they have disappointed, saying, "I don't need this," as if only interactions that make them feel good about themselves are bearable.

All narcissists have trouble with family life, but some varieties of narcissists are particularly at risk for making a mess of marriage. They don't see their partner as a fellow human being but as the embodiment of a fantasy in their heads.

A *Phallic Narcissist* evaluates a woman's worth on the basis of whether or not she turns him on. He is angry with his wife if she does not make him feel sufficiently in love, if she gains some weight or loses some tone and no longer corresponds to his physical ideal, or if her emotional state or attitude toward him fails to make him feel like a master of the universe. Sometimes he goes so far as to feel betrayed by his wife if other women turn him on.

A *Romantic Narcissist* is more often, but not always, female. She believes that if a man really loves her, he will only do, think, or say what would correspond to the romantic fantasy in her head. A Romantic Narcissist believes she has both a right and a responsibility to pout or carry on wildly if the guy does not conform to her fantasy.

A *Feminist Chauvinist* believes it is each man's personal responsibility to pay reparations for seven thousand years of patriarchy and to make up to her for everything other men have done wrong to her or to any of her ancestors. Whatever a man does wrong is proof of men's evil, and whatever she does wrong is because a man is doing something wrong.

Patriarchal Chauvinists are men who believe they deserve special treatment and entitlements by virtue of a Y chromosome that makes them much more special than any woman. They seem quaintly old-fashioned even though some of them are quite young. They may take Saint Paul's unfortunate "head of the household" remark literally and believe they are supposed to be the boss or "the captain of the ship" in their marriage. Some go as far as believing their wives are their employees or even their servants, and such men may do such outrageous things as treat their children as extensions of their wives while treating their paychecks as extensions of themselves.

Generational Narcissists believe the world in which they came of age, the world whose rules and boundaries they learned as a child, is the *right* world. They protest if the world changes in some way. They expect prior notification if a style or attitude changes, and they will call down the wrath of God if anyone tries to change anything substantial.

Linguistic Bullies believe that they should pass judgment on what other people are permitted to say and which words other people are permitted to use. They come in two varieties: the Politically Correct Bullies on our left, who tell us they speak for all the oppressed people in the world, and the Religious Right Bullies, who tell us they speak for God. Some merely speak for their own narcissism, telling people they cannot say certain things because it personally "offends" their delicate sensibilities.

Males of the baby boomer generation are more disoriented than the females. Since they came of age between the sexual revolution and the gender revolution, they are likely to be both Phallic Narcissists and Patriarchal Chauvinists. They may still be seeing themselves as the center of the universe, the creature God created first, and still believe that women were merely decorated ribs sent to serve and service them, to provide the perfect love their mothers tried but failed to provide, and to exult vigorously in the glory of their masculinity. They believe women have the power and the duty to make them feel man enough. But they may be so insecure about their sexual potency that they require women to correspond precisely to the centerfold images in their fantasies, hoping that will keep them in a constant state of sexual splendor.

In theories about narcissism, all but the most severe and extreme cases can be traced to children growing up feeling they were important just for their existence, quite apart from anything they might do in life, and feeling they were owed ideal love and would not have to return it. They might have grown up with the feeling that they were the center of the parental or social universe and would never be required to grow up and become parents or grown-ups themselves. The parents may have taken wonderful care of the children but failed to reveal themselves to them. So the children become princes and princesses, worshiped but serving no useful purpose. What they might have needed was more awareness of what their parents felt as they raised them. Narcissistic parents can teach their children to be narcissists as well by recruiting the children into their life of disdain for the outside world, but the surest way for parents to produce narcissists is to keep children as pampered but useless pets and neglect to teach them to identify with the adult world and to prepare to take their place in it.

Psychotherapists, as they try to explain what the parents did wrong in raising such people, dither over the details of parental love that was too much or too little or at the wrong moment. Nothing can warm the heart of a narcissist quite so much as the sound of psychoanalysts trying to figure out which parent is to blame for the narcissist's sense of entitlement, lack of concern with anyone outside him- or herself, and failure to appreciate and return the love he or she has been given. The thing about narcissists is that no matter how much love they get, it is never as much as they feel they need and/or deserve.

Needless to say, all of these narcissistic people have a hell of a time being married or raising children, since those are the activities that above all require people to show the maturity of considering other people's feelings as important as your own.

There is one way to stop narcissism dead in its tracks: The earlier children learn to do something useful and to give something back, the more likely they will grow up to become adults.

The Psychology of Victimhood

In addition to its role in enabling narcissism, psychotherapy has somehow become stylish as official sanction for irresponsibility. Victims get a psychoanalytic stamp of approval on their behavior. What they do is not their fault because of the behavior of others or even because of the strength of their own emotions. Woody Allen, the most psychoanalyzed man in America, couldn't live with his common-law wife and children. In fact, his family life was so chaotic, he didn't even know he was committing incest. His explanation, after decades of psychotherapy: "The heart wants what it wants."

Every day in my office I hear the stories of chronologically grown men who want to run away from home. It is not that they don't think they are doing a good-enough job and want my help in being better adults. They don't want to be grown-ups at all. They are angry at anyone who would expect adulthood from them and thus run the risk of making them feel guilt. To relieve that guilt, they want to declare that their immaturity is *not their fault*. They have bought so totally into the psychology of victimhood, they believe their character is the responsibility of their parents, the society, or even the neighbors. Some believe they would surely precipitate a neurosis if they did something they didn't want to do or were forced to act contrary to their feelings. These men may be aptly infuriating to those who try to depend on them, but they can't imagine that they are doing anything wrong. They just haven't been parented perfectly. They take literally the messages that come from the culture, much of it from the voices of mental health: "Me first!"

Gordon came in to tell me that he must leave his wife of

twenty years and their three children because he realized he had married a woman who was wrong for him. She didn't share his new interest in sea kayaking, and she liked to go to movies with subtitles. To top it off, he realized he was *not happy*. He had not had much success on any of his jobs and had not learned to be of much use at home. Mostly he worked out and exercised, and then he went home to show off the roundness of his muscles or the flatness of his belly. Sometimes his wife and children were unavailable for his daily worship. That made him unhappy. He wanted out of his family so he could find the happiness that he deserved. It was not his fault that he had had the misfortune of marrying the wrong woman.

Harvey was determined to leave his third wife and their two babies, as he had left his two previous wives and three previous children. This new wife had gotten mad and said some terribly insulting things about him when he failed to go to the hospital to see his latest baby. It was not his fault; he could not be expected to live with a woman who would talk to him that way. He didn't deserve that.

Irving called off his wedding and broke up with his fiancée of several years when she told him she wanted to have children. Irving had his regular golf and exercise routine, and he had seen children interfere with the lives of quite a few of his friends; he did not want that to happen to him. This was his life, and he didn't want it dominated by some squalling brats. It was not his fault; she had misled him into thinking he was as much of a child as she would ever need.

Jasper sneaked his barely postpubescent girlfriend into the hospital to see his new baby. He had been dating her throughout the pregnancy since his wife's pregnant body repulsed him, and he was afraid sex with her would punch in his son's head. He had even had some sessions with the young girlfriend's mother, a much divorced psychotherapist who encouraged divorce and remarriage with the happy news that research had shown divorce was good for children since it provided them with a rich diversity of parents. Jasper's wife was not so sanguine when she found the young girlfriend in the hospital holding her baby and demanding equal parental rights. Jasper could not understand why his wife would expose their child to the misery that would surely result if he were forced to stay in a marriage in which he was not completely in love. It wasn't his fault that he had gotten into an affair; his feelings had changed.

There are women as well who refuse to take responsibility for their lives. They may refuse to work, believing that men are supposed to provide for them, and also refuse to cook, clean, or tend, believing that such subservience is degrading. Few run out on their children, but many refuse to find a father for them or drive off an existing father. They may weave romantic fantasies of an ideal man and refuse to settle for anything less. They may demand total gender equality except in their own relationships, where they may waver between being a fairy princess and a wicked witch but never an equal partner. They may demand total control while insisting that their man achieve power, prestige, and wealth in the world. They may believe that whenever a man does wrong, it is because all men are jerks; whenever they themselves do wrong, it is also because all men are jerks.

Kyra left her loser redneck husband and married a man with a thriving business. He encouraged her to quit her job and keep the books for his business, but at the end of the first month, the books were a mess. He fussed at her, and she tearfully told him that it made her nervous to add and subtract. He laughed at her, and she started hitting him, though he was twice her size. He couldn't get her to stop and finally called the police. When the police arrived, she hit him some more and then hit the police, claiming he was abusing her by expecting her to add and subtract when he knew it made her nervous. The police carried her off, while she screamed that it was not her fault she was hitting them—her husband had made her mad.

Lois came into group therapy because she had been "abused" by her last boyfriend. When the group asked about the abuse, she explained that he would take her out any night of the week except Saturday, a time he liked to spend with his young son from a previous marriage. The group commented that that did not seem abusive, but she insisted it embarrassed her. Her friends, knowing she didn't have a date for Saturday night, might assume her boyfriend was out with another woman. Since it made her feel bad, ergo it was abuse.

Minnie's husband was handsome, successful, a great father, and good in bed, but he could not dance. Minnie had an affair with a man from the ballroom dancing school and left her husband and children. The dancer danced off, and her husband begged her to come home. She spent a weekend with him but reported that it would never work because, after all the pain of the divorce, he still hadn't learned to dance. "It's not my fault. If he really loved me, you'd think he would at least learn a fox trot and a waltz. If he really loved me, he would somehow get rhythm."

Nora called and interrupted me at the symphony with an emergency. I'd been seeing her and her husband for a while, and he was quite depressed over his financial difficulties. Nora reported that he had locked himself in the library of their mansion and wouldn't come to the door or the telephone. She said, "I climbed up through the bushes, looked in the window, and saw him sitting at his desk with a gun to his head. Does this mean he doesn't love me?"

These people who don't want to grow up can't seem to hold relationships together, can't manage family life, and don't really want to. Their narcissism is intense, but they declare themselves victims so it is not their fault. They resist adulthood and want to stay safely in adolescence, with all the rights and privileges of grown-ups but none of the responsibility.

A Typical Dysfunctional Family of the '90s

The Windsors may not be typical in most respects, but they seem to be suffering from a malady far more serious than mad cow disease. It is the same malady affecting most families on both sides of the Atlantic: They have lost their ability to raise children capable of raising children. They can raise children who look pretty good right up to the end of adolescence, and then they simply stop maturing. They stay stuck at that point of development and fall apart or pout if anyone tries to push them further toward adulthood. In them there is a coming together of postpatriarchal confusion, glorification of adolescence, toxic narcissism, and even whining victimhood.

The most public of all families in the English-speaking world has disintegrated before our eyes. Prince Charles told the press that his divorce from Princess Diana had nothing to do with his longtime affair with Camilla Parker Bowles. Instead, he insisted, he had to get a divorce because his father had made him marry his wife and have children and only afterward did he discover that his wife was not perfect but suffered from romantic notions of marriage and from bulimia. Worst of all, he was not in love with her, and having to be married to someone with whom he was not in love made him unhappy. Therefore, it was not his fault that he had to divorce his wife; his daddy screwed up his life. If Charles can't earn a throne through heroism, valor, or wisdom, perhaps he can earn one through victimhood, but he will always be remembered as the man who scorned the most loved woman on earth and thereby indirectly drove her to her death.

Princess Diana was even better at playing the victim game. During the messy divorce, she used her unparalleled celebrity, a wedding gift from Charles, to get the world on her side. She went on international tabloid TV to bewail the fact that she had to throw herself down staircases and have affairs with horse trainers, budding authors, and the like, because Charles—the man who offered her limitless wealth, even more limitless fame, and majesty in exchange for discretion, tolerance, and space—did not love her the way heroes loved heroines in the romance novels she had read (some of which had been written by her step-grandmother, Barbara Cartland). Diana never recovered from the realization that fairy tales do not come true. After the divorce, she continued to court the press, the world, and "a constituency of the rejected," to use a phrase of her brother's. She spent her time championing those who were dying of AIDS or stepping on land mines, and kissing more lepers than anyone short of Mother Teresa.

The world loved her and could not get enough of her. She took up with a billionaire Egyptian playboy who offered no protection from the ravenous press except speed. With a drunk driver at the wheel, she died in a Paris tunnel after a high-speed getaway to escape the ever-present photographers. She had bartered her life for, first, identity, then adoration, and finally revenge. But she ascended into sainthood while most of the English-speaking world, on TV or in person, gathered outside Buckingham Palace, wanting to show that they held Charles accountable for her death and to teach him and his mother how normal families grieved. The glass slipper was now on the other foot. But does Charles get it?

Charles is a baby boomer born in 1948, but unlike most baby boomers, he was not raised with the expectation of finding a way to make a living. He was born into his job and was raised to perform simple functions: marry respectably, stay married, produce and raise a prince or two capable of doing the same, and avoid scandal. Most of the world's people—even those born in poverty and squalor, with little or no education, and suffering from average or about half the time below-average intelligence—could manage to perform those tasks quite nicely. If they had not been able to do so, civilization and perhaps even the human race would not have survived. But the wealthiest, most privileged, and presumably most carefully nurtured and highly valued of princes cannot perform such simple and universal tasks.

Nor can any of his siblings. His sister, Anne, after years of adulterous rumors, dumped a husband who had mounted the wrong filly and married one of her mother's horsemen. His brother Andrew cavorted with porn stars and then married a wild woman he couldn't seem to keep up with. His bachelor baby brother Edward tries unsuccessfully to convince the world that he is not gay. Not one of the four Windsor children can do the simple job of marrying and staying married.

Some people looking at the decline of the House of Windsor and the potential collapse of the monarchy blame Queen Elizabeth for being too busy being queen to raise her children properly; presumably she should have quit her day job to stay at home with the kiddies. Others blame Prince Philip for being a rigidly patriarchal father with a wide streak of the philanderer in his behavior on the road. (Philip's philandering might explain why his children can't seem to do marriage, but the evidence for it is not very compelling; if he had been screwing around, surely someone would have cashed in on that lucrative piece of information.) Philip's job was to oversee the raising of the children despite the fact that he himself had not been raised in a family. His father had been a gambler and womanizer who left him and his mother when he was a mere lad. His mother was a deaf pseudo-nun who mostly prayed and sent the young Philip off to military school when he was two so he could be raised by soldiers.

Philip says he was careful never to be loving to his sons, since he wanted to toughen them up.

But blaming Charles on either Philip or the Queen is naive. Patriarchy—the system whereby God the Father was represented here on earth by a king who served as a model for the father in the family, the system that supported the divine right of kings and therefore of fathers—has been in much welcomed decline in the civilized world for at least two hundred years. And this is nowhere more evident than in Britain, where the reigning queens have always seemed to do better than the kings. While the Americans were overthrowing their kings and the French were beheading theirs, the British were redefining the function of their troubled monarchy, whose struggles over succession had led to wars and beheadings for many centuries.

The British had tried to get rid of their cumbersome monarchy in 1649 but found that Puritans were even more restrictive and a lot less fun. So they kept the monarch but took all his power away. When young George III succeeded to the throne in 1760, he actually tried to do what patriarchal kings were supposed to do: run things. He did that for a while and made such a mess of it that the colonists rebelled. He tried running things at home as well, and his sons ran wild.

So George III rethought the matter of royalty and decided his function was not to run things but to create the model of the ideal family. He and Queen Charlotte did so, and between his episodes of madness they produced fifteen children. This was a new and significant idea, that the way in which a king—or any other man—brings together the people and earns their loyalty is not by displays of power or even of competence or sanity but by functioning as a loyal husband and father, providing continuity of family life and an example of how a man and a family are supposed to behave. We have come to expect that from our elected leaders as well, and we often value it more highly than strength or competence.

This postpatriarchal definition of the function of the monarch was too late for George's wild sons, George IV and William IV, who succeeded him, but his granddaughter Victoria did it perfectly. And most of her successors—George V, George VI, and Elizabeth—have maintained model families as well. Victoria's son, Edward VII, who didn't ascend to the throne until he was sixty, entertained himself as he waited for his mother to die by chasing wild women and pursuing whatever other activities seemed masculine in a matriarchal world. He was a consummate philanderer, but he never let it wreck his marriage. (From the time of George IV until the current century, the sovereigns have done a good job of avoiding marital scandal.) Edward VII's grandson, Edward VIII, abdicated when he saw that he couldn't have the private life he wanted and the proper family life the job required.

Each of those men—George IV, Edward VII, Edward VIII, and Charles—who have been left in the prince position too long, with no function except to wait for their parent to die, seems to have had trouble growing up. That appears to be a formula for creating narcissism.

It appears to be either tragic or maddening that Charles, the centerpiece of his mother's *annus horribilus,* has failed to fulfill the postpatriarchal responsibilities that would seem to be requisite to the position he desires, yet he still expects his subjects to offer him the forgiveness and tolerance we give rock stars and ballplayers for similar behavior. Charles's job is to be the model of adulthood, and he can't do it; nonetheless, he wants all the rights and privileges of the job.

He is not alone. Something has gone horribly wrong, not just in this most public of families but all around us. More and more people of all social classes, of all economic circumstances, are running from family life, reverting to adolescence, setting up their emotions as the center of their life and the lives of their loved ones, and still finding some way to blame it on their parents.

What's going to happen to the children when there are no more grown-ups? We're about to find out.

It is tempting enough to do the stylish thing and put the blame on the parents or on the parents' parents. But here's the conundrum: How do we raise a better generation of children unless we first raise a better generation of grown-ups? Maybe adulthood is not the result of a wise choice of parents or a set of fortuituous circumstances. Maybe it is a choice people can make, a set of skills they can learn, a course of development they can attain. And maybe they can start choosing adulthood and learning its skills even if everything has not been just right up until now. Maybe it is never too late to have a happy adulthood.

3

How to Be a Grown Man

Beware the beast man for he is the devil's pawn.
Alone among God's primates, he kills for sport,
for lust, for greed. Yea, he will murder his
brother to possess his brother's land. Let him not
breed in great numbers, for he will make a
desert of his home and yours. Shun him, drive
him back into his jungle lair, for he is the
harbinger of death.

—Chimpanzee played by Roddy McDowall
in *Planet of the Apes*

Beware of men who cry. It's true that men who
cry are sensitive to and in touch with feelings,
but the only feelings they tend to be sensitive to
and in touch with are their own.

—Nora Ephron

The Job Description

The world is wary of the male gender lately despite our
substantial contributions to art, science, and civilization.
Michelangelo, Galileo, Shakespeare, Mozart, and Hank
Williams were all men, but regardless of our abundant good

deeds, men are in disfavor. We are accused of charging too much for our services. The world may not be able to afford us any longer. It is certainly unwilling to evaluate all other creatures on the basis of their value to the male gender. Instead, the world has begun to evaluate man on the basis of his value to everyone and everything else. We no longer think of man as the image of God put on earth to have dominion over all the lesser creatures, such as the fish of the sea, the fowl of the air, and women. But we don't know quite what he is for.

In *Manhood in the Making,* David Gilmore defines what a man has been expected to do in exchange for the privileges accorded him: "To be a man in most of the societies we have looked at, one must impregnate women, protect dependents from danger, and provision kith and kin." Needless to say, nowadays the woman must want to be either impregnated or protected before the man dare proceed with the operation, and she would expect to take part in the provisioning. In fact, the guy who insists upon doing it alone as a homage to traditional masculine bravado merely looks like a jerk.

As traditional man squirts the sperm, wrestles the bears, and brings home the tofu, he maintains a certain masculine attitude that, according to Harvard psychologist Ronald F. Levant in *Masculinity Reconstructed,* has the following seven dimensions:

1. the requirement to avoid all things feminine

2. the injunction to restrict one's emotional life

3. the emphasis on toughness and aggression

4. the injunction to be self-reliant

5. the emphasis on achieving status above all else

6. nonrelational, objectifying attitudes toward sexuality

7. fear and hatred of homosexuals

Boys are also encouraged to be big, loud, and smelly, though they needn't carry those qualities into adulthood. Still, in Alabama where I grew up, men who conformed to these seven standards might also grow large potbellies, smoke cigars, and drive trucks without mufflers to make themselves as big, smelly, and loud as they can be.

Traditional masculinity is a formula for making men sacrifice their lives (either the actuality of them or the awareness of the experience of them) for an outmoded and suicidal job description. It is the secret of unhappiness.

This model of masculinity is not intended for men who would live long enough to have relationships with women—it certainly would not attract or impress very many of them—and it would be a disaster for raising either sons or daughters. Instead, it becomes a mini-psychodrama that a man acts out for other men, a way of reassuring other men that he will be a reliable, indefatigable, and undemanding comrade-at-arms; will not require that his emotions be pampered; and will not try to get into the other guy's pants. Men flash this posture at one another as part of a greeting ceremony, but the guys who actually try to live by this code are either still practicing or just haven't caught on yet.

Such men are Patriarchal Chauvinists. They may not need to actively prove their masculinity in order to achieve some sort of entitlement to lord it over others; they believe it comes just from being a man. By accepting, without question, outdated gender notions and operating as if patriarchy were still in effect, they offend others without understanding what they are doing wrong.

These men—some of them fossils, others still wet behind

the ears—aren't necessarily mean-spirited or deliberately harmful. They aren't even trying to put down women. It isn't that they are trying to be the boss; they just assume God has placed them on earth to be "head of the household" and protect the "weaker sex."

Patriarchal Chauvinists may be quaint, harmless, and merely irritating, except to their loved ones. They can be dangerous if they get caught up in fundamentalist religion or politics and fight battles to maintain male privilege. But they can also destructively mislead their children by stifling a daughter's strengths and aspirations or setting up a son to make an unsatisfactory husband and a public fool of himself in an egalitarian world.

Sometimes I question their sanity. I remember one high school teacher and coach who gave up his career to become a gambler, hoping he could win enough money to enable his wife, a thoracic surgeon, to quit work and be a soccer mom, a plan to which she reacted with appropriate horror. He didn't even get it after she left him. His mother stayed at home, so surely that is what his wife would want. He never asked. The idea of eliciting an opinion from a woman was not part of the gender repertoire of his family.

It is strange that men who can memorize batting averages daily and can react to the most minimal fluctuation in stock prices can't remember the two hundred years of change that have taken place in gender relations; they act as if everything is just as it was when they were a child, when their grandfather was a child, and even when Henry VIII's grandfather was a child.

Boys who want to become traditional men have to learn this stifling male role and practice it with one another until they pass muster, and then they are sent out to risk their lives in football, war, or work. A boy must not seek the protected comfort afforded the "weaker" sex. He must not let his emotions interfere with his job. He must not stop until the job is done (and he will be honored if he dies in the process). He must not let any particular woman pussywhip him into caring about her rather than about the job at hand. And he mustn't molest the other guys and distract them from their jobs. He must always realize that the job he does is more important than he is. If the boy should by chance survive, he then gets to live as a man, though he has not been taught that role. He must learn it on his own or be taught by a woman.

Men who would live as men rather than die for their masculinity may then have the chance to learn the real postures of manhood. To their shock and disorientation, the postures of adult masculinity are almost the opposite of the postures they spent their early life learning.

A man spends much of his life as a grown man embracing and exploring things feminine, the things he was taught to disdain and the parts of himself that were suppressed by gender training; this is true especially if he raises daughters. A man opens up his emotional life to a woman, learning softness and cooperation, risking interdependency, and setting relationships, especially with a wife and children, ahead of status. And a man even talks about it. A man—and this is the crucial element in marriage—must learn to make sex so personal that he can commit it with only one woman. And he must overcome the homophobia of adolescence sufficiently to get close to the other guys; he doesn't have to sleep with them, but he does have to expose to them the pain and confusion of being a man and knowing he is not living up to the gender ideal.

But before he begins to learn to be a man, he has to go through boyhood with honor. Otherwise, shame will follow him, and he will be constantly recycling the tasks of boyhood until he gets them right.

Things a Boy Needs to Learn Before He Can Even Think About Learning How to Be a Grown Man

A male's survival among the culture of boys requires him to achieve a modicum of competence at rough-and-tumble sports or at least make a show of trying. There is much to be learned in the games of childhood and the adventures of adolescence, and I don't recommend that anyone forgo them. I also don't recommend—Kennedys and touch football notwithstanding—dragging them into adult life. There are other games for grown men to play. A boy who would be a man among men must first be a boy among boys, and then leave it there.

The games of childhood teach boys to follow the rules. The other kids will be only too happy to teach a boy the rules if the parents have failed to do so. In these games, boys learn to compete as well as cooperate. And they learn to lose as well as win. Most of us will do a lot more losing in life than winning. Rudyard Kipling, unlike Vince ("Winning isn't everything, it's the only thing") Lombardi, explained that you can be a man "if you can meet with Triumph and Disaster and treat those two impostors just the same." Kipling's words are inscribed over the doors to the center court at Wimbledon; Lombardi's words are on the souls of a generation of sports fans who confuse football with masculinity.

Boys being frantically taught to win may be so afraid of losing that they don't have fun when they play. Winning is nice, and everyone should get some experience with it. Life is difficult for people who don't know how to brag about victories. Those who are afraid of envy or who feel guilty for winning when others lose have both a social and a psychological problem. So do those who use their bragging not to share their joy and spread it around but to declare themselves winners in some contest with their fellows that the others didn't know they had entered. It is humble and friendly to tell one's friends of one's successes—once. The friends won't forget about the winning lottery ticket, the appearance on the cover of *Time,* or the big fish caught on the trip to Alaska; these things needn't be mentioned again, but it would be ungallant not to mention them once.

I once treated Otis who had spent his life playing on Little League teams that never lost a game. He was president of every club and valedictorian of every class. Every woman he ever smiled at leaped into his bed. His confidence was unbounded, and he thought he was invincible. He took a job making billion-dollar deals for a brokerage firm, interacting with clients who had little interest in maintaining his high-flying ego, and he promptly met his first failure. This did not surprise or bother his bosses or his colleagues, but it made him feel isolated and even suicidal. He had never learned to lose, and therefore he had never learned to cry on anyone's shoulder when he did so. And he wasn't sure that was a masculine enough thing to do. Men who don't quite feel man enough can be horribly lonely.

Masculine Impersonators

Any fool with a dick can make a baby, but it takes a real man to raise his children.

—Laurence Fishburne in *Boyz N the Hood*
by John Singleton

Most guys do not feel man enough, so they fake it.

In the natural scheme of things, masculinity is passed on from father to son. Women, no matter how wonderful, no matter how loving, no matter how heroic, can't teach it to us. If we don't have fathers, we should have grandfathers, uncles, or perhaps, under the right circumstances, careful stepfathers to raise us from boys into men. Boys absorb masculinity from a man who is invested in the boy's apprenticeship into masculinity by standing beside the man as he lives his life and does whatever a man does (usually nothing very different from what a woman does, though it may look different and may even smell different when a man does it) and by seeing, hearing, smelling, and feeling what a man sees and hears and smells and feels.

But if there is no man to stand beside the boy, to lead him into manhood, and to tell him when he has achieved his destination and can now relax, the boy gets his images of manhood from the movies or from other boys, so he grows up as a masculine impersonator, faking it for a lifetime, pretending that he knows what a man feels and trying to act the way he thinks a man is supposed to act. He is not likely to get it right.

Carol Gilligan explained in *In a Different Voice* that men and women seemed different not because they came from different planets or developed from different species but because they were both raised by women. Dorothy Dinnerstein reveals in *The Mermaid and the Minotaur* that "male rule of the world has its emotional roots in female rule of early childhood."

Women are likely to assume that masculinity is learned as automatically as femininity has seemed to be, but the seeming naturalness of femininity may be an artifact of female-dominated child raising. What is automatic for a girl with a mother may be a daunting struggle for a boy without a father. The problem with men who can't grow up is never too much mother; it is always too little father.

When a mother raises a son, she knows he is destined to grow up and leave her. She can teach him three things to help him in his life as a man. She can try to keep him out of trouble by teaching him to follow the rules, always with the hope that he will in time be able to make and enforce the rules. She can try to prepare him for some success in life by teaching him to compete successfully with the other kids, using whatever talents he might have. And she can try to prepare him for the time when some other woman will come along and mold him to her needs by teaching him to seduce women. If he can master these three things, he may get along just fine without his mother. Much of the rest of what he must learn he must learn from his father.

If the boy does not learn from a father how to love a woman, the boy may grow up knowing only how to seduce a woman. He may run in shame from the woman he should love and seek out new conquests—women who do not expect equality or totality in the relationship and are not angry when they fail to get it. *Philanderers*—men who reaffirm their shaky masculinity by escaping the domestic woman and seducing the strange woman—might have gotten by with this approach toward marriage in a patriarchal world which really believed that the most important function of family life was to support the man's sense of masculinity. Postpatriarchal women don't have to tolerate these betrayals and threats, so a man who takes this approach toward marriage may find himself divorced, disgraced, dethroned, or bobbited.

Phallic Narcissists are often philanderers. Their response to a woman—whether she is running for office, serving him food, painting his house, teaching his children, removing his gallbladder, or sharing his bed and his life—concerns her physical appearance. He really can't think of a woman as a fellow human being or a functional member of society but only as a contestant in some sort of sexual beauty contest in his head.

Even if the woman's appearance passes muster, her behavior must correspond to his fantasy, too. If she says or does the wrong thing and he loses his state of sexual arousal or reverie, then she is a witch or "ball buster." Phallic Narcissists have such delicate sexuality, they must never let the reality of a woman interfere with their sexual fantasy. This can be hard on them, but it is just as hard on the woman who tries to live up to the fantasy.

If a man is to be happy for all his life, he must learn to be turned on by wrinkles, liver spots, and cellulite.

If a boy does not get to study a father who is living in peace in a family, he may miss the masculine presence so intensely that he may exaggerate its uses. He may become a *controller,* a man who thinks he has been appointed boss or head of the household and who feels responsible for keeping everyone else playing by his rules. Some controlling men try to keep their own emotions low; other controlling men try to keep other people's emotions low, even if they have to have temper tantrums and outbursts of anger to get the emotional level within their comfort range. Some controlling men actually think they know what is right; others just believe it's their responsibility to decide what is right and to prove they aren't wrong, even if they haven't the foggiest notion what they are talking about.

In a patriarchal world, men were pacified by being told they could be the boss if they just didn't get in the way of the real work being done. In a postpatriarchal world, women have the same need for respect as men, and men who try to enhance their own status by reducing the status of the women in their family will eventually foment an appropriate and necessary rebellion.

If the boy is never quite anointed as a man, he may continue the competitive games of childhood far into adulthood, striving to become a champion and a star. He may become a *contender,* looking for contests to enter in which he can prove to his audience that he is indeed man enough. If he is lucky, he will find men to emulate, and he may identify strongly enough with his heroes to absorb some of their successes and some of the qualities for which they are admired. If he feels he is a loser, he may cringe in shame and envy the guys who seem to be winners. He may, of course, bypass the competitions with the other boys and instead vie against the forces of nature, taking risks and going places others haven't been, doing things other men haven't done. He may be so absorbed with making a living and the identity that comes from doing so that he may become a workaholic, continually doing what he has learned to do well and avoiding the messy business of leading a life or living in a family.

Masculine impersonators—philanderers, controllers, and contenders—go through their puberty rituals interminably. They may run away from Mama over and over again to join the other boys. They may reassure themselves of their puberty by escaping the woman at home and rescuing damsels in distress to whom they may still appear to be a hero.

They may try to affirm their maleness by bringing other people under their control. In their insecurity they may even try to be the boss over their wife and children, beating or berating them into submission and thus sacrificing them to their fragile masculinity.

They may play the games of boyhood, the sports, the wars, and the competitions in order to pile up the most toys. They may become tycoons or street fighters as they struggle to win victories, both real and imaginary.

Underneath this absurd behavior of desperate masculine impersonation, which makes such men unfit for family life, is the boy's furtive hope that he will get love if he makes a big enough show of his manliness. Sadly, no one benefits from or is impressed by death-defying macho displays when we have a world filled with women who need to be partnered and children who need to be fathered.

Postpatriarchal Men

It is clear to men that the images of adult manhood given by the popular culture are worn out; a man can no longer depend on them.

—Robert Bly, *Iron John*

Guys can spend most of their lives trying to develop, test, display, and defend their masculinity, and precious little of their lives actually doing anything useful with it. The boy who would be a man has to stop taking masculinity so seriously. We are merely being called upon to be a man, and once we get past the macho bullshit, a man is just a man— not that much in the scheme of things and vitally important only to his family.

Mercifully, the job description for men is changing since the traditional posture of masculinity has become increasingly incompatible with the role men are called upon to play now.

Yet while the job of being a man is far less suicidal in this new world, it is certainly no easier. It comes in four parts, the four mythic archetypes of masculinity: the King, the Warrior, the Lover, and the Magician.

The King, in pure form, is the father figure, the character Spencer Tracy and Jimmy Stewart played with such strength and tenacity in movies, and Robert Young and Bill Cosby played on television with such humility and integrity. The King has been satirized on stage by Yul Brynner and, in recent decades, cut down to the size of Ward Cleaver and Homer Simpson.

The Warrior in pure form is the fiercely macho movie hero, exemplified in the 1940s and '50s by John Wayne; more recently and more cruelly and inhumanly by Sean Connery and Clint Eastwood; and finally, disconnected from anything human, by Sylvester Stallone and Arnold Schwarzenegger.

The pure Lover can be as exotic as Rudolph Valentino, as glamorous as Cary Grant, or as homespun as Robert Redford, but his passion transforms him into whatever romantic fantasy his beloved favors.

The Magician has been to mysterious places and has come back with knowledge and understanding that others have not achieved. Magicians include wise men and scholars, men who have been into space, such as Chuck Yeager and the astronauts, or men who have been into the underworld, such as Humphrey Bogart and Jack Nicholson in their various film noir exposés of the rottenness in the human soul.

Obviously, each real man must contain all four archetypes.

Traditional masculinity training prepared boys to be Warriors. But there aren't very many opportunities nowadays for men to use their Warrior skills; they have to create incidents, pick fights, find adventures. They go around taking offense at strangers, often drinking or using other drugs to get themselves more out of control and aggressive as they prepare themselves for battle with the world.

But Warrior energy, like any other power, is not inherently evil and may be put to many uses, good and bad. A man who is ashamed of his fierceness, who must apologize for being a man, who must pull back from using his physical and moral strength in deference to women, who subordinates himself to women as affirmative action or penance for his ancestors is not showing respect for women, for men, or for himself. The goal is equality and respect, not demasculinization as sacrifice to the bitch goddess. Even in a postpatriarchal world Saint George may still have to rescue his damsel in distress from her dragon, and she may appreciate it. A man must be a Warrior on those rare occasions when he must stand up and speak out for what he believes to be right, usually by voting his conscience or writing a letter to the editor rather than by going "postal" or pulling a Travis (*Taxi Driver*) Bickell and blowing away those who offend him.

Every man must become a Lover, though he need not be a stud or hunk or heartthrob. What fuels romantic fantasies in high school girls has little to do with what it takes to partner a grown woman. A boy who would be a man needs heroes who love living and exploring life's mysteries, who find beauty in the world and bring it to their loved ones, and who know that their love is valued and will be returned.

Most of what an up-to-date hero does is love in all manner of ways. A man can't really give himself in love to a woman until he gets past his puberty rituals; then he no longer has to prove his masculinity and his heterosexuality by seducing more women. Love is a quite personal relationship, but a man cannot love a specific woman if he dislikes women in general. A man who would love a woman personally must come to love womankind, though not so personally.

Every man must become a Magician; he must know the tricks of life, be aware of what lies below the surface, and be unafraid of it. He must know how things work—not just mechanical things but nature and relationships as well. The boy who would be a man must seek out teachers and mentors who can unfold the world's mysteries and who can share their delight in the process of learning. And then he must be prepared to pass on that knowledge. He may go on adventures to learn new things to bring back to others. A man must be both student and teacher, must be a lover of lore and know-how.

The most important thing the new Magician must reveal to his loved ones is the inner world of life as a man. The secret that has been kept from women and children throughout patriarchy is the truth about what it feels like to be a man—the doubts about strength and courage; the fear of women's power to define a man's masculinity and to grant it through sexual response or take it back through anger; the fear of risking one's life for one's masculinity, and the greater fear of not doing so; and the awareness that almost every honest man (except apparently those gay men who insist they have known they were gay since the age of four) has had to struggle with doubts about his sexual identity. Only men who are Magicians can process this secret knowledge and relax their flexed masculinity long enough to step up from masculine *candidate* (trying to prove manhood) to masculine *practitioner* (doing the things a man does as a man).

The postpatriarchal hero must also find in himself the King, not the boss but the exemplar of Boy Scout virtues, the strong and steady source of calm wisdom and judgment, of patient, tolerant loyalty—the guy who is always there for his loved ones. Under old-fashioned patriarchy, kings and heads of households, as worldly representatives of God, would bring fertility, blessing, and order to their realms. The postpatriarchal counterparts to fertility, blessing, and order are more subtle: producing and performing good works that will make life better for others; creating with an equal partner an atmosphere in which each family member can achieve maximum physical, intellectual, and emotional well-being, plus security, productivity, and creativity; and embodying the virtues and strengths that will hold the family together and be emulated by others. It has nothing to do with being the boss.

Fertility is not valued in an overpopulated world, and a father figure is not appreciated for creating babies but for raising and nurturing the children he creates and any children he finds along the way. I.e., the world does not need his sperm as much as his milk. Once a baby is weaned, a man can provide just as much nurturing as a woman can, and his nurturing means more because it is rarer; it comes from a man, the gender the child is in danger of knowing less intimately.

A father figure's *blessing* is still crucial to the well-being of his loved ones, even if he has little of a more tangible nature to give. If, in his shame and failure to see his own value, he fails to anoint and bless his children, he does great harm. Unanointed boys, trying to become men, are particularly likely to pursue the labors of traditional masculinity to the end point of suicide or homicide, while unanointed girls are likely to sell themselves into various forms of slavery in order to get the overpriced and overvalued attention and approval of a man.

Every boy needs a man who will tell him he can relax the masculine striving and start living his life. The father figure's anointment may be as terse as the laconic Farmer Hoggett's final words to the porcine Babe, who has just won the Australian sheepdog competition: "That'll do, pig." Or it may be as celebratory as it was in *My Left Foot*, in which Christy Brown's father, who had refused to acknowledge the existence of his son severely handicapped with cerebral palsy, watches in amazement as the boy spells out the word "Mother" on the concrete floor with a piece of chalk grasped between his toes. Realizing that the boy is not profoundly retarded after all, the father picks him up off the floor, hoists him onto his shoulder, carries him to his regular pub, and bursts in announcing, "This is my son, Christy Brown, genius."

A father figure must still bring *order* to his world, in part by honoring the earth, in part by guiding and respecting others, in part by embodying the virtues he would have others emulate, but primarily by controlling the only person he is permitted to control: himself. As he desperately tries to prove his manhood, man has become the greatest danger on earth, the greatest danger in each home. If a man is to make the home safe for his family, he must do it by controlling himself, not others. And one thing he must particularly take care to control is his selfish longing to be "head of his household" and lord it over his loved ones.

In a postpatriarchal world, men have to strive toward the kingly virtues without the need to be crowned. We don't have to know best all the time. We don't have to restrict ourselves to the tasks and emotions that were traditionally male. We get to screw up; we don't get to pretend that we didn't. We get to be full-scale human beings, and what's more, we get to talk about how we feel as we go through our lives.

In a postpatriarchal world, we get to give up the splendid isolation that has kept us barricaded in our cave, fearing that contact with others will bring forth emotions and needs and vulnerabilities we were supposed to be too strong and self-reliant to show. We don't have to keep ourselves separate from any woman we are not actively screwing, beating, or rescuing at that moment. We don't have to keep ourselves separate from other guys we aren't fighting with or against at that moment. Since we are not expected to sacrifice our lives for our masculinity, we can go ahead and value the experience of our life and even let other people know what it feels like to be us.

The great advantage for postpatriarchal men, then, is that we don't have to die for our masculinity. The disadvantage is that we cannot expect, much less demand, that we be worshiped for it. It seems like a small price to pay, but men who languish and pout because they can't be macho heroes anymore just don't get it.

The mythopoetic men's movement, inspired by Robert Bly, brought men together, often in the woods, to comfort one another, to mourn their fathers, and to cherish the planet. It has been a coming together of fatherless sons for male nurturance. Men may never before have revealed the commonality of the secret shame of life as a man. Despite the talk of Warriors and the ever-present fear of feminist rage, the mythopoets have not been much concerned with restoration of men's patriarchal power. What made their coming together possible was the shared acceptance, and even welcoming, of men's diminished postpatriarchal state.

More recently, the fundamentalist Christian group Promise Keepers offers the same male sanctuary, with men hugging one another and bonding through the revelation of their shameful weaknesses—only these guys are doing it in football stadiums rather than under the trees. Bill McCartney, the group's intense football-coach founder, makes much of man's need to take spiritual responsibility and serve his family, and the primary emphasis is on reversing men's irresponsibility in family life.

But there seems to be a voice in Promise Keepers calling for men to become head of the household again. While it isn't quite clear what a man is supposed to do as head of the household, McCartney (who seems to be more of a revival leader than a thinker) suggests it may mean serving and taking family responsibility as their first priority without having to be nagged into it. The idea still scares the National Organization for Women, since some of these men seem to be calling for a patriarchal revival and telling their families that if they can't be boss, they'll run away from home—that is, if they can't pitch, they won't play.

I'm sure most of the Promise Keepers are doing something admirable: They are asking to be let back into family life and are promising to behave themselves as grown-ups this time around. A lot of good men, disoriented by the changes in their world in recent decades, are turning to this group. I hope that on their way back to responsible family life they don't get sidetracked by a need to be the boss or to speak for God.

It seems to me that after these decades of running from family life, men have enough of a job just being responsible adults and learning how to be fully sensitive human beings. The effort to resurrect patriarchy seems suicidal and can be destructive to men's families and men's lives as well as their spirits and their efforts to learn to love the experience of life. In the emerging postpatriarchal world, we men have lost little—only our illegitimate power and, with it, our isolation. But we have gained much—our lives and the opportunity to experience them. In a postpatriarchal world, women can be equal partners and men can be compatriots and confidants rather than just competitors. We never have to be lonely again.

Masculinity That Works

The great question which I have not been able to answer, despite my thirty years of research into the feminine soul, is "What does a woman want?"

—Sigmund Freud

I, being far too ambitious, am seeking someone with the body of a boy, the soul of a woman, the wisdom of a father, and the strength of almighty God.

—Anonymous female novelist

Men do not get around to asking themselves Freud's ultimate question until they have already been trained to be unconcerned with what a woman wants but still terrified of her displeasure when she doesn't get it. The answer to the question is of course obvious: She wants to be asked personally what she personally wants (unless she is one of those Romantic Narcissists who only feels loved if some guy can read her mind. Such women are nuts. Avoid them.)

Routinely, in my practice I ask women what a man has done in her life that has made her love and value him. They all tell me pretty much the same thing. While most men think that women would be attracted to bigger bankrolls, bigger peckers, or bigger pecs, the names of H. Ross Perot, John C. Holmes, and Fabio rarely come up. A few women, bloodthirsty creatures who require human sacrifice, have appreciated a man's willingness to give up his wife, his children, or his mother for them, but almost all the rest say the same few things: They want a man to talk and listen to her, to show attention to her rather than inhaling all the oxygen in the room himself. Sure she expects him to work and she hopes he enjoys it, but that's not his only job. He needn't be a master of the universe, just an equal partner to her. And that runs contrary to much that he has learned up until now.

Betsy, my wife of thirty-seven years, is clear on it. She's pleased with me when I cook fabulous gourmet delights for her and clean up my own mess. She is not pleased when I cook fabulous gourmet delights for company, bask in the praise, and then leave the mess for her to clean up. She is pleased with her son when he tells her how wonderful she is. She is displeased with him when he tells her interminably how wonderful he is. She was pleased with her ninety-three-year-old father when he thanked her for what she did for him. She was displeased when he thanked *me* for what she had done for him and took *her* good works for granted because he felt nurturing and care were expected from a woman. She is mildly sympathetic when I have to go to the trouble of feeding my ego with trophies and goodies and fan mail. She wants to be appreciated and loved by her loved ones, not by strangers in the world.

After asking "What's a man ever done for you to make him worth your trouble?" one answer came from Pauline, who grew up poor in a black ghetto up North. She told the story of her father getting up early when it snowed, shoveling the snow, and then gathering all the kids in the neighborhood to take them to school. He never made much money but always kept a little "Popsicle change" to give the kids a treat. He was renowned in the neighborhood for his magical ability to fix bicycles. He went to all her sporting events and took her and her brothers and sisters to work with him when he could and took them fishing whenever he went. He taught his children to work and play, delighting in doing it with them, and he taught them to get along on very little. He was loving and much loved, and got dressed up and took his wife dancing once a week. Pauline found a man much like him to marry, but eventually he died. After raising her kids, she is now raising her grandchildren and has become famous in the neighborhood for her skill at fixing bicycles. She hopes to find another man but doesn't need a man to define her, support her, or give her life meaning, only to share the experience.

Pleasing a woman is certainly the most frightening task a man ever tries to perform, especially if he tries to do it from the traditional male posture of demonstrating his disdain for all things female, his restricted emotional life, his toughness and aggression, his lack of need for her, and his rabid homophobia. Most men, though, are less concerned with pleasing a woman than with pleasing the other guys, those from his past and those with whom he seeks sanctuary from the confusing world of women who scare men by trying to get them to forget the masculinity training of their youth and act like grown-ups. Most guys are better prepared to run through a ton of opposing linemen out to crush them or a barrage of machine-gun fire than to face a woman's displeasure. Death, war, and football feel like play for a boy; a woman's anger feels like work for a man.

A lot of men, even in their state of disorientation about the job description for men and the function of their masculinity, do a good-enough job of keeping relationships together over the long haul, of raising their children to be able to share a world with them, and of making themselves rea-

sonably happy without imposing too much on everybody
else. A lot of guys are man enough but wear themselves out
trying to do it right or trying to find some way to win at it.
If they only knew how little masculinity it takes!

We're not likely to know that unless we talk about it with
the other guys, compare the experiences, and swap the secrets
of being a man. The greatest tragedy of men's lives is our
loneliness, our failure to share the experiences of life with
others. We live our lives with women and do things with
other guys; we tell jokes and tall tales, and brag to one another and insult one another (as a form of affection), but we
don't often reveal to one another what it feels like to be a
man. And because we don't talk about our lives, we don't
get a perspective on life. Jane Smiley described it in *A Thousand Acres*: "[Men] all had misbehaved, and failed, and suffered. . . . I had suffered, too, and all the women I knew, but
there seemed to be a dumb, unknowing quality to the way
the men had suffered, as if, like animals, it was not possible
for them to gain perspective on their suffering."

Of course it is possible for men to gain the perspective that
will make sense of their suffering, that will make their pain
part of the human condition, to be shared with others rather
than their individual defeat and shame, one of Pa Joad's
"jerks." All we have to do is talk about it with one another.
We talk about our suffering with women and expect forgiveness for not being heroes and we expect nurturance as com-
pensation, but we gain perspective when we talk about our
suffering with other men who can comfort and understand
us. Masculinity that works is lived in the company of other
men rather than secretly, hiding behind the nurturance and
protection of women.

Secrets of Being a Happy Grown Man

As we move from a patriarchal to a postpatriarchal model of
masculinity, a man need not feel ashamed for failing to

match the macho myths, but he must not be ashamed, either, for finding in himself primeval male characteristics and drive: a dedication to getting the job done even if it hurts; a spirit of adventure even if it is dangerous; a longing to see what is over the next hill; a love of nature and all things earthy and raw and wild; an itch for physical activity and turning thoughts and emotions into action; an exhilaration at the smell of sweat and blood; a fascination with games; a tendency to classify and make things predictable and ordered. All those things that seem part of man's nature are quite compatible with adulthood, with family life, and with civilization. Never apologize for being a man. It may not be the thing on which you stake your pride, but it is not something to be ashamed of, either. It is a fact of both nature and nurture.

Your job as a grown man is to get past the contests of adolescence, declare yourself a man so you don't have to keep proving it, do your life's work, and embark on life's adventures. You don't have to be master of the universe. You don't have to be the boss at home or at work. You don't need more than one woman and can't have more than one equal partner. You don't have to die for your masculinity. You can relax the model of masculinity you learned growing up; it is outdated. What the world needs is for you to live your life as a man and tell your loved ones what you experience, what you learn, and what it feels like to be you.

I've written more extensively about becoming a man in *Man Enough: Fathers, Sons, and the Search for Masculinity*, but here are a few hints and exercises on how to do it.

1. If you want to be treated as a grown man, dress the part. Dress the way you'd like to feel about yourself rather than the way you experience yourself inside. But to be a grown man takes even more: You have to change not

only your clothes and hairstyle but your values and attitudes. Get your thinking straight.

2. The world is changing rapidly for all of us. We are all scared, and we are all faking it. You are not alone even though you may feel alone. Tell other men what it feels like to be you. Take down the barriers between you and other men. Closeness to other guys will not make you gay, but you would be no less a man if it did.

3. One of the tragedies of being raised primarily by women is that we men are led to believe we must give up our mothers in order to become grown men. We are led to fear that our mothers will keep us from becoming men. They won't. We still need them. Make your mother a friend and a peer, and talk things over with her. She knows you better than anyone else. Avoid the temptation to run from her when she sees the child that you try to keep hidden inside you.

4. You can't understand yourself as a man until you understand your father and how he learned to be a man. Understand your father even if he is more or less dead and stuffed in front of the TV set with a beer can in his hand. Find out what he was doing and feeling that made him too busy to show you how to be a man. He is the most important person in your life as a man and will always be the prime determinant of your masculinity. In addition, find some grown men, older men in your family and outside it, and get to know how they think and what they feel. You need elders and mentors as well as a father.

5. But the world of masculinity has changed since your father's day. You have more freedom than he did. Do the things your father was afraid to do, the things he

would have considered dangerously feminine: cry, hug your male friends, change diapers, read a romance novel (one is quite enough), do the dishes, knit a sweater—whatever it was that he was afraid to do because he was holding tightly to his more rigidly patriarchal, dehumanizing model of masculinity. When you do something he considered women's stuff, you set yourself free without giving up one drop of testosterone, one Y chromosome. Before you are your own man, you must do this and also notice that your balls don't fall off.

6. Expose yourself to the half of the world you were taught to fear. Go to movies that are not about car crashes and broken glass and things exploding but instead are about people baring their hearts and souls to one another.

I'm quite sure that the second most important thing (after actually listening to a woman) that men can do to get themselves past the stifling limits of our gender training is to see a better class of movies. For men who have overdosed, whether they know it or not, on tales of heroism and macho glory, there is an antidote: classic films about flawed men and their relationships, such as *Citizen Kane, All About Eve, Ordinary People, Terms of Endearment, Moonstruck, Hamlet,* the *Godfather* trilogy, and *Bull Durham.* There are also more recent masterpieces of psychological wisdom such as *Secrets and Lies, Marvin's Room, Ulee's Gold, The Full Monty,* and even *Jerry Maguire,* whose insights are far beyond *Cheers, Home Improvement,* or *Seinfeld.* Every man who would be an adult should memorize the father-son classics *I Never Sang for My Father, East of Eden, Kramer vs. Kramer, Field of Dreams, The Rack, A River Runs Through It, Boyz N the Hood, Nobody's Fool,* and *Dad.* And the male-bonding flicks *Women in Love, Gallipoli, Stand by Me, Diner, Bye Bye Love, City Slickers,* and even *Of Mice and Men* might take a guy a few steps past *The Three*

Musketeers, The Man Who Would Be King, and *The Dirty Dozen.* And if a man wanted to understand the lives of women, he could try *Out of Africa, The Piano, Howards End, Thelma and Louise,* or *Waiting to Exhale* as well as those ultimate chick flicks by Jane Austen, *Sense and Sensibility* and *Emma.* It's a whole different world from John Wayne, James Bond, and Rambo.

7. Rethink how you learned what you did learn. Watch again the movies of your youth and rethink what those films taught you about men and masculinity. Redo your models. The most efficient way to change yourself as a man is to choose more relaxed heroes.

8. Overcome your fear of reliance on others. Stop at a filling station and ask for directions. You may find it less threatening the first time you do this if you are not actually lost but know the way quite well; however, don't let the service station attendant in on your little secret.

9. It is wrong to be right; it puts other people down and keeps you from learning anything new. Practice telling people that you may be wrong about the subject under discussion. Practice saying "I don't know. What do you think?" to your loved ones and those you care about. The rewards will amaze you.

10. Part of our masculinity training involved playing sports. That's great; keep it up. Another part of it involved watching other people play sports. If the players are your children, that's okay. But watching athletic events creates a druglike state: Brain-numbing adrenaline rushes lead us to see life as a series of win-lose contests. Don't read the sports page or watch any sports on television for a month and see what you find yourself doing and talking about with others.

11. Money costs too much. Put some money in a bowl and set it on fire. Keep doing this until you stop crying and realize that heat and light are worth more than money. So is your life. Once you have done this exercise, anytime you feel you don't have enough money, give some of what you have to someone who has less. Give money to the symphony, for example; if you make the world a more beautiful place, you'll feel rich.

12. Winning is not everything. Deliberately lose an actual competition and practice being happy about it. Just think how good your children are going to feel about you and themselves when you can still be happy even after you lose a contest (especially to them).

13. Learn about women. In addition to talking to your wife, your mother, your sister, and your daughter about being a woman, read women's magazines. You will be shocked, but you'll learn that women are very different from how you thought they were.

14. Also read the hard-core feminist literature. It will change your view of women forever and ultimately for the better. But at first it will anger and depress you because these women who are telling everyone how things ought to be don't have the foggiest notion what a man is about. They assume that we have amazing powers and nasty motives, while we know that we are powerless despite our very best intentions. This exercise will be disturbing, but that is the point. We can see ourselves clearly only when we see how half the world's population sees us.

15. Stop fantasizing about sex with other women; try imagining their emotional lives instead. If you must interact with a woman who turns you on, talk to her about how much you love your wife or your girlfriend.

That may make her lust crazily after you, so if she throws herself at you, turn her down, go home, and tell your honey about it.

16. Of all life's adventures, the most magical, the one that will teach you the most about yourself and your fellows, is raising children. It isn't the only thing you can do in life and doesn't interfere with anything else that is worth doing, but I definitely commend it.

17. Live your life as a model for your grandchildren, imagining the world you hope your grandson and your granddaughter will inherit. Change the world for them.

18. If you have been the boss at work too long for your own humility, volunteer to do some work at which you are definitely not the boss. I know CEOs who do some weekend carpentry with Jimmy Carter at Habitat for Humanity, building solid homes for the poor. On the other hand, if you haven't been the boss at work, find some project in which you can be the boss. Shelters for the homeless never seem to have enough people who are willing to take on some responsibility. Everybody needs to experience both leading and following, both winning and losing, both success and failure.

19. Get in touch with the guys you envied when you were growing up. Find out about their lives as men. You'll be surprised.

20. Think of yourself as a success and act accordingly by treating other people as if they thought you were important and your treatment of them mattered.

21. Never let your masculinity interfere with your humanity. Practice thinking of yourself not as a man but as a human.

4

How to Be a Grown Woman

*Feminism is no longer a group of organizations
or leaders. It's the expectations that parents have
for their daughters, and their sons, too. It's the
way we talk about and treat one another. It's
who makes the money and who makes the
compromises and who makes the dinner. It's a
state of mind. It's the way we live now.*

—Anna Quindlen, "And Now,
Babe Feminism"

The Job Description

"Femininity, in all its contrivances, is a very active endeavor," Susan Brownmiller says in *Femininity*. She goes on:
"The masculine principle is better understood as a driving
ethos of superiority designed to inspire straightforward, con-
fident success, while the feminine principle is composed of
vulnerability, the need for protection, the formalities of compliance and the avoidance of conflict—in short, an appeal of
dependence and good will that gives the masculine principle
its romantic validity and its admiring applause."

Women have always had power in personal relationships
but have been taught to wield that power indirectly. Under

patriarchy, femininity was often a set of illusions to keep from scaring men and making them feel unmasculine; it may even have been a trick, but it was presumably based on women's biological capacity to create and sustain life, and thus to tend and monitor relationships. Femininity has always required great sensitivity to what was going on inside and between people, and perhaps a higher priority was given to the relationships and the long-range goals than to the competition or contest at hand. It may look to men like weakness or passivity. It is not.

In *Dangerous Liaisons,* a modern play adapted from Laclos's 1782 novel, John Malkovich as malevolent sensualist Valmont asks Glenn Close as seductress Madame de Merteuil: "I've often wondered how you managed to invent yourself." Her reply:

> I had no choice, did I? I'm a woman. . . . I've always known I was born to dominate your sex and avenge my own. . . . When I came out in society, I was fifteen. I already knew that the role I was condemned to, namely to keep quiet and do what I was told, gave me the opportunity to listen and observe, not to what people told me, which naturally was of no interest, but to whatever it was they were trying to hide. I practiced detachment. I learned how to look cheerful when under the table I stuck a fork into the back of my hand. I became a virtuoso of deceit. It wasn't pleasure I was after but knowledge. I consulted the strictest moralists to learn how to appear, philosophers to find out how to think, and novelists to see what I could get away with, and in the end I distilled everything into one wonderfully simple principle: Win or die.

When women were condemned to dutiful passivity, they had to learn to deceive and manipulate, to wield power and exact revenge indirectly. In a postpatriarchal society, if a woman knows femininity is an illusion, it is a useful skill for her armamentarium, but if she takes it literally, it will destroy her. The greatest power women have over men is that women know gender is just a game and femininity just an illusion, while men are likely to take their masculinity as seriously as a war or a heart attack and defend it with their lives.

In our society a good little girl is called upon to obey and comfort her mother, please and delight her father, subjugate herself to her religion and cloak her expectations of others in the authority of its mantle, find a way to nurture her children—without getting close enough to smother them—and still have plenty of time and energy left to titillate and oh-so-subtly structure her husband. On top of that she may hold down a job or two and keep in such glorious shape that the man she serves and supervises will never notice any other woman of any age. And her therapist will demand that she assert herself fiercely. The patriarchal job description for women was degrading and restrictive, but the postpatriarchal job description for women is absurd and overwhelming.

Clearly, negotiating life's obstacle course amid the debris of patriarchy can be confusing at best. Many people—women as well as men—yearn for a patriarchal revival in which they no longer have to think about or even listen to one another.

Gender fundamentalism is seductive. We've been raised within a strongly gendered world, trained to conform to rules and roles specified by gender. Each of us carries powerful outdated gender restrictions and commandments inside us. These old defining ideas may get just enough reinforcement here and there to keep them alive within us like a giant tapeworm even after the modern world has granted us permission to pass and bury them. Indeed, while patriarchy may be considered illegal by the courts, it is still alive and feeding on us in our gut; the patriarchal ideas inside us influence, limit, and enslave us far more than any of the patriarchal artifacts and throwbacks we are likely to encounter in the world.

Our gender training stripped away whatever did not fit with the fashion of the era and turned each of us into half-persons. We have a lifetime struggle to recapture the parts of ourselves that were lost. Becoming a full-scale postpatriarchal adult involves not just mastering the steps of our own gender's dance but learning the skills and emotions that were reserved for the other gender. The postpatriarchal job for women as well as for men is to learn the other half without losing our identity. Each of us is at a different point in that tricky and delicately personal transition, coming at it from different directions and without a clear end point. But each step away from gender absolutism, however scary, is a breath of freedom.

If women are to understand what is going on, they must speak what they feel and consider it worth hearing. If men are to understand what is happening to their world—or what they had thought was their world—they must emerge from their caves and hear the voices of women.

The Voices of Women

That image of the madonna-mother . . . has disabled us from knowing that, just as men are more than fathers, women are more than mothers. It has kept us from hearing their voices when they try to tell us their aspirations.

—Lillian Breslow Rubin,
Women of a Certain Age

One of the first things that happened when the stranglehold of patriarchy began to loosen and men began to assert their inalienable rights to life, liberty, and the pursuit of happiness was an assertion by women that they had the same rights. Mary Wollstonecraft wrote *A Vindication of the Rights of Woman* in 1792, between the American and French revolutions, arguing that if women are not as well educated as men, they can never be equal partners and true companions to each other. As she put it, "I do earnestly wish to see the distinction of sex confounded in society, unless where love animates the behaviour. For the distinction is, I am firmly persuaded, the foundation of the weakness of character ascribed to woman . . . and the same cause accounts for their preferring the graceful before the heroic virtues."

When women found their voices and began to read and write, they read and wrote about their own lives. The greatest female writers wrote only of domestic and internal affairs, and found the world contained within those narrow boundaries. Women novelists such as George Sand, George Eliot, and the Brontë sisters, writing about freedom to choose sexual and romantic partners, took male pen names in the hope of attracting male readers. If men could understand the inner lives of women, then both could find happiness.

Jane Austen (1775–1817), generally considered the greatest English writer after Shakespeare, was our most trenchant social observer of life under enlightened patriarchy. She could step past the restricted life of a woman in her times and expose the power of the social order to referee the gender rules and the mating games; she saw their passionless underpinnings.

As the nineteenth century proceeded and women increasingly had more say about their lives, they could still enslave themselves to men with fantasies of romance. Women often preferred to fight for freedom from their fathers' privilege of choosing a mate for them rather than for freedom from the mate that was chosen. Dying for a love of one's own choosing was the ultimate emotional self-determination.

But it was a man, Henrik Ibsen, who noticed the dead end for women in traditional marriage. Nora in *A Doll's House* walked out on her husband and kids in 1879. Her husband had told her, "First and foremost, you are a wife and mother." Nora did not agree and replied, "I believe that first and foremost I am an individual, just as much as you are." She declares, "If I am ever to reach any understanding of myself and the things around me, I must learn to stand alone. That's why I can't stay here with you any longer." Not many women followed Nora out the door, though family life of the time prevented women from being full adults, much less happy ones.

Women acquired the right to vote in 1920 in the States, in 1928 in Britain, and in time essentially everywhere. But this did not free women to pursue happiness, and gradually women decided the traditional family was part of the problem. In *The Second Sex* in 1949, Simone de Beauvoir said, "As long as the family and the myth of the family . . . have not been destroyed, women will still be oppressed."

Women were enfranchised to take on more jobs and more responsibilities but without giving up the ones they already had. Women, still burdened with interminable reproduction and child care, gained the right to become more stimulating and sexually uninhibited partners for men, who competed with their own children for their wives' nurturance. Stephanie Coontz said in *The Way We Never Were* in 1992, "The hybrid idea that a woman can be fully absorbed with her youngsters while simultaneously maintaining passionate sexual excitement with her husband was a 1950s invention that drove thousands of women to therapists, tranquilizers, or alcohol when they actually tried to live up to it."

Betty Friedan faced *The Feminine Mystique* in 1963: "American housewives have not had their brains shot away, nor are they schizophrenic in the clinical sense. But if . . . the fundamental human drive is not the urge for pleasure or the satisfaction of biological needs, but the need to grow and to realize one's full potential, their comfortable, empty, purposeless days are indeed cause for a nameless terror."

A deluge of feminist literature quickly followed as women made themselves aware not only of the oppressive nature of the society but the oppressive aspects of their most personal relationships. Friedan and her followers were not man-haters. The problem was patriarchy, not men themselves. As Friedan quipped to the *Christian Science Monitor,* "Men weren't really the enemy. . . . They were fellow victims suffering from an outmoded masculine mystique that made them feel unnecessarily inadequate when there were no bears to kill."

In 1996 I was on a panel with Friedan discussing the healing of gender wounds. She explained that women are three generations ahead of men in awareness of the gender system and what it has been doing to them. Many women are getting tired of waiting for men to grow up.

What's A Poor Girl to Do When the Men Refuse to Grow Up?

The problem began with boys refusing to grow up, but soon grown men were lapsing back into adolescence, defining a new period of irresponsibility, the *midlife crisis,* in which men dump their wives and children in the hope of rediscovering youth with a woman who is younger, thinner, dumber, poorer, and beset with more problems. This is insane, of course, but it is based on the furtive hope that an aging man with a woman he hasn't hurt yet may still become a hero in someone's eyes.

Women tried responding by increasing their levels of self-sacrificial nurturance, but that didn't lure the men into adulthood. It merely made them see mothering as a source of guilt, and they ran away even harder from women who would trap them into grown manhood.

Mothers found themselves stuck at home alone while first the men and then the children preferred to conduct their lives almost anywhere else. Men went to bars, golf courses, offices, or up into trees to wait for deer, all to keep from coming under the control of the wife-mother at home. Children slept all day and stayed up all night in cars, on street corners, or in crowds so that they didn't have to spend time with Mother and take lessons in growing up. Men and children, struggling to avoid adulthood, dreaded Mother and her competence, virtue, and adultness that made them feel guilty because they had no interest in reciprocating.

One way that women tried to turn men into parents was to stop being available to protect them from moving up into manhood. Depressed and exhausted Meryl Streep left workaholic Dustin Hoffman and their son in *Kramer vs. Kramer* in 1979, and the poor man had to learn to be a father when he didn't even know what grade his child was in. Droves of women began running away from home, attending to their own needs, and shedding the burdens the men had imposed on them. Some heroic men picked up the job; most didn't.

As the exodus from family life gathered steam, there was soon no one to raise the children, and only Macaulay Culkin was left at home.

In the space of two generations we have effectively destroyed the human family, made the home a place no one wanted to be, and raised a generation of men and women unfit for family life. We're now burdened by a generation of petulant geriatric adolescents who demand everything and give little back. Each generation which runs from adulthood means another generation that is raised without adult parents and that sees adulthood from a greater and greater distance.

Both men and women are facing a whole new world. Both are confused about the roles of women because both have had mothers, been overwhelmed by mothers, and have taken mothers for granted. Not too many years ago my strongly feminist niece constantly wore a button announcing: I AM NOT YOUR MOTHER.

Learning Adulthood from Mothers

THE COUNTESS: What are you hiding from me?
HER FRIENDS: The world has changed, Madame.
THE COUNTESS: Why wasn't I told?

—Jean Giraudoux, *The Madwoman of Chaillot*

Everybody else in a woman's life, even husbands and gods, can be exchanged or ignored when they're outgrown, but her mother is with her always—sitting on the shoulders of her psyche proclaiming what she is doing wrong, according to the mother's dated instruction book, and occasionally, if she is lucky, what she is doing right (even though it may not be). A woman never escapes her mother, so she had better get her into perspective.

From the moment of birth a mother teaches her children about gender, and while she can only guess at masculinity— thereby producing sons who can only fake it unless there is a father around to model it—she can confidently understand what it looks like and feels like to be a woman, or at least a woman of her own era. Mother sends sons out to play the ballgames of boyhood that form the basis for the money games of adulthood, and while the boys are safely out of earshot, she tells daughters the secrets of life and demonstrates the really useful skills for the care, feeding, beautification, and pacification of the family and the world.

Few girls grow up without mothers or mother surrogates.

But many will, at the stroke of puberty, reject what their mothers have taught.

Lyn Mikel Brown and Carol Gilligan's research on female self-esteem (*Meeting at the Crossroads*) revealed that girls whose childhood worlds, in environments like school and home, are dominated by seemingly powerful women have higher self-esteem than boys until around puberty. Then boys develop muscles and athletic skills that thrill the adult world, while girls' bodies grow vulnerable, and they are suddenly expected to subordinate themselves to the egos of the boys they had so recently bested and disdained. The girls realize their fate in life may be to make men feel strong and successful, and their status in the world may depend less on their own accomplishments than on how well they can satisfy men.

Girls at that point experience a precipitous drop in self-esteem. They may begin then to see their mother's life more clearly. The daughter notices and scorns the mother's lost career; the mother's inhibition in grasping and wielding power in the world; her failure to sustain or equalize marriage; the disregard, abuse, and contempt she receives from men in her life; the disregard, abuse, and contempt she shows for the men she serves, abuses, or tolerates. And her terrifying unhappiness.

Girls (not in all cultures but in our own) get a lot more mothering than boys get fathering, but they don't tend to value it as much. The girl who rejects her mother's life rather than building on it remains as disoriented as the boy who fails to know his father well enough to use his model as a starting point. Most girls do get a dozen years or so of modeling from mothers before they run from home toward the trendier models of their generation. And they revive an appreciation of their mother's life once they start a family of their own.

Queenie's mother raised her beautiful and talented daughter to be a sexually repressed socialite and the wife of a doctor or lawyer, and when the daughter leaned toward passion and self-expression, the frantic woman countered with powerful assaults of guilt. But Queenie dismissed all her mother's anxieties and spoiled her mother's plans for her. After a couple of failed marriages, she built on skills she had learned from her carpenter father and became a successful builder, with a supportive, entertaining, intermittently employed husband. Once she was free and successful and clearly out of reach of her mother's panics, she could finally love her mother and get close to her again.

Daughters, no less than sons, may have to escape Mother before they can safely appreciate her, stop differentiating themselves from her, and put into operation her many messages. Yet when daughters exercise the freedoms their mothers didn't have a few decades before, they are likely to feel guilty, as if they are betraying them by going into territory that was forbidden to them. If they can feel they are fulfilling their mother's dreams, their adventures may tighten the bond between mother and daughter, but if the mother protects herself by disapproving the new opportunities in a changing world, the daughter's exploits may loosen that bond. Of course, if the mother is happy, the daughter will be happy and will want to be like her. If she's unhappy, her wisdom and nurturance are for naught.

Mothers should not be discarded cavalierly; even the craziest, meanest, and most miserable of them have a lifetime of learning to teach. Once you are grown, it is not necessary to obey or please her, but you must listen to her and understand her life, her times, and the reasons she sees things as she does. Mother generally knows best but only if she knows the whole story, and you must know how to translate her advice from her life and generation to yours. Know her and let her know you. Come on, she's your mother.

Learning Adulthood from Fathers

Why must they do everything their mothers do?
Why can't they turn out like their fathers
instead?

—Henry Higgins in Alan J. Lerner's
My Fair Lady

Girls receive even less fathering than boys do if that is possible. Fortunately for girls, they are not nearly as dependent on their fathers as boys are. In contrast to the crippling devastation wreaked on boys' lives by a shortage of fathering, fatherless girls can grow up fine and can be successful and productive adults—unless, of course, they try to date men, marry men, raise men, or work with men. If men are foreign and mysterious to women, they may be overvalued. What is more, the most excessively hypermasculine behavior of philandering, controlling, or contending may seem desirable and proof of masculine power rather than a sign of weakness and shame, stupidity or psychosis.

"Fathers are the first men daughters ever love. Fathers teach what men are and what sort of treatment daughters can expect from them. They give the first inkling of what the world expects from women. As children, daughters fight for their attention, bask in their praise, rebel against their authority, hide from their anger, weep over their rejection, delight in their smiles, and thrill to their manliness." This is according to Barbara Goulter and Joan Minninger in *The Father-Daughter Dance*. If fathers knew how important they were to their daughters, they would do things differently, but men's fear of women affects how they deal with daughters as well as mothers and wives.

Fathers of daughters have several crucial jobs:

The best father respects things that are traditionally female and shows it even as he forgets, at least some of the time, that his daughter is a girl. He teaches her all the things he knows about being a human being living a life in the world.

A father needs to teach his daughter, as much as his son, to move and challenge her body and claim the world as her playing field. At one time the world taught women they were the weaker sex, too delicate with their natural femininity to build and train their bodies for sports and games and adventures. It was a dirty trick. Each Olympic year the women who are active from childhood and are trained to use their bodies move closer to the performance levels of the men. And even more important than winning, an unexercised body cannot support a happy brain.

As the first man in his daughter's life, a father must make his daughter feel she is attractive and then not make an issue of it. Looks mustn't take priority over matters of real substance. His delight in his daughter must not center on her appearance. Victoria Secunda warns in *Women and Their Fathers:* "The line between flirtation and carnality gets murky when Daddy is *too* responsive to his daughter's appearance, when his admiration becomes *too* personal, when he is more complimentary toward her than toward his own wife."

Fathers nowadays often run from their daughters because of fears of incest. Men who do hands-on child care and change a lot of diapers become immune to incestuous impulses; it is hard for anyone to sexualize a little thing in a dirty diaper. If a father sexualizes the relationship with his daughter, even without acting on it, she in turn is at risk for sexualizing herself and every encounter she has subsequently with a man. But if the overly cautious father pulls away from her and fails to make her feel attractive, the girl's sense of herself as a sexual person may end up being left to the mercy of eighth-grade boys.

A father must stick around. A girl's experience with her father prepares her for dealing with the men to come later. If he abandons her, she may expect to be abandoned and may protect herself by aloofness, anger, infidelity, clinging, jealousy, or any of the techniques a distrustful woman uses to destroy a relationship before it destroys her.

A father must be pleased with his daughter. His greatest gift to her is making her aware that she makes him happy, not by doing things for him but by living her own life and pursuing her own goals.

A father must show respect for his daughter's mother, in her talents and skills, and in her career. If he shows no interest in either woman's career and talents and does not get excited about plans for her future, the girl may have a hard time imagining that she will have one. Because a father is likely to feel more expert at the things he can pass on to his son and may ignore his daughter's future, the woman who is most likely to have spectacular career success is the brotherless daughter of a doting father. She becomes his honorary son and heir.

Just as boys need to learn what women have always known as well as learn all the arts and crafts of masculinity, girls need to learn the other half of the world's lore that their fathers best teach. A woman who didn't get it from Daddy needs to apprentice herself to other men in order to learn the valid lore of manhood. And she needn't give up an ounce of womanliness to do it.

A woman needs male mentors, but she doesn't have to marry stronger, older men to make up for her deficits in being fathered. She needs nonsexual friendships with men who don't feel protective or romantic. If she lets them get sexual, the relationship is ruined (see the movie *Yentl*), and the guy will stop teaching her what he knows and will show it off instead of sharing it. Men are at their most infantile and narcissistic in sexual relationships; they get weird when sex rears its rosy head. If sex is not a factor, men get normal and can even treat a woman as one of the guys, which is one of the experiences she needs in order to become whole.

It is not enough for an adult in a postpatriarchal world to know only half of what a human being must know to be complete. No one has to give up one half for the other half. Only the sort of flat-footedly literal people who get sex-change operations feel compelled to choose between absolute stereotypical maleness and absolute stereotypical femaleness. The rest of us are past that, but boys and girls won't know that soon enough unless their parents know it and teach them. Otherwise, they have to learn it on the street.

Bosom Buddies

Being a woman. That's one career all females have in common, whether we like it or not.

—Bette Davis in Joseph L. Mankiewicz's
All About Eve

Women must learn from one another the things mothers and fathers do not know and do not teach about becoming a happy grown-up. The experiences of other women bring clarity and perspective to life as a woman.

Carol Tavris says in *The Mismeasure of Woman:* "Female friendships . . . are celebrated as being deep, intimate, and true, based as they are on shared feelings and confidences and on women's allegedly greater capacity for connection with others."

Surveys on friendship show that both men and women will name a woman as their best friend. Everyone wants to be close to women (except husbands with secrets). Friendships with women can be safe. Emotions need not be hidden; women want to hear more, not less, about what others—particularly other women—feel. As women have more choices about their lives, they may seem to be going in directions that are far different from one another, juggling the conflicting demands of love and work. But women know they are making choices, and they need to compare lives, the roads they take, the roads not taken. What they have in common is the career of being a woman in a barely and incompletely postpatriarchal world.

The woman who is always a bride and never a bridesmaid is at risk for loneliness and unhappiness, and for letting a man or a series of men define her. It is not safe for a woman to expect a relationship with a man to provide all the human companionship and communication she needs in life. No man, as my daughters and nieces and other critics tell me constantly, can ever understand fully what it is like to be a woman. And none of us can maintain our sanity in life unless we know we are understood.

One of the great advantages women have over men is that women acknowledge and talk about all the tricks and artistry that go into playing out femininity, while men think all the other guys feel the masculinity they are only faking. So women talk about it to one another and bond around it. When women impersonate femininity, they know they're not alone.

Female Impersonators

Women struggle to find models that will permit them access to personal happiness without scaring off men and engulfing children. It is exhausting, and the efforts have led down a variety of dead ends. Women have created a few cherished ways of making themselves miserable.

BEAUTY CONTESTANTS

*The ideology of beauty is the last one
remaining of the old feminine ideologies that
still has the power to control women. It has
taken over the work of social coercion that
myths about motherhood, domesticity,
chastity, and passivity no longer can manage.*

—Naomi Wolf, *The Beauty Myth*

Women have been tortured, scarred, bound, starved, and painted to mold them into the stylish shape that would arouse men and keep them potent, or keep alternatives available. When men started their escape from family life, women began torturing their own bodies in the hope of attracting and holding the increasingly elusive men. As women got more powerful in the world, the masculine ideal of female beauty began to center on littleness, skinniness, and youthfulness. Skinny, barely pubescent-looking women, patterned after Audrey Hepburn, Jacqueline Kennedy, Nancy Reagan, or fashion models, became the prototypes.

Among the things women give up when they try to pass for harmless, weak virginal children are their strength, their mature wisdom, and especially their sensuality. The women who fear looking full-grown are afraid of their own power and opt to abdicate it. It is hard to imagine much sexual abandon and energy from someone self-loathing enough to abhor her own flesh and tolerate only her skin and bones. And some women will have any extra skin cut off and even have a few bones, like ribs, removed.

This death-defying style has conferred status. Tom Wolfe in *Bonfire of the Vanities* talked about "social X rays" who were "starved to perfection," women so thin they were devoid of mass or depth, and you could see right through them.

Horrifyingly, adolescent girls equate thinness with beauty and encourage the anorexia of their peers. Yet while anorexia is stylish, zaftig sex symbols with watermelon breasts, such as Playmate of the Year Anna Nicole Smith, reign supreme in pornography.

Aging in women, even normal maturity, has been declared a deformity to be treated by surgery. Women assure one another they look young even if what they do to keep themselves looking young keeps them from looking healthy or happy.

A potentially happy woman has gotten past her beauty pageant fixation and is willing to be big and muscular even if that makes insecure men feel small and weak. She has learned to love her body for what it can do, can experience, and can create, rather than how stylish it is. She keeps her body healthy, giving it a high priority; she dresses for comfort, action, or whatever catches her fancy, rather than for faux sexuality. She doesn't have to be a female impersonator to be happy. She doesn't have to give away her power.

When I was teaching in Greece recently, a very tall Norwegian couple came to my workshop on the development of sexual identity. The man was dressed in high heels, a flouncy flowered dress, a fluffy wig, and a pound or two of makeup. When he went to the ladies' room, an army of Greek women protested and called the police. At the banquet later that evening, he kept losing his balance on the dance floor. He tottered back and forth to the bathroom and was unable to eat anything; his wife explained that both phenomena were caused by the tightness of his corset. Nonetheless, over the hubbub of the protests from the Greek women, he smiled beatifically at Betsy and me across the table and insisted, "I feel so much better dressed this way." There must be simpler ways of being happy than turning gender appearance into an obsession or a cause célèbre. Most women have been brainwashed into doing what our Norwegian friend was doing:

sacrificing freedom and comfort for gender appearance. It is no less cruelly absurd for women than for men to do it.

FEMINIST OUTRAGE

All men are not slimy warthogs. Some men are silly giraffes, some woebegone puppies, some insecure frogs. But if one is not careful, those slimy warthogs can ruin it for all the others.

—Cynthia Heimel

The First Women's Rights Conference in Seneca Falls, New York, in 1848 proclaimed:

[Man] has compelled her to submit to laws in the formation of which she has no voice. . . . He has taken from her all right to property, even to the wages she earns. . . . In the covenant of marriage, she is compelled to promise obedience to her husband, he becoming to all intents and purposes her master—the law giving him power to deprive her of her liberty, and to administer chastisement. . . . He closes against her all the avenues of wealth and distinction which he considers most honorable to himself. As a teacher of theology, medicine, or law, she is not known. He has denied her the facilities for obtaining a thorough education, all colleges being closed against her. . . . He has created . . . a different code of morals for men and women by which moral delinquencies which exclude women from society are not only tolerated, but deemed of little account to man. He has claimed it as his right to assign for her a sphere of action, when that belongs to her conscience and to her God. He has endeavored in every way that he could to destroy her confidence in her own powers, to lessen her self-respect, and to make her willing to lead a dependent and abject life.

Few of the conditions of 150 years ago apply now. Legally, women are fully enfranchised and hold positions of great power. But there are still men who believe there is a different code of morals for men than for women, who believe men should assign for women a sphere of action, and who set out to destroy her confidence and her self-respect in order to keep her under their control. They haven't updated their worldview lately—but are more to be censured than pitied.

I recently saw a man who was trying to decide whether to marry. His hesitancy had to do with his discomfort over the woman's language. He explained: "Sometimes she uses words that are only appropriate for men to use, and only then when there are no ladies around. You just don't hear a woman say things like 'The Packers sure kicked ass this weekend.'" I laughingly commented that I thought it quite appropriate for women to say things like "I don't think I could live with a man who expected me to care whether or not the Packers got their fucking asses kicked this weekend when he doesn't grant me the voice to say whatever damn fool thing I think or feel." I gently explained that he wasn't ready to marry any woman until he realized that the same rules that apply to him also apply to her, and she must have an equal voice in making the rules. He wondered if I might be "one of those feminists." I assured him I was and warned him that it isn't really safe for a man to marry or raise children of any gender until he is a feminist—that is, committed to gender equality and especially to an equal marital partnership. As he thought it through over the next few sessions, he came to see gender in a quite different way.

There are, sadly, women who are so accustomed to thinking patriarchally that they will subordinate themselves to such attitudes, perhaps because they are misguided enough to want such a man but more often because they have not updated their own worldview lately.

Women who do think about it are understandably angry. But female anger at all men—as if each of us personally created and enforced patriarchy rather than being fellow victims of it—makes relationships with any one man nearly impossible, just as men whining about women's enfranchisement and independence makes relationships with women adversarial. A feminist narcissist may want each man to make up to her for everything other men have done wrong to her or to any of her ancestors. She believes that whatever a man does wrong is proof of men's evil, and whatever she does wrong is a man's fault.

While a woman's anger at men can bring about tighter bonds with other women, it keeps her from realizing the power she has to make her life and relationships more to her liking. It keeps her from noticing that the feminist agenda has been largely achieved in her world, and the most challenging remaining work needs to be done in her own head. Anger is exhausting, weakening, and infantilizing. It makes people feel helpless. It is a sure route to unhappiness.

VICTIMS

Freedom is what you do with what's been done to you.

—Jean-Paul Sartre

Increasing a woman's choices and opportunities is not an unmixed blessing. A woman faces challenges for which she has not been prepared by family or by history, and for which she may receive little support from men or women in her life. A woman who can't grasp the power within her reach may feel defeated and revert to the victim position.

Victims are saying, "This is not my real life. This is a mere shadow of the life I would have had if I had been treated right. My real life was taken away from me by

—my father who left me;
—my mother who beat me;
—my third-grade teacher who humiliated me;
—my uncle who molested me;
—my neighbors who were prejudiced against me;
—my first husband who left me;
—my second husband who collapsed on me."

Females do suffer traumas as they are growing up, just as males do, but they are less likely to have been taught how to fight back effectively. We have all suffered physical abuse, most of it at the hands of males. Every boy has been beat up, picked on, and humiliated by other boys. As females enter former male sanctuaries, they are expected to play by the male rules. Boys' physical and verbal abuse of one another, and respect for one another's ability to tolerate abuse, has been considered a necessary part of masculinity training and preparation for a life as a soldier, athlete, or budding master of the universe. It is no less so for women with those aspirations.

The first young women entering military environments such as The Citadel face boys who go there to be toughened up and trained as military men who can't get their feelings hurt. The boys resent the idea that this is something girls can do as well; girls who go there are going to have to show their toughness. Girls who fight for their right only through the court rather than also on the field, who are out of shape, and whose emotions are too close to the surface to endure pain and humiliation without crying and running away cannot expect respect from guys whose lives have been devoted to making this sort of sacrifice of emotion and individuality.

Equality of opportunity can be legislated, but equality cannot. Women who set their minds and bodies to it can play essentially any game as well as guys can, but can ask no quarter. They don't get to yell foul and play victim when somebody hurts their bodies or their feelings.

Even sexual abuse cannot be viewed from a gender orientation whereby women are victimized in ways that men are not. Most of us—male or female—encounter unwanted, inappropriate sexual treatment before we are grown. Those who were sexually abused by adult members of their families remember it vividly, often with shame and/or rage, and may obsess over the episodes, building a self-image and a worldview centered on those unforgettably horrifying experiences. Some become psychic basket cases; most do not because they process those awful memories and see that they now have powers and freedoms they did not have then. They see that they are no longer weak, helpless, and vulnerable.

If a woman is to become a happy grown-up, she must have a sense of her own power and judgment; she must also have trust in the world around her and trust in her toughness and resiliency when others don't treat her properly. Women who can function only when treated just so are too delicate for either adulthood or happiness.

When we visited my niece Virginia, who was working on her master's in eighteenth-century feminist literature at the University of London, she took us to see a tombstone on the floor of Dorchester Abbey that commemorated Sarah Fletcher, who departed this life at the age of twenty-nine in 1799. It read:

> Reader! If thou hast a heart famed for tenderness and pity, contemplate this spot in which are deposited the remains of a young lady whose artless beauty, innocence of mind, and gentle manners once obtained her the love and esteem of all who knew her. But when

nerves were too delicately spun to bear the rude shakes and jostlings which we meet with in this transitory world, Nature gave way. She sunk and died a martyr to excessive sensibility.

ROMANTIC NARCISSISTS

New lovers are nervous and tender, but smash everything—for the heart is an organ of fire.

—Michael Ondaatje, *The English Patient*

A Romantic Narcissist overvalues a man and expects him to bring her happiness. She believes she has a right and responsibility to pout or carry on wildly if the guy does not conform to her fantasy. When a Romantic Narcissist says she "loves" the man she rages against, she means only that she has tolerated him and expects him to reward her for it. The reward she expects is perhaps his undivided attention forever, or perhaps his head on a silver platter.

One of the most frightening romantics was Cathy in *Wuthering Heights,* who believed that her glowering stable boy could show his love for her by bringing the universe to her feet. She meets him on the windy moors and says, "Heathcliff, make the world stand still. Make the moors never change and you and I never change. . . . No matter what I ever do or say, Heathcliff, this is me—now—standing on this hill with you. This is me, forever." Heathcliff reciprocates by loving her far too much: "I want to crawl to her feet—whimper to be forgiven for loving her, for needing her more than my own life, for belonging to her more than my own soul." None of this stops Cathy from marrying a rich neighbor and making life miserable for those she loved and those she didn't. Heathcliff apparently failed to make the moors stand still.

If a Romantic Narcissist does not achieve utopia—that is, a constant state of ecstatic wonder—then clearly the person sent by the gods or the stars to make her happy is an impostor. Not only does he have to make her happy, but he has to guess just what she wants and deliver it at just the right moment without any hints or clues from her. She could of course be happy if she would tell a man, sweetly and lovingly, what she wants him to do and what she wants him to stop doing, but that would be cheating and would take all the magic out of it. He doesn't "really" love her unless he gives her just what she wants, not because she asked for it but because he loves her so much that he reads her mind.

Sometimes, at least for a moment, it happens that way. The in-love state is intoxicating and disorienting, akin to a manic episode in its insensitivity, its obsessive refusal to be distracted, and its inability to see the situation and the pitfalls clearly. In our culture the in-love state is a sacred form of insanity, as sacred as cows are in India, and those who suffer from it are permitted to wander around loose, creating all manner of mess that someone else has to clean up. But as reality breaks through and melts this double stranglehold and replaces it with a less stifling and more flexible bond, one partner is bound to feel some betrayal. As Louis Jourdan angrily sang in *Gigi*, "She is *not* thinking of me!"

The beauty contestants, the victims, the raging manhaters, and the Romantic Narcissists are losers at the task of becoming real women. Real women, no less than fictional ones, are juggling the conflicting archetypes that merge into our models of masculinity and femininity.

Postpatriarchal Women

Age can not wither her, nor custom stale her infinite variety.

—Shakespeare, *Antony and Cleopatra*

What's a woman to be now that all roles, all emotions, all activities are open to her? Even if the family could provide stirring and soothing models of femininity for its daughters, girls may also look to the culture to find images she might aspire to. In mythology and imagination woman exists in the four classic archetypes. Woman can be Mother or Queen, the giver, nurturer, and sustainer of life. Woman can be Lover or Virgin, the bestower of sexuality. Woman can be Magician, Witch, or Wise Woman, with forbidden knowledge of the world's secrets. And woman can be Amazon or Warrior, who has the strength and courage to right wrongs or provide protection. Obviously, every woman embodies all four and spends a lifetime keeping the four in a workable balance. But the times are changing, and in our postpatriarchal era the styles of femininity are getting richer and broader. Women get less predictable every day.

THE MOTHER

Under patriarchy, the Mother archetype became weak and passive, a source of warm milk, creamy goodness, mystical faith healing, and totally benign selflessness. She was incarnated as Mary, the mother of God. Movie mothers in the old tradition were selfless saints who facilitated other people's lives but had little life and no agenda of their own. On television, Harriet Nelson, June Cleaver, and Donna Reed were horrifyingly selfless. But those sainted mothers were so inhumanly immaculate and beyond sin and selfishness that they could make anyone feel as if they were dirty and needed to brush their teeth and go to bed—and sometimes could make anyone feel like a sexual pervert or a budding serial killer. They were fountains of warm milk, but often flavored with guilt.

In reality, a totally selfless mother becomes terrifyingly guilt producing, bonding her children to her because she has nothing else in her life. It is not strong mothers but weak ones who hold their children hostage. A weak mother, who has nothing to look forward to except her children's visits, makes the children feel responsible for her and ties them down with her. A mother may only become safe for her children, who are trying to become grown-ups in their own right, when she is too busy leading her life to run the lives of her children. Obviously, a mother who is all Mother is far less desirable than a mother who is a bit of a Warrior, a Lover, and a Witch in her spare time. The Mother must be part of the archetypal mix, but it is only safe if the woman gets some of her identity and fulfillment from other directions.

By the 1960s we had stopped fearing that our mother wouldn't love us enough to let us live and began to fear she'd love us too much to let us grow up. The mother who had nothing else in her life but us was especially dangerous.

For two decades, from *Psycho* in 1960 through *Mommie Dearest* in 1981 right up to *Terms of Endearment* in 1983, there were few sympathetic mothers on the big screen. *Terms of Endearment* was a turning point. The Warrior Witch Mother played by Shirley MacLaine had dedicated her single life to hovering over her daughter, Debra Winger, who marries a weak man, has three children, and dies, leaving the kids for their grandmother to raise. Before the daughter can trust the mother with her kids, MacLaine has to have a sex life with the astronaut next door so that she is no longer just a mother. Before the daughter can die in peace, she has to convince her children that they love her and should feel none of the guilt she has always felt for not loving her mother as much as her mother loves her.

Of course, a woman can safely love anyone too much except her own children—for instance, Susan Sarandon's undaunted death-row nun in *Dead Man Walking*, Juliette Binoche's radiant nurse in *The English Patient*, and Diane Keaton's loyal daughter and niece in *Marvin's Room*.

We fear the power of mother love because we never out-grow it. It is powerful enough to keep us going for a lifetime, and in times past we always carried it with us as a source of strength rather than a proof of weakness. I often think back to my father's deathbed; his ninety-three-year-old mother sat beside him, stroking his hand as he lay there delirious. She turned to me and said, "It's times like this that I miss my mother most." Her mother had died when she was eight.

THE LOVER

One traditional counterbalance to the Mother energy is the archetype of the Lover, which comes in at least two forms: active temptress and passive virgin. Throughout patri-archy, active Lovers were potentially threatening to men—they might want more than the man had to give—and so they were considered bad girls and were condemned. Good girls, the passive Lovers who were preferably virgins with no experience with which to compare the man's capacity for loving, never wanted more than the man had to offer and were satisfied just to satisfy him.

Wives were once pictured as faithful supporters, standing in the background being stalwart—part Mother, part Wise Woman, and potential Warrior, but rarely much of a Lover. Myrna Loy, the "perfect wife" to William Powell's hard-drinking socialite detective in *The Thin Man* series of the 1930s and '40s, was a sassy, witty, drinking and working companion, but she slept in a separate bed. Marriage brought a partner, playmate, and workmate more than a bedmate.

The woman who desired men too fiercely created a prob-lem for herself as well as for him. Anna Karenina's obsessive, possessive love of Count Vronsky led to the breakup of her marriage, the loss of her son, and the end of Vronsky's ca-reer. When Vronsky finally broke free enough to go back to work, Anna didn't get a volunteer job, go back to college, or join a women's group; instead she threw herself in front of a train, which butchered her and upset Vronsky. The woman who expects a man to fulfill her and give her life meaning will soon exhaust herself, him, or both of them.

The most enduring screen sex goddess, Marilyn Monroe, was supremely passive. Her public persona was so naive and innocent, she was always a Virgin no matter how many men she experienced. With her baby voice, fleshy, pale, almost transparent body, and apparent lack of intelligence or will, she was not a threat to any man. Marilyn is with us always and can't really be improved upon as the preferred sex object for men who fear the power of women.

Our reigning postpatriarchal sex subject is a Warrior Lover who represents sexual aggressiveness and independence from men. Madonna is hard in every way that Marilyn was soft and, unlike Marilyn, determined not to be a victim. Boys are toys to her. She's a mix of the monumentally self-mocking Mae West, the trashily physical Jean Harlow, and the fearsomely armored Darth Vader. With Madonna, postpatriarchal sex is no longer a male victory but an expression of female power. She has even produced a more or less fatherless child, using her young personal trainer as sperm donor. Her model is both liberating and terrifying, and certainly a drastic change from what went before.

WITCHES AND WISE WOMEN

Every woman who is paying attention as the life cycle flows through has much wisdom to pass on. The sadder but wiser femme fatale of film noir has been around the block a few times and has come back with a deeper understanding of it all. She may not actually be a Witch, but like Glenn Close in *Fatal Attraction* and Sharon Stone in *Basic Instinct,* she has been around enough to see right through any man, and if he doesn't give her what she wants from him, she'll take it. A terrifying moment in *Fatal Attraction* comes when

Glenn Close threatens to reveal adulterous husband Michael Douglas's secrets to his wife. In *Basic Instinct* it comes when Sharon Stone reveals to Douglas his own secrets from a book she has been keeping on him. Men fear women because women understand them.

Fairy tales and even operas center on men's fears of being known and exposed by women. Wagner's Lohengrin makes his bride promise that she will never ask him who he is and where he comes from. She does, so he hops on the next swan and sails away. Puccini's Turandot asks each suitor riddles. If he answers them, he will win her hand and the throne of ancient China; if he fails, he forfeits his head. Calaf answers the riddles and courageously offers his head to her if she can find out his name before dawn. How can she not love a man brave enough to reveal himself to her?

Wise Women in the movies are usually kind and heroic. Doctors, teachers, and nuns are rich in this archetype. Healers, from psychiatrist Ingrid Bergman in *Spellbound* through psychiatrist Barbra Streisand in *Prince of Tides,* had magical wisdom but were not pure Wise Women. They could only heal the patients with whom they fell in love.

More motherly and less sexual Wise Women include the likes of Billie Burke as the benevolent good witch in *The Wizard of Oz,* who could create magical transportation for Dorothy by having her click her heels together three times and recite "There's no place like home." Margaret Rutherford, as Agatha Christie's homey village sleuth Miss Marple, used her familiarity with her neighbors and her sensitivity to human nature to solve any crime. In *Resurrection,* Ellen Burstyn died and came back to life with the magical power to heal others by hugging them.

Knowledge is power, as Glenn Close explained in *Dangerous Liaisons.* Some women are so afraid of being seen as a Witch that they fail to use the power of their knowledge.

Any woman who can't be a Witch isn't using the power nature and culture have given her.

AMAZONS AND WARRIORS

Most images of Woman on screen tell us only about the men who create them. But heroines of independence, the female warriors, tell us much about the psyches of real women, as they have fought for a place in a world in which men have become increasingly unreliable and women have had to learn to go it alone. Katharine Hepburn laughed it off in the 1930s and fell back on family wealth; Doris Day put a sunny face on it in the '50s, but the tragedy of the woman whose man has got away—and the fear of putting her life in the hands of a man who might not value it—is the subtext of films about Warrior Woman. In these films Bette Davis got mad, Joan Crawford got even, Jane Fonda got fitter and more politically conscious, Barbra Streisand got sassier, Sigourney Weaver got bigger, and Emma Thompson got more sensible—all in their determination not to be the victims of weak men.

Meryl Streep gave up her marriage and child for the sake of her sanity in *Kramer vs. Kramer,* and she gave up one child to save the other in *Sophie's Choice.* But she didn't leave her husband, children, and the bridges of Madison County to go off in Clint Eastwood's dirty truck to watch the dhows come up in Mombasa, even after he peeled carrots with her at the sink and stood in the rain with tears running down the creases of his weather-beaten face. Heroines of independence no longer throw away their lives for love.

Emma Thompson revived Jane Austen, the Enlightenment voice of reason, to usher in the nonromantic era. When women start to value men less, they will scare men less, and gender egalitarianism will be easier to reach. Women will be free to pursue their own happiness, though they may still find, as men are beginning to find, that happiness is more likely to come from loving than from being loved.

The most important heroine of independence may have been Jodie Foster in *Silence of the Lambs:* For one woman to gain the insight to save other women from a serial killer, she went into the dungeon and faced the monstrous cannibal-psychiatrist who could lead her into the mind of the killer. The message: If women are to recapture the world or any part of it and achieve happiness, they must overcome any lingering fear of the power of men.

Femininity That Works

Man may work from sun to sun,
But woman's work is never done.

—Anonymous

Patriarchy was built not only upon the suicidal self-sacrifice of men but also upon the slave labor of women. In Edward Albee's play *A Delicate Balance,* a mother explains to her daughter the differences between the lives of men and the lives of women:

> I do wish sometimes that I had been born a man. Their concerns are so simple, money and death, making ends meet until they meet the end. If they knew what it was like to be a wife, a mother, a lover, a homemaker, a nurse, a hostess, an agitator, a pacifier, a truth teller, a deceiver. There's a book out, I believe, a new one by one of the thirty million psychiatrists now practicing in this land of ours, a book which opines that the sexes are reversing, or coming to resemble each other too much at any rate. It's to be read and disbelieved. It disturbs our sense of well-

129

being. If the book is right, and I suspect that it is, then I would be no better off as a man, would I?

When men and women were half persons, they had only half as much to do. Traditionally, many women already had too much responsibility for too much stuff, too many lives, and, above all, too many relationships. Now, in a postpatriarchal world where all roles and careers are open to her, it is compelling for a woman to try to have it all. But she'll drive herself nuts if she tries to do it all, have it all, and do it all perfectly.

Their biology is no longer their destiny; women have choices. They don't have to attach themselves to a man. They may have to find a way to support themselves, but they don't have to marry and/or have children if they would rather not.

Our two daughters, our three nieces, our daughter-in-law, and our nieces-in-law are postpatriarchal women. They all have graduate degrees and fascinating careers and families. They include two psychologists, a nurse, a sociologist, an obstetrician, a physical therapist, a mathematician, a college professor and a former cable company executive, a marketing director, and a TV host and carpenter.

They all have strong and determinedly equal marriages with men who have professions and businesses and very busy lives themselves. Seven of these ten young women have children, one has stepchildren, one may opt out of reproducing, and one is waiting until she has completed her doctorate. They use day care and nannies for their children, and the fathers do about as much of the parenting as they do. They exercise a lot, climb mountains, and run marathons. They take care of relatives and maintain close friendships with other women. Not one of them has ever been bored for a moment, but they all get exhausted. They talk a lot about their lives and their choices. They laugh about their casual approaches toward the housekeeping and social activities their mothers and grandmothers took so seriously. Their houses are often a mess, but their lives are together. They are full-scale human beings who could get along fine without men (even though their children might not) but prefer a man as a partner.

They haven't always had it easy. My nephew Harrison's wife, Catherine, was a widow; her first husband died before the birth of her son, Wes. As a single mother she gathered her parents and her mother-in-law around her for support and assistance, learned to live cheaply on Social Security, and worked and went to school part-time while she raised Wes. She taught exercise classes, obtained a master's degree in education, was a news reporter for National Public Radio, had a weekly TV show for years, framed houses for Habitat for Humanity, raised funds, did marketing, and took whatever challenges came along. Nobody ever told her she couldn't do something. Even when things were at their worst, there were always options, always opportunities. "You just do what you have to do. You just do it. Good grief," she said, "you can't sit around wailing that you don't have a man to do it for you."

Since Catherine didn't need a man, she waited until she found one who was seeking a woman as strong and independent and resourceful as his own determinedly postpatriarchal mother. Catherine didn't have to train Harrison to respect and value femininity at its fullest and most powerful. But as she says, "The love and companionship of a man, while not necessary for survival, is important—even if men don't always make life easier." Fortunately, Harrison is an eager, active father to both Wes and their new son, Pitt, and Catherine has an opportunity to be a full-time mom. She says it has been the best challenge of all her jobs so far.

Betsy and I just got back from a week with our psychologist daughter Tina, two-and-a-half-year-old Justin, and our newest grandson, Christopher. Our son-in-law Ken's software company has been booming recently, and a week after Christopher was born, he had no choice but to go to London on business. Tina, knee-deep in diapers, spit-up, toy trucks, and sibling rivalry, was fielding phone calls from suicidal patients. She laughed when anyone asked her if she was going back to work after the latest baby was born and replied, "Of course I am. And so is Ken." Tina went on:

> Most weeks I get through by the skin of my teeth while I'm up to my eyebrows in things that need to be done. I can't do anything as much or as perfectly as I used to, but you do what you can do. I don't have a Martha Stewart house or a coiffed yard. I wear clothes I don't have to iron. I don't have time to wear makeup often. I don't cook fancy meals. But I'm happy with my busy life. I'm also happy with my marriage. I rely on Ken to be an equal partner in parenting. But I'm responsible for making my life interesting, and I'm not going to depend on just one person for that. I have friends, male and female, a job, my research and teaching, and organizational projects to make my life interesting. No matter how busy I get, I'm not going to give that up.

Our daughter-in-law Gaybie is a full-time plastic surgery nurse with a four-month-old, Frank V, and a husband, Frank IV, who also has a demanding job as a CPA, a demanding after-hours duty tending the family business, a demanding house that is currently an unfinished carpentry project, and a demanding night school program to get his master's degree. Fortunately, he is still a hands-on father and has arranged his schedule so he can do most of his work at home. Gaybie is the first woman in her family to continue working while she has a small child at home, so she has no models for it. She has concluded that survival for a postpatriarchal woman, which includes protection from either total exhaustion or total rage, requires personal security so you don't shrink back from setting your own goals or from speaking your mind; a partner who welcomes open and ongoing communication; and ways of telling him what you need without humiliating him and making him feel deficient when he can't read your mind. She has decided that "the art of femininity involves the skill and grace to get the job done without messing up the relationships."

Gender arrangements and role assignments aren't automatic anymore. Men and women have to talk about it, and talking about it is a traditionally female thing. What seems superficial to a woman may be a profound and life-changing conversation for a man. Talking about the experience of life lifts the veil of mystery and detoxifies the relationship.

Women don't have to live with men in order to have a life, but men and women can live together happily and equally only if they do talk about it.

Secrets of Being a Happy Grown Woman

Here is some of the advice I have been given by my daughters, my nieces, and many decades of patients.

1. Love your gender. There is nothing a man can do that you can't except maybe piss off the porch standing up—but you can create and sustain life, and he can't. So there.

2. Love your body. Keep it clean, healthy, well exercised, and well fed, and value it on the basis of what it can do rather than how it looks. The pursuit of happiness is not a beauty contest.

133

3. Honor your mother. All that advice she keeps giving you is what she needs to hear, but it is said with love, so accept the love and then apply the wisdom in your own way. And it is always possible that she is wiser than you think.

4. Don't idolize your father. Identify with him instead and learn what he knows about the world and how it works.

5. Make sure you have something in your life that makes you feel powerful and connected to the world in a functional way. Have a career, not just a job. Only then is it safe to sink deeply into the relationships of your life without fear of drowning.

6. Love your children too much. It won't hurt them. It will hurt them if you expect them to love you too much in return.

7. While "a woman needs a man like a fish needs a bicycle," a child needs a father, and that alone may be a good enough reason to keep a man around the house.

8. Don't take men so seriously. They are useful, especially as partners in raising children, but they can't be expected to make you happy or even entertained. If men were as entertaining as many women think they should be, no one would have invented cable TV.

9. Don't blame any particular man for the inequities and stupidities of human history.

10. Don't expect men to read your mind: they weren't even taught to read their own.

11. There is no danger in loving a man unless you fancy yourself in love with him, whereupon you are in danger of losing your head as well as your body because you will begin to let him define you. You may be loved by a man, supported by a man, employed by a man, and befriended by a man, but you must never let yourself be defined by a man.

12. You cannot imagine how much your anger terrifies men. If they treat you badly, it is because they are afraid of your power, not because they fail to see it. They see it, they smell it, they hear it, they feel it. But don't worry about the man who is afraid of you unless it is your boss, your son, your husband, your friend, or someone to whom you're trying to sell something.

13. We all get hurt and we all get abused, so when it happens, get up, dust yourself off, and stop whining. And if necessary, call the cops; they're on your side. But whatever you have experienced is just one more thing you know you can survive. What doesn't kill you makes you stronger.

14. You need female elders as mentors. When you conquer new territory, you don't have to be the Lone Ranger. There are other women who have been there, and you need to learn all you can from them.

15. Make sure you have female friends. Don't throw them over or break dates with them for a guy; you'll need them later. You can be yourself with a female friend; there's not as much danger of scaring them. No one will ever understand you as well as another woman who partakes of the same struggles and the same triumphs that you do.

16. Martha Stewart? Who the hell is Martha Stewart?

17. There is not much of interest in movies and books made for men, but experience them once in a while just to understand what sort of things men have been taught to think about. If you keep it in perspective, you may work up some sympathy for them.

18. Learn to enjoy sex yourself, to give yourself pleasure, and teach someone else how to give you pleasure as well, so you won't be at the mercy of some clumsy man who is so orgastic about his penis that he thinks you should be, too.

19. The sexual revolution did not give you the right to be a cheat and liar and a fool. Use your sexuality sensibly and in the service of relationships; it can hold relationships together, and it can blow them apart.

20. If you feel compelled to model yourself after men in a man's world, model yourself after nice men. Men who feel compelled to make a show of power do so because they don't think they have it. Disdain them; don't emulate them.

21. As it says on the airplane, when the oxygen pressure falls and the oxygen masks drop down, put on your own mask first, make sure you are breathing comfortably, and only then worry about the men and children who haven't learned to breathe without you yet.

5

How to Be a Grown-up Even Around Your Own Parents

You know what my scenario was for this whole thing? I was gonna move away. I was gonna get rich and move into a luxurious mansion. My parents were gonna come visit me— once—and say, "Oh, what a nice mansion. We love you, Dave." And I was gonna say, "I love you, too, Mom and Dad." And then they were gonna go away and die. Does this make me an asshole?

—Tom Hanks in *Nothing in Common*
by Rick Podell and Michael Preminger

Hello, Arthur. This is your mother. Do you remember me? . . . Someday, Arthur, you'll get married and you'll have children of your own, and Honey, when you do, I only pray that they'll make you suffer the way you're making me. That's a Mother's Prayer.

—Mike Nichols and Elaine May,
Mother and Son

The Fear of Parents

In Mike Nichols and Elaine May's *Mother and Son* skit from the late 1950s, the son is a NASA scientist interrupting a countdown at Cape Canaveral to take an emergency telephone call from his mother, who is calling to tell him she's going into the hospital to have her nerves X-rayed because he hasn't called lately. Within minutes this competent adult is reduced to infantile blathering. The message that makes the skit such a classic is that none of us, however powerful and successful, can function as adults if our parents are not satisfied with us. In the presence of an angry parent, don't even the best of us become a child again?

Similarly, even the best of us, like Tom Hanks, feel awful guilt when we realize we don't want to repay our debts to our parents. All of us have at times wanted our parents to give us their blessing and their approval—and then leave us alone. Parents seem to come from a different time, a world that is now past, and nothing they can say would be relevant to understanding the world now. Our parents may understand nothing about the world we live in, but they understand everything about us and where we came from and how we got here. And they surely understand the universal truths that in any generation get buried beneath the novel, the trendy, and the stylish. The more confusing and foreign the world, the more we need their grounding—even if we fear they'll drive us crazy.

The problem is simply this: We cannot feel like the CEO of our life in the presence of the people who toilet-trained us and spanked us when we were naughty. We may have become masters of the universe—accustomed to giving life and taking it away, casually ordering people into battle or out of their jobs, comfortably cutting up and rearranging people's brains or machines or governments or corporations—but we may still dirty our diapers at the sound of our mommy's whimper or our daddy's growl. At least in part we are still children all of our lives, but never so overtly as when we are in the presence of our parents.

The Terrifying Power of Parents to Strip Off Our Masks of Adulthood and Expose the Child Underneath

We never really are the adults we pretend to be. We wear the mask and perhaps the clothes and posture of grown-ups, but inside we are never as wise or as sure or as strong as we want to convince ourselves and others we are. We may fool all the rest of the people all of the time, but we never fool our parents. They can see past the mask of adulthood. To her mommy and daddy, the empress never has on any clothes— and the empress knows it.

Parents can make us distrust ourselves. Around our parents we are not masters. In fact, to our parents we seem always to be "works in progress." A parent's work is never done: We are never finished and ready to face life on our own; there are always little nips and tucks by which we can be made better. I remember going to see our oldest daughter off on the train to college. As the train pulled out of the station, one of the other mothers took off running behind it, trying to catch the train and stop it. She had suddenly remembered a piece of advice she hadn't given her daughter. A mother's failure to understand the new world in which her child lives does not reduce one iota her responsibility to give advice about how to deal with it.

Parents can make us distrust the world around us. Parents can intimidate their children, sometimes bullying them into submission, sometimes awing them and making them feel weak and foolish by contrast, sometimes terrifying them into doubting their ability to get along on their own. The dangers parents see might be the real dangers of the world or just the fear of any distance coming between parent and child. A child of any age who feels intimidated by a parent loses the ability to determine what is dangerous and what is safe, and instead absorbs the parents' fears rather than opening up the world for both generations.

Parents may undercut our sense of mastery by making us distrust our values. Each generation's job is to question the things the parents accept on faith, explore the possibilities, and adapt or accept the last generation's system of values for a new age.

The world is changing more rapidly with each generation; there has never been a generation gap as wide as that between you and your parents. The only one wider is the one that will eventually come between you and your children. The enormity of the change is painful for those on either side of the generational divide. Fathers who won World War II single-handedly and have strutted around as head of the household ever since may never understand sons who want to be house husbands. Mothers who have sucked it in and pretended to be mentally retarded and emotionally unstable in order not to threaten their patriarchal husbands may enormously resent their daughters who get to be full-scale human beings.

Parents may feel betrayed when their children adopt different styles and habits, when the daughter chooses a different kind of career or language or sexual expression than the mother, when the son grows long hair and wears earrings instead of the crew cut and tattoos that signified manhood for the previous generation. Matters of style may turn into matters of morality, health, or safety. To the parents, various things done by their children may mean the death of the longed for and as yet unborn grandchildren, while to the child, homosexuality may be a lifestyle choice, suicide may be a political statement, and joining the foreign legion may be an interesting career move.

No parent a generation ago could have anticipated the world we find ourselves in now. Children don't get to be grown-ups until they understand that grown-ups don't have a magical ability to see the future and aren't always going to understand and accept their children's choices; it is childish to fear and resent parents for the cultural limitations of their well-intentioned advice and counsel.

Techniques for Turning Grown Offspring into Blathering Children

Parents who want to strip away their children's mask of adulthood and expose them as still imperfect children who are in need of parents in attendance have a variety of time-honored techniques at their disposal to keep both generations firmly in place.

Parents can simply remind you that you are not quite who you pretend to be. They can bring up stories from your childhood at the most amazingly deflating moments, such as telling stories about your toilet training at your wedding reception or telling your new boss how your kindergarten teacher thought you didn't have enough sense to get out of junior high. My father insisted the most awful moment of his life came when he was making his first high school touchdown and heard his mother's voice above the roar of the crowd calling "My Sonny Boy," a name he never lived down.

Parents can offer a sanctuary, not just a pit stop on the road of life but a permanent alternative to adulthood. They can devote their lives to making it possible for you to never grow up. They can give you or offer to leave you more money than you can make; this way you never have to plan an adult life and cannot truly respect the adult life you have been able to achieve. One of my patients is a man who is almost forty, doesn't work, dresses like a college kid, and centers his life on his college. He didn't graduate from the school (he cut too many classes), but he hasn't missed a football game since he left. His father, who left school at an early age to start working on the fortune with which he keeps his son infantilized, keeps telling the son how lucky he is to have a life of leisure as a full-time college "boy."

Parents can make regression to childhood so inviting that nothing in life appears sweeter. There are domestic horror stories about the mother-in-law who can bake better biscuits than any wife and insists on bringing them over to show off the wife's deficiencies, or the father-in-law who is so handy, the young husband begins to feel and look as if he has ten thumbs and no brain. A young woman in my practice caught her husband in an affair, saw a couples therapist, confronted the contrite young husband, and reconciled. She then told her parents what had happened, whereupon her three-times-divorced father gave her the money for the best divorce attorneys and her two-times-divorced mother offered the other half of her fancy duplex. They insisted that she needed time with her parents before choosing her next husband. They hinted that taking her in and raising her and her children might bring them back together again.

Your parents can lay claim to your children and tell you how to raise them. Seemingly adult children can feel so frightened by their parents' interference in their parenting efforts that they carry on wildly when they get advice. They don't have to take the advice, of course, but the more rattled they are by the challenges of child raising and the less secure they feel that they are doing the right thing, the more they seem to resent efforts to help. Frankly, such advice can be useful. Every child needs more than two parents, so grandparents can come in handy. Finding out how your parents

or your partner's parents thought out the issues of child raising—how they came to do what they did and how you came
to be who you are—can give wonderful insights into both
them and you. Of course it can rattle you. I know I'm more
comfortable getting advice when I know what I'm doing
than when I am trying to fake competence. We are all amateurs at child raising.

Parents have subtle ways of humbling you by reminding
you of your origins—perhaps by showing up at the moment
of your greatest glory to remind you where you came from
and demonstrating that you still have some of it between
your toes. They can just show up and be themselves, or,
worse, they can try to be something they are not. Everyone
has a few relatives who are closet cases because they are so
real, so truly of the family and the heritage. But sometimes
such humbling is a blessing. I went to a wedding in which
the grandfather from the old country cut through his family's
WASP pretensions by not only making a toast introducing
the family by the old family name, before it had been
changed, but bringing pictures of the old family nose before
everyone in the family except himself had had it carved
down. Before the evening was over, the old man was leading
the crowd in spirited Mediterranean dancing. It was a wonderful beginning for the new couple.

Parents can criticize you sensitively and astutely, reminding you that you aren't perfect yet. Even as the world ap-
plauds, your parents can take your victory away by
suggesting you might have done a better job in some way.
Many people have told me the story of an incident in their
lives that I thought had happened only to me: bringing home
a report card with four A's and one B, and having the parent
ask only about the B. "That's nice, but what did you do
wrong in calculus?" When I was about thirty, I called
Mother to tell her I had been written up in *Time* magazine.
She said, "Nobody in Autauga County, Alabama, reads *Time*

anymore. Why didn't you get written up in *U.S. News and World Report?*" That meant, "Don't get too big for your britches around me, Sonny Boy. I knew you when." After a few minutes of sympathetic reflection, I realized that it also meant, "I'm so afraid you'll be so successful and so acclaimed by the world that you won't need us anymore, that you'll feel too good for us, that you'll be ashamed of us. Please love me even in your moments of glory." I might wonder why she didn't put it that way, but I'm grateful that she cared whether I cared about her.

At any time your parents can call in their investment in you and demand repayment for giving you life. The classic approach to this is guilt; as Erma Bombeck put it: "Guilt, the gift that keeps on giving." King Lear was our expert at this, bewailing about "how sharper than a serpent's tooth it is to have a thankless child." His kids fixed him.

Parents vary in their sense of what would be suitable repayment for creating, sustaining, and tolerating you all those years and what circumstances would be drastic enough for them to present the voucher. Obviously there is no repayment that would be sufficient. The debt is there, inescapable and even irreducible, and with it the guilt. We need to remember that the debt of life is too outrageously enormous to be treated as anything other than a joke. My mother used to tell me, as often as needed, how she had to lie in bed flat on her back for nine months in order to give birth to me. If I displeased her, she'd remind me that all she would have had to do was stand up and I would be a messy spot on the floor, so I should be eternally grateful that she didn't do that. I'd thank her and assure her it would be okay for her to stand up now.

Parents can write the family history, putting you wherever they choose, preferring perhaps to keep you in the family mythology as a child. My mother, for example, was clearly ambivalent about my successes. When I went to give a widely publicized talk to dedicate Alabama's first mental health center, I was about forty, and the picture of me she sent to the newspapers was from high school. I was a middle-aged man but was still Little Frank, my mother's boy wonder.

The Awkwardness of Adolescence and How It Becomes a Permanent State of Immaturity

We give parents the power to take the wind out of our sails when we are in adolescence, when we are so seriously self-conscious that we become adult male and adult female impersonators, trying to convince everyone, mostly ourselves, that we are no longer children. We have enough trouble carrying it off when we are doing it in front of a mirror, but it becomes impossible to look like an adult when our parents are telling us what to do. Our parents know how immature we are. In response, we pose as grown-ups by making a show of not needing our parents—at just the point of greatest confusion and disorientation of our lives, right when we need them most.

Our parents' style and values, their ideas about how the world works, are likely to seem old-fashioned on principle, but the real issue is that as adolescents we are too scared to tolerate doubt about ourselves and our beliefs.

Our parents might have money or things to leave us when they die, but this may not make us value them; it may make us impatient with them for continuing to live. If we can't find a use for them and they don't have anything for us, we might want to find an escape from them. We might even come to fear them, as if their active involvement in our life were proof of our weakness in character and maybe even dangerous to our mental health. We often try to escape from them.

It is hard to look like a grown-up, much less feel like one, when you are busy running away from home. Yet we have a society in which adolescence, for some insane reason, is seen as the most desirable time in life. We have a world full of people who get into the middle of the stream of life and paddle like hell trying to stay in the same spot while the life cycle and the world flow past us, leaving us equidistant from childhood and adulthood. Blaming the way our parents raised us for the choices we're making now is a sure way to keep us stuck in the middle of the stream as life and its opportunities for maturation pass right past us.

Imperfect Parents

One of the most highly valued functions of used parents, people who are kept around for sentimental value, is to be the villains of their children's lives, the people the children blame for any shortcomings or disappointments. This approach to escaping guilt is an effort to protect the victim from taking responsibility for his or her own life. But if your identity comes from your parents' failings, then you remain forever a member of the child generation, unable to move on to adulthood in which you identify yourself in terms of what you do rather than what has been done to you.

Indeed, there are great advantages to seeing yourself as an accident created by amateur parents as they practiced. You have been left in an imperfect state, and the rest is up to you. Only the most pitifully inept child requires perfection from parents. It might help for the parents to apologize a few times, but the child who would become an adult must finally get off the parents' back and get on with the job at hand.

I know your parents made a lot of mistakes—like most parents including my own, and including me. That was then; this is now. A lot of parents reached adulthood as they raised you and are better people now than they were then.

Some parents, though, got stuck in childhood and adolescence, and the process of raising you did not turn them into grown-ups. Some parents were awful back then and are awful still. But if you are going to grow up, you still have to forgive them for the things they did to you when you were a child.

Clearly, all the things parents do are not so lovably and forgivably benign. Parents sometimes do horrendous things to their children—beating them, raping them, selling them into slavery, even trying to kill them. Many parents abandon their children, breaking up their children's family to run off with someone who did not have the best interests of the children at heart and leaving the children with someone they could not tolerate living with themselves. Those things must also be faced, and when they are finally understood, they must be forgiven. Otherwise the child may never feel secure with the imperfect love and imperfect investment the parents made in him or her or with his or her own inability to reciprocate that love. An angry, unforgiving child going through life feeling like a victim of imperfect parenting has no way of moving into the adult position in relationships. Unrelenting anger at parents is a developmental dead end.

It is interesting how people blame parents much more for overdoing their jobs than for underfunctioning as parents. People seem tolerant and forgiving of fathers who love too little, while they spend a lifetime fearing mothers who love too much.

A patient of mine was loved too little. Rhoda's father disappeared when she was born and was never heard from again. Her tight-lipped mother raised her all alone. When she was eighteen and had finished high school, Rhoda chose not to go to college but to work and save money to find her father. A private detective she hired eventually found her father, who was working at an optical shop. She introduced herself, and they went for a cup of coffee. He was rather silent, but he explained that he had run away because he feared he would not be a good enough father for her, and he had been ashamed of that ever since. He told her he had little he could offer her, but he gave her a package of eyeglass wipes and advised her to keep her eyeglasses clean. That little box of wipes was the only thing Rhoda had ever gotten from her father—except for his explanation that he had run away because he felt she deserved more than he had to give. She never saw her father again, but that explanation helped her set a goal of hanging in and raising her own children. She realized that she didn't have to be wonderful to raise children, but she did have to be there. Rhoda was forever grateful to her father for that insight, and she always kept her eyeglasses clean. We don't know what their meeting did for her father; he ran away again after that.

Parents who were clearly imperfect can be helpful to you. While you were trying to grow up despite their fumbling efforts, you had to develop skills and tolerances other kids did not. Some of the strongest people I know grew up taking care of inept, invalid, or psychotic parents—but they knew the parents were not normal, healthy, and whole. Children of imperfect parents might be grateful to their imperfect parents for the opportunities to develop unexpected strengths. My sister and I are firmly convinced that our mother's alcoholism made us stronger people and better caretakers. Such a tragicomic existence certainly did wonders for our sense of humor.

Therapists and Adult Children of Imperfect Parents

Therapists often abet our inability to grow up because they are frozen in the child generation themselves. If a therapist agrees, sight unseen, that the parent who gave you life and sustained you, albeit imperfectly, through your period of real vulnerability is going to be the death of you now that you're grown, that therapist is condemning you to a life in hiding. If a therapist is so frightened of parents that he or she is convinced only perfect parents should be permitted to share the world with their children, then that therapist should rethink his or her choice of career—after resolving matters with his or her own parents.

Child-generation therapists might think that guilt is a killer, and set out to protect grown children from guilt by helping them shuck the relationships, realities, and responsibilities of adulthood. They may encourage you to blame your life on the mistakes of your parents rather than encourage you to find out what the experience was like for your parents, how they learned to be the people and the parents they were, and whether they would do it differently now. That exploration brings parents and children together, and can set both free.

An adult-generation therapist (of any age) will see both you and your parents through the eyes of an adult rather than through the eyes of a child and will know that you must forgive your parents if you are ever to be free of your sense of childlike helplessness.

The point of exploring your parents' deficiencies is to correct the misinformation you've received, not to blame your life on them and then avoid them. You can't escape them anyway. Your biological parents are present in every chromosome in your body. The parents who raised you are present in every word you speak, every action you take. Your job is not to satisfy your parents or to fix them but to understand them. Only through understanding them can you finally understand yourself.

You must understand their life and yours from their perspective before you can truly forgive them. It may take a lifetime. Some of it will happen automatically as you raise your children, but some of it can happen only if you examine your parents, living or dead, present or absent.

If your parents are not available, you may have to learn about them through the eyes of those who knew them. Seek out these people and talk to them while there is still time. Find out what your parent was doing when he or she was not there for you. Some of the stories you'll hear will be fanciful or romantic, but that is generally the case with family lore.

On the other hand, if your parent is a homicidal maniac, you may have to have armed guards present as you hang out with him and demystify him or her. Even if your father has to be kept in a cage like Hannibal the Cannibal, you cannot continue to avoid him and come to peace with the world. As long as you believe your parent wants to do you in, you can never feel safe in the world. No matter how awful the incestuous or homicidal parent, he must be faced and understood, not for his sake but for yours.

There is nothing in life so therapeutic as coming to peace with your parents.

Acting Like a Grown-up

To move into the adult position with your parents, you must do several things. Your parents can't do these things for you. They cannot grant you your adulthood; you must claim it for yourself.

It is worth repeating that to be an adult a child must forgive his or her parents for all the ways in which they didn't raise him or her just right, whether their errors were in loving too much or too little. If you have children, you'll do some of the things your parents did, too, and eventually laugh about them.

The child who would be an adult must take responsibility

for his or her own life, not necessarily doing it perfectly but accepting the blame for the missteps: "I did this, and I did it wrong. Now I want to learn from my mistakes. What do you think I could do different next time?" As a newly proclaimed adult, you are eager to accept well-intentioned counsel from those who know and love you, even if neither their love for you nor their understanding of you is ideal. One of the hallmarks of maturity, and surely the biggest factor in success, is the willingness to seek and accept coaching and supervision from those with expertise and then be willing to make your own decisions. People, especially parents, love to give advice, and they will respect your sign of maturity in asking for it.

The child who would be an adult must relinquish any lingering childlike sense of parental power, both the magical ability to solve your problems for you and the dreaded ability to make you revert to being a child. When you are no longer hiding from your parents or clinging to them and can accept them as fellow human beings, then they can do the same for you. They know by now (I hope) that they have no magical powers, but it is up to you to make yourself aware of that. They cannot turn you into a child; that is something you are doing to yourself when you collapse, run, or hide under the spell of your childlike awe at their presumed power. You must move in close and unmask them as Toto did the Wizard of Oz, who turned out to be a silly old man hiding behind a lot of sound and lights. As he said when told he was a bad man, "No. I am a very good man, just a very bad wizard." Parents and wizards are all faking it.

Dismantling the Family Hierarchy and Becoming Peers

Grown children who expect respect from their parents must accept responsibility for their own lives and act like grown-ups. Grown children who are still trying to blame their lives on their parents cannot expect this.

Moreover, you need to achieve something that will make your parents feel that their investment in you has paid off. If you are not reinvesting in others what your parents invested in you and you are not doing anything with your life that your parents can value, you are still in their debt. It can feel tyrannical, but it is really just your parents' effort to use their influence to push you into doing what will bring you success, honor, integrity, security, and grown-up happiness.

You must understand that your parents may be ambivalent about your becoming an adult or remaining a child. This is because they fear they will lose you if you grow up and feel secure and independent. It will be less threatening to them if your security and independence don't carry you too far away from them. They can treat you as an adult if they know you'll still be around for any fine-tuning they need to provide.

Members of the child generation can feel sure the debts are paid if they get to take care of the parents when they are old, sick, or terminally ill. Nursing your parents through to the end liberates you from parental guilt and empowers your adultness. It can make you feel wonderful when your parent needs you more than you need him or her. But if you are still feeling guilty—that you have not paid enough, achieved enough, reinvested enough, or suffered enough for the parent—you can come to feel like a slave. You must decide when you have bought your freedom, and then you must give a bit more just to be sure. When you have paid back your parents for your life and paid more than you owe, then you are indeed your own person.

In considering the ledger equal, it must be understood that the greatest gift you have given your parents is the opportunity to raise you. What a child gets from parents can't compare to what a parent gets from raising a child. Only by having the same experience can you understand the degree to which children give meaning to the lives of parents.

While it is not the only way to do it, the traditional way for someone to move from the child generation to the parent generation is by having a child and becoming a parent. Child raising—hands-on, fully invested child raising—is the main event in life. It is the experience that takes you out of the child generation, where you are only able to *take,* and puts you squarely in the parent generation, where you are able to *give* as well. You thus become able to take deservedly and unashamedly, without the nagging guilt that children feel about taking more than they are giving back.

The end product of child raising is not only the child but the parents, who get to go through each stage of human development from the other side, to relive the experiences that shaped them, and to rethink everything their parents taught them. In effect, they get to re-raise themselves and become their own person.

Secrets for Getting Parents to See You as an Adult and Treat You with Respect

Meanwhile, there are secrets—techniques, really—for achieving hierarchical equality with your parents. Here are some techniques my children taught me that I didn't learn when I was entering adulthood because I wasn't mature enough to face my parents head-on. These techniques are guaranteed to work better than whining childishly or raging adolescently at your parents that they don't treat you as an adult.

1. Tell them about you. Tell them what you like and don't like. You be the expert on you.

2. When your parents try to tell you more about you and your shortcomings than you really want to hear, ask

them about themselves at your age. Explore them, not you.

3. Thank them for their criticism and ask them what their experiences were that led them to their opinions.

4. Ask for their advice before they have a chance to give it. If they know you are taking it seriously, they may give more sympathetic advice.

5. Explain how much you value their opinion, being sure to add that you will particularly value it as you make your own decision.

6. Don't hide anything from them. Secrets and lies will make you ashamed of yourself and will make them think you are hiding things from them, as a child does.

7. Invite them to do things with you, whether they like to do them or not, and accept their invitations in return. Include them in your social life.

8. Ask them to do favors for you now. Give them ample opportunity to feel useful.

9. Alternately, put them in situations where they are dependent on you rather than the other way around, but be careful not to rub it in. Break the familiar patterns of the interaction.

10. Travel with them, getting out of their familiar territory and out of yours; encounter together some new experiences, new people, new places, and new challenges. Different patterns of interaction should evolve.

11. Find things to thank them for, especially memories from the past. Thank them randomly.

12. Ask them to tell you family stories. When they tell family stories about you, give them the necessary information to change your position in the family lore.

13. Tell them whether you need cheerleading or criticism at the moment. Remember, they want above all to feel needed and to be good parents. Help in structuring them to do so.

14. Reveal secrets you have kept from them. Blow their minds. Actually, they will probably be surprised that you weren't worse.

15. Call them more often than necessary. Try to call during their favorite TV show so they will be in a hurry to get you off the phone.

16. Don't criticize them to others. Get into the habit of praising them to your friends. That won't change them, but it will free you from your adolescent pout with them.

17. Name your children after them.

18. Don't name your pets after them.

19. Take them to movies about parents and children. *Mommie Dearest* and *The Great Santini* are good choices. Then talk about the movie, taking the parent's side. Since they've been children longer than they've been parents, they might just counter by seeing the conflict from the child's perspective.

20. Give your parent a copy of this book with appropriate passages underlined—very faintly.

21. Take your parents with you to your therapist and tell the therapist what wonderful parents they have been. If you don't have a therapist, use casual neighbors or even passing strangers. In time even the most hidebound parents will have to start telling these people what a wonderful child you have been. And even if they don't, the therapists, neighbors, and strangers you do this with will think of you as a wonderful child to your ungrateful parents. And that is all you want, isn't it?

Whose Life Is It Anyway?

There may be situations in which it is possible to be overinvolved with your family—when you can't marry and have your own family because you have a full-time job taking care of your parents or when you aren't free to leave home to get the training and experience you need to pursue your own talents or when the family traditions trap you in an occupation or gender role that doesn't suit you. But when your family can make use of your special talents and can make you part of something bigger than yourself, it's great. The problem is not "overinvolvement" but losing your individual voice in the collective whole.

I increasingly question those extremely popular and influential mental health theories of the '60s and '70s that found closeness and interdependency between the generations unhealthy. But I believed it back then, too. I'm not convinced now that most people are better off if they differentiate a lot, as Murray Bowen would have had us do, break free from all their warm, cozy enmeshment, as Sal Minuchin advised; and leave home, the way Jay Haley encouraged us to do. Maybe the family has become safer and wiser in the last generation, or maybe I simply graduated into adulthood. But I like being as close to my children as I am, talking over cases and writing papers with my psychologist daughters and working out with my triathlete son. My wife, Betsy, has run my psychiatric practice for the past twenty-five years. Our son is our accountant and Betsy's primary source of business advice. My ninety-three-year-old psychiatrist father-in-law lived with us for four years and let us do a few things for him, a pitifully partial payment for all he had done for us. In addition to everything else, he was a source of much of my clinical wisdom. I've looked at a lot of families over my thirty-plus years as a therapist, and I want a normal three- or four-generation family, not one of those skinny little nuclear things.

As we raise our children, as we invest our hopes, our energies, our futures, and our very beings in them, we are all hoping we will get something back from them that will make up for any deficiencies in our parenting. Each life carries within it all the generations that came before and all the generations to follow. In whatever we do, we must be aware of both. During my adolescence I felt connected only to my generation, and I felt oppressed when anyone required my allegiance to anything outside myself. Having lived through the adolescent sense that my family and the human race began and ended with me and now seeing myself connected on both ends, I no longer feel lost and alone.

I wish the same for you.

6

How to Have a Grown-up Marriage

Marriage is our last, best chance to grow up.

—Joseph Barth

I didn't marry you because you were perfect. I didn't even marry you because I loved you. I married you because you gave me a promise. That promise made up for your faults. And the promise I gave you made up for mine. Two imperfect people got married and it was the promise that made the marriage. And when our children were growing up, it wasn't a house that protected them; and it wasn't our love that protected them—it was that promise.

—Thornton Wilder, *The Skin of Our Teeth*

MARRIAGE IS THE PROMISE—NOT THE EMOTIONS, NOT EVEN the relationship, but the commitment. To be worth anything more than a vacation together, a boarding arrangement, or a temporary job, a marital promise must be made to withstand and weather all human emotions, and inhuman ones as well. It must withstand cruelty, neglect, and innumerable subtle forms of abuse that frightened people use to protect themselves from recognizing the equal rights of others. It must withstand periods of separation that may occur when the reality of war, work, school, illness, imprisonment, duty, or vacation comes between people. It must withstand cooling-off periods when one person's behavior requires that the other escape to safety or distance. It must withstand change, aging, loss of youth, loss of beauty, loss of youthful hopes, and a lifetime of disappointment. But if that promise is made to hold, one is never alone, never in despair, never lost in the universe. One always has a home.

Jessie Bernard stated in *The Future of Marriage*, "One fundamental fact underlies the conception of marriage itself. Some kind of commitment must be involved. . . . Merely fly-by-night, touch and go relationships do not qualify." In Louisiana a new state law gives couples a choice between regular marriage that permits no-fault quickie divorce and "covenant" marriage that requires counseling, cause, and patience to escape. I worry a bit about those who would choose "marriage lite" rather than the real thing. People who marry "till death do us part" have a quite different level of commitment and therefore a quite different level of security and a quite different level of freedom and a quite different level of happiness than those who marry "so long as love doth last." The "love doth last" folks are always anticipating the moment when they or their mate wakes up one morning and finds the good feeling that holds them afloat has dissolved beneath them.

Marriage is not about being in love. It is about the agreement to love one another. Love is an active, transitive verb. It is something married grown-ups do no matter how they feel. It is nice when married people are in love with each other, but if they are loving enough to each other, that magic may catch fire again.

There is a relationship between love and marriage, but it

is oblique. Judith Viorst, author of *Necessary Losses*, explained, "One advantage of marriage, it seems to me, is that when you fall out of love with him, or he falls out of love with you, it keeps you together until you maybe fall in again." Paul Tournier said in *The Meaning of Persons*, "It is a lovely thing to have a husband and wife developing together and having the feeling of falling in love again. That is what marriage really means: helping one another to reach the full status of being persons, responsible and autonomous beings who do not run away from life."

Marriage is not supposed to make you *happy*. It is supposed to make you *married*, and once you are safely and totally married, then you have a structure of security and support from which you are free to make yourself happy, rather than wasting your adulthood looking for a structure.

The state of marriage can make people happier even if the particular partner is a disappointment or an irritant. The state of marriage seems to offer security in lives that would otherwise be obsessed with either the deficiencies of the unpartnered state or the search for a partner. The marriage does not have to be very fulfilling to offer comfort and structure and the sense that life is going on. But when the marriage is threatened by either partner, the sanctuary of domestic life is lost, triggering intense insecurity and disorientation. Some marriages are so abusive, degrading, unequal, or insecure that they offer no sanctuary at all, but even then people rarely leave before finding a potential partner who offers a more hopeful alternative. The human animal resists being alone.

Her Marriage, His Marriage

The responsibility for recording a marriage has always been up to the woman; if it wasn't for her, marriage would have disappeared long

*since. No man is going to jeopardize his present
or poison his future with a lot of little brats
hollering around the house unless he's forced to.
It's up to the woman to knock him down, hog-
tie him, and drag him in front of two witnesses
immediately if not sooner.*

—Preston Sturges, *The Miracle of Morgan's
Creek*

Does marriage "jeopardize" a man's present and "poison his
future"? On the other hand, does it enslave women? Under
patriarchy, every effort was made to undercut the basic
equality of marriage. In the patriarchal book of Genesis, God
tells Eve, "Thy desire shall be to thy husband and he shall
rule over you." Men were warned to keep women unequal.
In 215 B.C. in Rome, Cato the Censor warned: "Suffer
women once to arrive at an equality with you, and they will
from that moment become your superiors."

Under patriarchy, a woman was treated as property to be
passed from a father to a husband without ever achieving an
independent adulthood of her own. There was a time when
the job description for a wife—that is, a helpmate to a
man—was close to that of a servant.

Yet even in those patriarchal times, just as in these as yet
imperfectly postpatriarchal ones, marriage offered the closest
possible situation of equality to men. "Traditionally, marriage involved a kind of bartering, rather than mutual interdependence or role sharing. Husbands financially and
economically supported wives, while wives emotionally, psy-
chologically, and socially supported husbands. He brought
home the bacon, she cooked it. He fixed the plumbing, she
the psyche," Bettina Arndt wrote in *Private Lives.*

Under patriarchy, according to Elizabeth Fox-Genovese in
Feminism Without Illusions, "marriage did subject women,

inluding their property and their wages, to the authority of a man upon whom they depended for support. [But] for many women . . . marriage constituted a viable career, a more promising source of security than anything the individualism of the public sphere could offer." If the relationship could become personal, then it could be flexible enough for inter-dependency and a measure of equality to be achieved.

Marriage has become far more personal in our postpatriar-chal society as people have increasingly demanded their rights to pursue happiness. As the roles, no longer prescribed by gender, became negotiable and interchangeable, "a suc-cessful relationship rested on the emotional compatibility of husband and wife, rather than the fulfillment of gender-pre-scribed duties and roles," according to John D'Emilio and Estelle B. Freedman in *Intimate Matters*. But of course as people began to take their marriages more personally and realized they had more say in how things went, they began to complain and tinker with the relationship more and concern themselves with matters of automatic compatibility.

Men have been accustomed to believing that women get a better deal out of marriage than men do. Men have tended to complain more about what they give up in order to be married. For instance, Rock Hudson in the movie *Pillow Talk*, explains:

> Before a man gets married, he's like a tree in the for-est. He stands there independent, an entity unto him-self. And then he's chopped down. His branches are cut off, he's stripped of his bark, and he's thrown into the river with the rest of the logs. Then this tree is taken to the mills. Now, when it comes out, it's no longer a tree. It's the vanity table, the breakfast nook, the baby crib, and the newspaper that lines the family garbage can.

Women have had their say as well about the inequities of marriage: Mildred Natwick explains to her daughter Jane Fonda in Neil Simon's *Barefoot in the Park,* "Take care of him. Make him feel important. Give up a little bit of you for him. If you can do that, you'll have a happy and wonderful marriage—like two out of every ten couples."

Actually, the data indicate that both men and women benefit from marriage (quite aside from the overriding benefit to children). Jessie Bernard's findings on that subject, and her collection of the relevant research on the matter (compiled in *The Future of Marriage* in 1972 and updated in 1982), have been widely quoted and divergently interpreted. For instance, in *The Family Interpreted,* Deborah Leupnitz states, "Looking at a host of variables, from rates of psychiatric admissions to self-reports of happiness, Bernard found that married men were better off than single men, but that single women were better off than married women." It is not quite that bad. Certainly men have benefited more from patriarchal marriage than women have, but women have benefited as well. Married women do have more psychological distress than single ones, and women with children at home are more stressed than those without them, but married women are more likely to consider themselves happy. Women who marry and stay at home have more psychological symptoms than single women with careers, but married women who also work are healthier. Working mothers and wives may be exhausted, but they are healthy and happy.

In these surveys, separated, divorced, and widowed women had higher levels of unhappiness than those who were still married even if the marriage was not too great. Women complained about their marriages more than men did and found the specific relationships with their husbands less satisfying than they had wished, but they found the state and institution of marriage a source of satisfaction as well as security. Perhaps one of the pleasures women get from marriage is the opportunity to complain about it, just as men who sacrifice their lives to work delight in complaining about doing so.

The concept of "unhappily married" is misleading. The person so described is both unhappy and married at the same time, but I think it dangerous and presumptuous to assume that the marriage is causing the unhappiness. Only foolish romantics assume that their marriage partner should make them so happy that they will not have periods of unhappiness—or, for that matter, feelings of attraction to others or longings to live in a different place or time or situation or century.

Anne Morrow Lindbergh said in *War Within and Without,* "Marriage is tough, because it is woven of all these various elements, the weak and the strong. 'In loveness' is fragile for it is woven only with the gossamer threads of beauty. It seems to me absurd to talk about 'happy' and 'unhappy' marriages."

Simone Signoret, married forever to Yves Montand in a marriage that survived his notorious affairs with Edith Piaf and Marilyn Monroe, explained, "Chains do not hold a marriage together. It is threads, hundreds of tiny threads which sew people together through the years. This is what makes a marriage last—more than passion or even sex."

Still, Bernard concludes, "To be happy in a relationship which imposes so many impediments on her, as traditional marriage does, a woman must be slightly ill mentally."

Men have consistently been happier and more satisfied with their marriages than have their wives, but that is probably because men have been less likely to expect their marriage to be the primary source of their happiness. Men expect more service but less joy from marriage because they look to their careers for their major source of satisfaction.

Bernard notes: "There are few findings more consistent, less equivocal, and more convincing than the sometimes spectacular and always impressive superiority on almost every index—demographic, psychological, or social—of married over never-married men. Despite all the jokes about marriage in which men indulge, all the complaints they lodge against it, it is one of the greatest boons of their sex."

Susan Faludi, in *Backlash,* summarizes: "The suicide rate of single men is twice as high as that of married men. Single men suffer from nearly twice as many severe neurotic symptoms and are far more susceptible to nervous breakdowns, depression, even nightmares. And despite the all-American image of the carefree single cowboy, in reality bachelors are far more likely to be morose, passive, and phobic than married men."

And according to *Sex in America,* by Robert T. Michael and others, single men have a lot less sex as well.

Even if traditional marriage was a greater boon to men than to women, marriage makes both men and women happy, and the breakdown of marriage makes both men and women miserable. Still, men don't always do a very good job of meeting the psychological needs of their wives and making women happy, especially women with a romantic turn of mind. In our postpatriarchal society, men are having to change, of course, but so are women. Women need more in their lives. It is not surprising that better educated men and women are happier and more satisfied with marriage. But it should also not be surprising that married women who work outside the home are healthier than housewives in almost every category of psychological symptom. Women can't look to men any more than they can to children for the total meaning of their lives, and many have been erroneously socialized to expect that.

Marriage worked fine—in fact, probably better—before it got saddled with fantasies and expectations of romantic love. Marriage was always a necessary economic and social arrangement that provided an atmosphere in which children could be raised and sex regulated, and in which adults would have a partner and companion to share the work and keep them from feeling alone in the world.

Samuel Johnson, who was right about most things, was quoted by Boswell in 1776: "I believe marriages would in general be as happy, and often more so, if they were all made by the Lord Chancellor, upon a due consideration of the characters and circumstances, without the parties having any choice in the matter." I regularly see people who have come to the conclusion that they married for the wrong reasons or at the wrong time in their lives; and therefore, they feel their marriage is emotionally invalid and they owe no loyalty to their commitments or the basic structure of their life. This is immature and irresponsible, and is a guarantee of unhappiness for somebody, probably everybody.

Above all, it does matter how marriage partners treat each other. Contrary to the theories of the 1960s, such as those expressed in *The Intimate Enemy* by George R. Bach and Peter Wyden, fighting a lot, spewing emotions on one another, and "expressing" every damn fool thing you feel as if it were pus in an abscess does not make marriages happier. John Gottman reported in *Why Marriages Succeed or Fail* that contempt, criticism, complaining, and withdrawing forebode gloom for marriage.

Kindness seems to be the heart of a happy marriage. What marriage partners need is less encounter-group-style "mental health" and better manners. There is little in life that ever needs to be said, from "Your breath stinks" to "I shall surely kill you if you ever do that again," that cannot be said politely, even lovingly.

The primary task for postpatriarchal marriage, however, is to keep it not just personal—focusing on the ability to make each other happy—but equal. It is hard for marriage to be equal when the impact of divorce might affect the two partners unequally, might have different financial consequences for one than the other, might have different impacts on their relationships with the children, and might put one in a better position to remarry. So one step toward equalizing a marriage is to preclude the possibility of divorce. Another step is to provide equal access to money and to decisions about money. Still another necessary step is to divide the work equitably, which requires ongoing negotiation of chores and tasks and responsibilities. Even if the jobs aren't equal in some way, the voices must be.

The Equality of Marriage

Virtue can only flourish among equals.

—Mary Wollstonecraft, *A Vindication of the Rights of Men*

Equality is a platitudinous concept that practically everybody supports because it can be given any meaning we like. . . . Formal agreement on equality as a value masks the fact that we haven't a clue as to what is supposed to be equal to what, and in what way, or to what degree.

—Phillip E. Johnson, *Stanford Law Review*

Equality is a process. Pepper Schwartz in *Peer Marriage* (aka *Love Among Equals*) studied egalitarian couples who "based their marriages on a mix of equity (each person gives in proportion to what he or she receives) and equality (each person has equal status and is equally responsible for emotional, economic, and household duties). . . . These couples were distinguished by more than their dedication to fairness and collaboration; the most happy and durable among them had refocused their relationship on *intense companionship.*"

167

But the pursuit of equality can become tyrannical, as money, diapers, dishes, and choices of TV shows are carefully tabulated so no one can take advantage of the other. The equality must be in the spirit and the atmosphere rather than in the balance sheet. As Schwartz puts it, "The point of the marriages was not to share everything fifty-fifty. Rather, the shared decisions, responsibility, and household labor were in the service of an intimate and deeply collaborative marriage . . . a collaboration of love and labor in order to produce profound intimacy and mutual respect."

Equality is in the attitude. People who are so competitive that they fear their partner will win at the marriage, and thus they will lose, aren't going about it with the right attitude. Couples either both win or both lose; they are partners, not opponents. They are on the same side of the net. If they achieve equality, their team wins. (I've known at least one marriage that ended in divorce because a woman and her therapist concluded that the husband's greater happiness meant he was getting a better deal than she was and was thus exploiting or abusing her.)

There are many ways in which people can destroy the equality of the marriage and turn their sanctuary into a war zone. Some tactics are brutal, some are subtle, but men or women who resort to them must be doing so because they feel themselves overpowered in other ways.

The most desperate of these tactics for winning at marriage is *violence*. The violence does not have to be extensive or frequent to create a reign of terror. Violence is never forgotten, and from that point on, the threat of its recurrence hangs over the relationship. The truce of civilization is broken; one or both of these partners will resort to physical force to gain control of the relationship. Needless to say, the violent partner is not always male, but male violence is more likely to do damage and create a state of terror. The way to equalize a violent relationship is to call the police each time it happens.

Money can easily unbalance a relationship. When it is inherited, when it is earned, when it is spent, when it is saved, it represents power. He, or she, who has the gold makes the rules. Control of the money is control of the relationship. Men who get the pride, satisfaction, and status of earning the money often demand the satisfaction of saving it, blowing it, or counting it as well, thus doubly unbalancing the relationship. Poor wives of rich men have little access to power except by spending the money, and if they can't charge things, they can just wreck cars, go to doctors or hospitals, or otherwise throw money away. Of course, divorce is another option for gaining access to money and escaping the control of a financial bully.

Alliances with the kids create a majority in the family and with it the desired state of inequality to punish or override the partner who is outside the alliance. This is a popular but particularly cruel way of winning at marriage, since it sacrifices the children for a short-term advantage.

Secrets and *lies* drive the other partner to distraction. Those who have been lied to are disoriented and can't trust their own reality testing. They become increasingly confused, insecure, and dependent. Lying to a marriage partner, perhaps about an infidelity, perhaps about the price of a pair of shoes, perhaps about one's whereabouts or activities, can be crazy making. In the classic film in which Charles Boyer tried to drive Ingrid Bergman crazy, it was known as *Gaslight*ing. The only defense against it is to decide the lying gaslighter is some sort of nut and ignore whatever he or she says.

Withdrawal is a cruel form of control and inequality. It brings out the latent dependency in just about anyone. It doesn't work with people who have plenty to entertain them elsewhere and have stopped caring.

Threats of divorce, sometimes quite subtle, are used by bullies to scare their partners into compliance.

Insults and *emotional pyrotechnics* unbalance the relationship when one person carries on abusively and ends up humbling, humiliating, scaring, unbalancing, or just overwhelming the other. Unlike muscles and wealth, insults and emotional fireworks only work if the other partner cringes before them. Delicate creatures who collapse when they feel "verbally abused" are easy targets.

On the other hand, impeccable *manners* and airs of *superiority* can be disarming and can gather outside support to unbalance the marriage. Those who are unperturbably polite have a distinct advantage and make those who resist them feel shabby, crazy, crude, or out of control.

Those who fear equality may forfeit their chances for happiness by trying to win at their marriage. Those who persist in trying to win at marriage and who can't see that equality is in their best interests may be very selfish or competitive. Perhaps they have unresolved sibling rivalry that turns any encounter into a competition. Perhaps they had faulty gender training and can't imagine someone of another gender being an equal partner. Perhaps they just have infantile aspirations and want to enslave some man or some woman to take care of them.

If in doubt about the equality of the relationship, men should overcompensate. It may not be necessary for men to pay reparations for their grandfather's offenses, but it is necessary for men to make sure they give at least as much as they get. They can pride themselves on giving more and maybe get more in return.

Like so much else about marriage, equality does not come naturally. It has to be worked at. We may fall into love, with it all happening magically and automatically, but we don't fall into marriage like that. We adapt to it. It is a conscious process that takes a fair amount of effort and involves a fair amount of conflict and crisis.

Compatibility and the Life Cycle of Marriage

Seldom, or perhaps never, does a marriage develop into an individual relationship smoothly and without crises; there is no coming to consciousness without pain.

—Carl G. Jung, *Contributions to Analytical Psychology*

All marriage partners are incompatible. Much of the incompatibility comes because they have been raised as members of different genders, indoctrinated in a different set of roles and rules that left each partner as a half person. These roles were supposed to have been complementary, making each person compatible and essentially interchangeable with any other member of the same gender. They weren't compatible, of course, in part because each partner's personal individuality would keep breaking through, in part because they were raised in different families with different emotional styles and different interpretations of every word and action, but in part because the roles and rules have been changing so rapidly that they are outdated before they can be put into operation.

Even those who are members of the same gender—and I see more and more such couples in my practice and in the world—are incompatible. There are many reasons why gay marriages are at risk for volatility and instability, including the frequent absence of family support for the relationship and the relative absence of a safety zone of same-sex, nonsexual friendships. But a major stressor is that each partner has been trained to be a member of a gender that is not self-supporting but only half of a functioning unit, and even if they each reject certain aspects of their gender expectations, they can never escape their gender training completely. They may understand each other far better than marriage partners of different genders can, but their roles and expectations are not complementary and fewer parts of the marriage are automatic and relatively conflict-free. The keys just don't fit the locks smoothly.

When marriages are incompatible, there is conflict; there is a need to discuss things and compare perspectives in order to know one another and oneself. That is the source of a marriage's energy. If both partners are paying attention as they examine their differing instruction books on life, and if one does not dominate the other and insist upon being right, then in time they will come to know each other. They will begin to hear each other's voices in their heads and even see what the other would see in each situation. In effect, they will develop binocular vision and, with it, depth perception that will free them from the two-dimensional worldview with which they were raised.

Of course, the magical development of depth perception—and, for that matter, the creation of partnership, companionship, and even friendship—is impossible if one or both partners insist on being right. As a patient once realized, "You're telling me that I can't be right and married at the same time." Right. A married person must respect the partner's opinions, emotional reactions, preferences, and points of view without applying a standard of right or wrong to them. The fact that an opinion is logical, right, true, standard, or popular should not be the final determinant of the issue. Emotions are equally valid and must be if a man and a woman are going to be happy with the choices they make. The process of understanding this is rich and enlightening.

Incompatibility is good and right and proper, but it is greater at some times than at others. Presumably people are attracted to each other because they find similarities that make them comfortable and differences that make them fascinated. Either the similarities or the differences can begin to irritate them after a while. This irritation can be greatest at times of crisis when the two people must come together to first disagree, and thus enlighten each other, and ultimately to agree, and thus take action. The course of marriage, like the course of true love, never did run smoothly and isn't supposed to.

But there are specific and predictable turning points of marriage, intersections along the course of the life cycle when the incompatibility can feel too intense for comfort. Generally one partner enters these crises or becomes aware of the need for change before the other does. I've come to call these turning points Falling in Love, Prenuptial Panic, the End of the Romance, Joining a Family, Becoming Parents Together, Sexual Cooling, Reaching the Summit, and the Facts of Life.

FALLING IN LOVE

For a few years I've written an advice column in *Psychology Today* aimed at people who have painful personal problems, have no one in their lives whom they can consult for wisdom about intimate matters, and who don't go to therapists. The majority of the people in our world fall into that category. People write to me asking painful questions and revealing lives of terrible loneliness and confusion; they misunderstand the self-help literature and the information related by the mental health professions. Many of these tragic people believe their relationship with the universe would be righted if only someone would fall in love with them. Here is a summary of one such letter:

Dear Dr. Frank:
I am having an extremely difficult time with women. I'm 44 years old, and I've had very few dates

173

and no sex. My last actual date was in the spring of 1978, and that lasted one night. In March of this year I ate a pizza with a woman but, like the woman 14 years ago in February, she ran out the door never to return and never to speak to me again.

I have a measured IQ of 215, and maybe that is not helping. I don't use drugs of any kind or tobacco. In the past 20 years I have never had a cavity and have no personal bad habits. I have never been in prison or jail. I have no friends of any kind, male, female, work, or social.

I have tried the local mental health center and I have read self-help books, but you know theory must correspond to experiment; without experiment theory is useless. I've tried every method to gain companionship but nothing works.

What is my problem?

Lonesome

I wrote back to explain to this painfully lonely man:

"You want women to fall in love with you, even if you have no personal interest in them—or in anyone else. You want love, but love is highly personal. If you can get women to sit down with you, but then they run away when you start eating pizza, the problem is not your physical appearance but may be your neediness, your insensitivity, or your table manners. You need someone to tell you when you are repulsing people; that is one of the functions friends perform for all of us.

"Until you hang out with people and make friends, you really aren't ready to fall in love yet. You seem to have much free time and few interests to share, so join groups of active, interested people. I can't imagine groups for people who brush their teeth a lot, but Mensa caters to people with very high IQs.

"You must learn to enjoy people. Ask your mental health center about a therapy group. It's something between psychotherapy, and a band of friends, and charm school. Good luck!"

The gist of my advice was simple: Falling in love is something people can't really do until they first learn the skills of friendship. Lonely people who look around for someone with whom to fall in love are comparable to friendless, unemployed, starving people who spend their last dollar on a lottery ticket rather than a meal or a bath.

Yet in every relationship one prospective partner is still enjoying the friendship and making plans for Saturday night while the other is hearing Mendelssohn in the background. Therapists diagnose people as having a borderline personality disorder when they fall in love too easily and then get furious when the new friend or relative stranger does not fall in love in return. Life can be very lonely for those who cannot enjoy friendships without in-loveness. Such people are known as Good-bye Girls or Good-bye Guys. They drive people away with their hunger for love. Yet haven't we all been there? One of the greatest pains of love is that one of us always gets there first and must patiently wait for the other to catch up. We can work on our friendship skills while we are waiting.

We dare not try to fall in love in order to be made happy. We get happy, and then we fall in love to share it.

PRENUPTIAL PANIC

In a 1988 movie, *She's Having a Baby,* Kevin Bacon, facing Elizabeth McGovern at the altar, is hearing:

"Wilt thou, Jefferson, have this woman to be thy wedded wife? Wilt thou comfort and keep her in sickness and in health? Wilt thou provide her with credit cards and a four-bedroom, two-and-a-half-bath home with central air and professional decorating, a Mercedes-Benz, and two weeks in the Bahamas every spring? Wilt thou try to remember the little things that mean so much, like flowers on her anniversary, a kind word when she's had a rough day, and an occasional "Gee, Honey, you look pretty today"? Wilt thou be understanding when she feels ugly or when she has a big pimple on her chin? Wilt thou not be such a pig when you shave and shower? Wilt though listen patiently to long stories about kids' colds, kitchen towels, shoes, makeup, and decorator checkbook covers?"

The laugh comes when the sweating, panicky Jefferson nonetheless says, "I will."

Anyone who doesn't feel a bit of panic at the point of making such a total permanent commitment either doesn't mean it or is not paying attention. Yet, years later, in the throes of an old, open conflict or a new, secret romance, those who would run from their marriage always remember the sprint not taken on their wedding day. They don't realize it is universal. The function of all the well-dressed wedding guests is to keep the bride or groom from cutting and running as Katharine Ross did in *The Graduate,* and Hugh Grant did in *Four Weddings and a Funeral.*

If the panic occurs *before* the wedding day, it may simply be an effort to step back from your beloved to make sure you have not lost the parts of yourself you have put into the relationship—that you still exist outside the relationship as well as inside it.

In the romantic 1984 film *Splash,* Tom Hanks, exhausted by the brutalities of life in the big city, goes underwater with mermaid Daryl Hannah. As long as he is touching her, he can breathe through her gills. That level of dependency could disturb the basic equality of a relationship, and Hanks might feel the need to come up for air from time to time.

If your prospective mate panics when you come up for air and refuses to let you have enough distance to take stock of yourself and to breathe on your own, then the relationship is as dangerous as you had feared. Marriage, if it is to be other than mutual hostile dependency, must permit both people to be whole.

THE END OF THE ROMANCE

Romance and marriage are basically incompatible. Romance is about escape from reality, while marriage is a format and structure for facing and dealing with the random obstacle course of life. There is a moment in the whimsical long-running musical *The Fantasticks,* after the young couple has fallen in love and their fathers have become friends, when the lights come on starkly bright and the characters emerge from their enchantment. One of them notices by saying harshly, "This plum is too ripe!"

I recall a teenage girl who had gotten herself involved with a druggie ex-con and was plotting with him to kill her father for money. What saved the older man's life was his daughter's discovery that her idealized *innamorato* had grown a pimple on his back that was "icky." She decided, "I just don't love him anymore."

I expect grown-ups, whose psyches are presumably tied together more tightly, to need more than a pimple or two to turn them against their mates, but I have seen people who fell out of love when a wife gained a few pounds or a man shaved off the beard that hid his weak chin. One woman could not live with a man who masturbated; a man could not tolerate a woman who was not a virgin; and another fell out of love the first time his wife showed her anger at him.

In Neil Simon and Elaine May's remarkably insightful

1972 comedy *The Heartbreak Kid,* horny Charles Grodin idealizes and marries Jeannie Berlin while so much in lust and love that he fails to notice the reality of her. He freaks on their honeymoon when he is faced with her sloppy eating habits and the egg salad on her chin, is repulsed when he hears her on the toilet, and is driven to distraction by her use of baby talk as she pulls at the hairs on his chest. When she points out a decrepit old couple and tells him, "That will be us in forty or fifty years," the incompletely married Grodin knows he must escape his insensitive but totally married bride. He promptly falls in love with Cybill Shepherd. Grodin is a Romantic Narcissist, demanding that the women in his life correspond with the woman in his dreams, while Berlin is in love with love and doesn't notice the man she is repulsing.

Many men and women are turned off by reality. The nineteenth-century British essayist and critic John Ruskin was unable to consummate his marriage after an engagement of many years when he discovered on his wedding night that women, unlike marble statues, had pubic hair. Others discover after marriage that their spouse has bad moods, bad odors, or bad habits, much as they themselves do. Whatever such people think marriage will bring, reality is not part of the fantasy. Many want perfection in their mate's appearance, behavior, and history, and what is even more outrageous, they want perfection in their own emotions.

For people who understand marriage, the end of the romance is the beginning of the relationship. Once people are past the point of having to appear ideal to each other, once they overcome their blindness to each other's weaknesses, reality can be noticed, negotiated, and faced together. A determinedly idealized relationship cannot permit much honesty, and even less reality.

If you find you are not feeling in love anymore, be more loving.

JOINING A FAMILY

In the cherishable 1977 movie *Annie Hall*, Woody Allen goes to meet Diane Keaton's family. As the upper-middle-class Wasps conduct their superficial conversation over the ham at Easter dinner, Woody pictures the contrast of his own noisy, constantly complaining Jewish family and sees himself in full Hasidic getup, with black hat and coat, uncut beard, and sideburns to his shoulders.

We are at home with our own families and hope to create a new family in which we are at home. Yet the incest taboo requires that we do it with a partner who grew up in a family in which we may never feel fully at home.

Everybody ends up with many more relatives by marriage than relatives by blood. If you extend it a little beyond the traditional six degrees of separation, you don't have to be Elizabeth Taylor to find that you are related by marriage to all the people on earth. This should be wonderful, creating one big happy family on the planet, but it doesn't work out that way. In-laws mess up your restrictive sense of family. They dilute and invade the atmosphere of informal family intimacy, the sharing of a common past and an agreed upon set of values and attitudes. And they constantly challenge your loyalties. Once the in-laws are included, it isn't "just us."

In-laws make life rich and full, and pull us out of the narrow bounds of our isolated family, but in-laws rank high among life's irritants in large part because they seem like family and must be honored as family, yet must be handled by a quite different and rather delicate set of principles. The crucial secret of dealing with in-laws is this: You have all the responsibilities and duties toward in-laws that you have toward your own relatives, but you can have none of the expectations. You have no rights and privileges with your in-laws; therefore, you must appreciate the good things they do for you and cheerfully overlook the bad things. You are not permitted to criticize your in-laws either to their faces or behind their backs.

The in-laws who are around the table are not as problematic as those who live inside each partner's psyche, interpreting life's events and demanding loyalty. Every family is a delicate exercise in multiculturalism, even those who give the family antiques to Goodwill and forget everything conscious about the family stories. It's inside.

The work of marriage is not only to make "one flesh" out of two separate people but to make one family out of two separate traditions and sets of rituals, where every symbol has a different meaning, every event a different set of implications and, behind it, a different history. Two people do not have to come from different parts of the world, different ethnic traditions, or different religions to have drastically different ways of doing things and reacting to things. I am currently seeing a couple who have been engaged for ten years and are in all respects ideally suited to each other, but they cannot get married because one comes from a family of diehard Georgia Tech fans and the other from a family in which anyone who missed a University of Georgia football game would be excommunicated.

The most problematic in-laws are not the notorious mothers-in-law, and certainly not ex-wives and ex-husbands, but "ex-children," the remnants of past failures at liaison who come and go in each new marriage, never being totally part of it and certainly never anchoring it as children do in their real families, but always there in the flesh or in spirit.

Stepparents get a bad name in part because the presence of a stepparent is a constant reminder that a real parent has been lost, and in part because stepparents have their primary connection with the other parent and not with the child. The stepmother who was willing to have an affair with a married father has already demonstrated her lack of concern for the man's children. The stepparent who brings his or her children into the family intrudes on the child's space and security. The stepfather who tries his hand at being an amateur disciplinarian, either because he dislikes kids or because he wants to be a hero to the beleaguered single mother, is the natural enemy of the child.

Stepchildren are lost in space, and their relationships with stepparents are among the trickier and more volatile realities that budding grown-ups have to master. Some do it well; in my practice I don't get to see them much. Instead I see people who can't figure out what the function of a stepparent is. They destroy other people's children as they practice one of the trickiest jobs in life. I often see men who dumbly assume that women are interchangeable, that each possesses an infallible maternal instinct which guides her in parenting. So he drops off his children of whatever age with his wife or girlfriend of whatever duration and expects her to know how to parent these children who are in post-traumatic shock from the parents' divorce and remarriage. These men may believe that child rearing is woman's work and should never interfere with their work or golf game.

There are women who dumbly assume the new man in their lives, who deserted his own children or avoided having them up until now. will know how to sensitively and lovingly beat her recently fatherless kids into shape for her.

I routinely see women who can't tolerate anyone's children but their own; in fact, it is a rare and saintly stepmother who will make no distinction between her children and those of the woman (or women) she has replaced. But I often see men who pay attention to the child at hand and forget about the children they left behind. Shakespeare reminded us that "it is a wise father that knows his own child." It is not necessarily a wise child but a lucky one who knows his or her own parents.

Stepparents must never forget that they have no authority over children except that which comes directly from the child's parents. Stepparents must never criticize or compete with the parent he or she has replaced and must never undercut the parent he or she is assisting. Stepparents are in a position to bolster the parents and offer an alternate environment and companionship to children, but they exert their influence not by authority but by friendship and loving involvement. In some ways stepparents are like aunts and uncles. Stepparents have to be at least as loving and a lot more accepting and generous than actual parents. The necessary degree of powerlessness is hard for amateur stepparents to achieve. Stepparenting is an intermittently humbling and ultimately rewarding investment, but it is not a position of power.

BECOMING PARENTS TOGETHER

In the movie *Raising Arizona,* convenience-store armed robber Nicolas Cage and cop Holly Hunter, unable to get pregnant and blocked from adopting, kidnap a baby. Instantly, Hunter becomes the expert and Cage the amateur. He is required to watch his language, to hide his *Playboy* magazines, and to put himself under his wife's tutelage as she civilizes him and trains him to be a proper parent.

Nothing unbalances a relationship quite like the introduction of children into it. Sometimes the children get there first. When there are children from a previous liaison, the entering stepparent is an intruder, a competitor, and a minority.

If the children come from this marriage, they don't unbalance it quite so much, but a pregnant woman is a "we," with the rights and privileges of a majority. Even after a baby leaves the mother's body, the child is more connected with the mother for a time afterward. Thus it seems only natural for the mother to speak for the child, and for the father and husband to be peripheral to the central relationship of the family. This has disastrous consequences on the father-child relationship, which is distanced from the get-go; the mother-child relationship, which is enmeshed all along; and the marriage, which is marginalized to the back burner. If the mother speaks for the child, she is the grown-up, and the father becomes a selfish and intrusive child.

For the relationships to work out right, fathers must be just as involved as mothers in child raising from birth, and certainly from weaning. In olden days, children were apprenticed to their fathers as soon as they could walk, but now that fathers do their work away from home and family, they are at risk for becoming merely absentee landlords to whom complaints and requests may be made but who are not quite emotionally part of the family. There is nothing in life that can make a man happier, more emotionally whole, or more adult than hands-on child raising. The man who avoids it is trying to guard his own childishness. He is a fool and, unfortunately, will remain a fool because he is skipping the experience that would give him grown-up wisdom.

Many women, perhaps women who failed to develop other skills and talents, are Maternal Chauvinists, championing the idea that "mother knows best": Some sort of internal information system gives her the correct answer to any issue involving children. I recall a pediatrician's wife who, despite her profession as a CPA, was convinced that her gender gave her far more information about the illnesses of children than her husband might have.

Another Maternal Chauvinist, who mostly slept, drank, and screwed around between the time her husband took the older kids to school and the time he brought them home and fixed dinner for the family, resisted his theory that she should not go off and leave the three-year-old at home alone. She insisted that since she was a mother, she knew best, and anyway, because of her maternal instincts, she would know instantly, wherever she was, whether her children needed anything. Her husband might be sober, clearheaded, and responsible, but he was not a mother, so what did he know?

Such Maternal Chauvinists are balanced by Patriarchal Narcissists who think their own wishes or opinions should prevail on any subject, even the activities they disdain. They know best not because of competence or wisdom but because they are men and have

—a bigger paycheck;
—greater upper-body strength that makes them more effective at throwing things when they have a temper tantrum;
—a last name that belonged to their father rather than to their husband;
—a favorable comment about their gender from Saint Paul;
—a penis;
—a belief that their penis might fall off if a woman should be right and they should be wrong about anything, however insignificant.

In some families, men become the boss because no one expects them to do anything more useful. If the mother, getting little love and attention from a marriage in which the two partners do their work in separate arenas, requires her husband's attention whenever he is around, the amount of fathering he can give and his children can get from him is drastically reduced. The father's competition with his children is thus encouraged, and his life becomes increasingly meaningless. If the father does not father, everyone in the family is likely to end up unhappily angry. If the mother does nothing except mother, everyone in the family is likely to end up unhappily guilty.

Marriages in which parenting is going on may be more

gratifying in the long run, but they seem more frustrating and strangely enough more fragile than marriages without children or those in which the children are grown and gone. A marriage in which parenting is going on is going to be in trouble on several levels unless both grown-ups are giving top priority to the child raising, at least during the time when the parents are at home. Nondomestic men are a luxury few families can afford, though many men were raised to expect such pampering and feel cheated when they don't get to be the child in the family. However the couple assigns parenting tasks, it becomes apparent that the nuclear family is just not big enough or flexible enough to support a home, a career or two, a child or more, and a nonfunctional prince or visiting celebrity.

One or both of the parents may identify strongly with the little tyke and may react to the other parent as the child does. Either or both may reexperience traumas with their own parents, attributing the feelings to their mate. It is a disconcerting experience to watch a lover/playmate/fellow child turning into a parent/authority/adult. Both partners transfer feelings about their parents onto their partners, especially during adolescence when our sense of ourselves as separate beings got established through our necessary battles with our own parents. Unless we are astoundingly adult, we are at risk for identifying with our adolescent child against the more adult parent.

Not surprisingly, marriages with adolescent kids are the most fragile, and the less completely adult parent is strongly at risk for reverting to adolescence, starting an affair, and running off to go through puberty another time. As good as child raising is for those chronological adults who would be parents, it is frustrating for those who would be children again.

SEXUAL COOLING

I'm at the age where food has taken the place of sex in my life. In fact, I've just had a mirror put over my kitchen table.

—Rodney Dangerfield

Without sex, men and women might not seem like natural partners. They might not even consider trying to live together. Sex covers a lot of flaws in a relationship, at least as long as the sex is exclusive to the marriage, it works for both people, and each gets what he or she wants from it, which may be orgasms, attention or friendliness, affirmation of gender, or just a few moments of calm in the storm of the marital battle. If sex is important, then the partners will be constantly aware of each other and will be kind enough to make sex possible; if sex is not important, then distances don't have to be breached, barriers don't have to be torn down, and attention does not have to be paid. Sex is good for relationships, and it is rare for actively monogamous couples to find themselves either unhappy or divorced. Sex is one of the things that contributes greatly to human happiness.

Most people like sex, at least at first, but after the mysteries of puberty have been revealed and the adventures of adolescence and early adulthood have brought their necessary victories, sex settles in as a comfortable part of life. Many people then don't really like sex as much as they say they like it or even as much as they think they like it. Sex with a familiar partner requires people to be close, vulnerable, tender, unselfish, and even actively loving, and some people can't bring themselves to do that very often.

Happy people open themselves up completely to their

partner, revealing all they need and want. They would like to make themselves sexually happy, and they give whatever it takes to make their partner sexually happy—not necessarily at the same time. Few people marry these days without first working out a sexual relationship that rings both partner's chimes. They know how to do it. The problems people have now are due less often to ignorance, scruples, modesty, or anxiety than to laziness.

Women, even in today's postpatriarchal world, are still likely to need sex for reassurance of the relationship, while men are still likely to need sex for reassurance of masculinity. So, as the man's need becomes less pressing and he pursues sex with less vigor, the woman may doubt his love or her attractiveness, and thus may pull back further at just the time she needs to jump his bones in order to keep their sexual love alive. He may think he is getting impotent, which usually responds to either pornography or fellatio, or both—anything that takes his anxious focus off his shrinking penis. Urologists have amazing tricks up their sleeves these days if the simpler tactics don't work; but waiting anxiously will not restore life to a scared penis, and seeking a different partner will ruin the marriage and the life, and will probably not help the penis very much for very long anyway.

Couples can remain sexually active for a lifetime if they don't turn it into a competitive sport. As people age, sex, which had become efficient in a couple's forties, becomes mysterious and exciting again. People can relish the adventure of never knowing ahead of time what is going to work and what isn't. Over a lifetime, sex requires wondrous amounts of both humility and goodwill, and a fair amount of communication.

It is not generally good for relationships at any age to go too long without sex. Honestly, if you don't use it, you really will lose it.

REACHING THE SUMMIT

The intellect of man is forced to choose
Perfection of the life, or of the work.

—W. B. Yeats, "The Choice"

"Money and death, making ends meet until they meet the end," was, according to Edward Albee in *A Delicate Balance,* the simplicity of men's lives. Much has changed. Two-career marriages are the norm now, so the pressures on men and women are not drastically different or at least don't have to be. But he is still likely to expect his career to take top priority, while she is still likely to give a higher priority to family and kids. She is still likely to retain most of the instrumental jobs at home as well as the emotional and interpersonal ones. Once the kids leave home or need less attention and service, she may be set free to pursue her career, often just as he is ready to slow down and let her use her new leisure to take care of him. Old patterns die hard even in a new world.

A man is and always has been perfectly capable of doing whatever needs to be done, but he isn't likely to do it if she does it first. Part of it is his doubt about his competence in these roles and his reluctance to become mother's little helper while she shows him how to do things he should already know how to do. Part of it is sheer laziness. Once a man gets as spoiled by his wife as he was by his mother, he is not likely to be pushed into fully adult functioning without a bit of a battle. The battle is worth it for both him and her.

But if a man achieves less career success than he had expected or hoped, he may be crushed, humiliated, depressed, even if his life is actually going well. He sees himself as a failure and assumes all around him will see him that way, too. But if he achieves more successes than expected, he may be thrown into an even bigger crisis, especially if nothing in

188

his background prepared him to know how a rich and famous man acts. Most frustrating, he will find himself distanced from old friends, envied and pursued by perfect strangers, and thrown into greater dependence on a family that is not likely to be particularly impressed with it all since they have needs of their own. The need of a successful man to be understood, shielded, and pampered because of his success is not likely to be on top of others' lists. But either great success or relative failure is a crisis and can lead to affairs, addictions, and even suicide.

Women, on the other hand, are likely to take success or failure, even wealth or poverty, in stride because their vocational achievements are not likely to be the sole pillar of their identity and self-esteem. Some women are desperate for success; most aren't and are thus healthier in this area, more concerned with making a contribution and enjoying the process. Often women get little interpersonal reward for their successes; they may even be penalized at home and have to make it up to men who are less spectacularly successful.

Men must get this into perspective if they ever hope to be happy in midlife. If a man can learn to give a higher priority to family and relationships, he may avoid the crisis of reaching the summit and finding it is higher or lower than planned.

THE FACTS OF LIFE

Norma, you're a woman of fifty. Now, grow up! There's nothing tragic about being fifty—not unless you try to be twenty-five.

—William Holden to Gloria Swanson in
Sunset Boulevard by C. Brackett, B.
Wilder, and D. M. Marchman, Jr.

Growing old isn't so bad when you consider the alternative.

—Maurice Chevalier

We grow old. It's not so bad unless we try to keep it from happening. But after the children leave home and our attention is directed once more to ourselves and our life cycle rather than them and theirs, we notice that we are no longer young. Actually, we may first notice that our mate is no longer young. Our children leave us but are still dependent on us for anything from love to money to recipes; our parents fail and become more dependent on us; we join the "tween" generation. This seems like, and probably is, our last chance to change our lives. We may even daydream about the lives we could have had instead and perhaps the lives we still could have instead. Possible, but it could cost everything in life.

In *The Four Seasons* from 1981, Carol Burnett, as she applies lotion to her face, confronts her husband, Alan Alda, with his envy and competitiveness with a friend who is being waited on by an energetic new wife: "You wish you had some blonde nymph adoring you like he does. So, go on, go find one. How long are you going to hold on to these fantasies? The reality is you're married to a middle-aged woman with a good sense of humor and dry skin. If you don't like it, go find yourself a nymph. In other words, and I say this in the most loving way, shit or get off the pot."

When the younger generation leaves and the older generation dies, people in midlife have each other, and that can be the best time in life, but only if they have not gone too far away from one another in the interim to find each other now. One partner always accepts aging first, and sees its liberation rather than seeing only its disability. This stage of life lasts a long time, maybe as long as all the rest put together,

190

and it can be creative and fun for anyone who accepts it. Some don't.

Age is not just associated with dying or even with weakness and ugliness. It is also associated with becoming like one's parents. People who are comfortable with their parents seem comfortable turning into them. Those who are still adolescents in rebellion will surely rebel against this ultimate fact of life. The point of not growing up is to avoid growing old. Those who have not accepted adulthood yet may be horrified at the prospect of marriage to someone who is growing old inside as well as out. Even at the end, some people are determined to remain unhappy by refusing to accept the inevitable.

Marriage Among Adults

Much of the maturing that takes place in marriage comes from learning the half of humanness that was lost in gender training. It does not mean disdaining the things men do that are "just like a man" or the things women do that are "just like a woman." It means that we get past the "Me Tarzan, you Jane. Me hunt, you cook" or "Men are from Mars, women are from Venus" schools of gender relations and learn to value, appreciate, and even perform the arts, skills, and attitudes of our partners.

So far, more women are succeeding at this crucial job than men. In *Outrageous Acts and Everyday Rebellions,* Gloria Steinem noticed, "Many more women are becoming the men they wanted to marry, but too few men are becoming the women they wanted to marry. . . . Until men are socialized to raise children and care for the home as much as women are, this double burden will continue to restrict women, deprive children of nurturing fathers, and perpetuate gender roles." As couples grow old together it becomes especially crucial that they be functionally interchangeable and able to do whatever their partner can no longer do, regardless of such insignificant details as gender.

THE TOTALITY OF MARRIAGE

Never fear. A lifetime of marriage gives people plenty to talk about, plenty of changes and revelations to process. There is no danger of boredom if you're paying attention.

But marriage doesn't make you happy unless you are in it all the way. Every time I talk about marriage, I feel compelled to point out the similarities to swimming. Swimming instructors who teach drown-proofing have learned that drowning occurs when people are afraid of the water and struggle to stay above it. If they went ahead and immersed themselves in the water, they would find they could float securely, breathe comfortably, and relax totally. It is the effort to keep from being engulfed by the water that is exhausting and potentially fatal. Marriage is similarly frightening. Many drown rather than surrender themselves to it. They try to protect themselves from it or win at it, and are therefore doomed to failure at such a simple but completely engulfing state.

Those who try to protect themselves from their marriage are soon at war. It is a bit like seeking safety by keeping oneself partway out of an airplane or submarine.

MONOGAMY: MARRIAGE INSURANCE

Fidelity gave unity to lives that would otherwise splinter into thousands of split-second impressions.

—Milan Kundera, *The Unbearable Lightness of Being*

Fidelity is the single most important element in solidly enduring marriages.

Married couples fight. They go through the full range of human emotions toward each other. Often they hate one another. Sometimes they kill one another. But they're not likely to get a divorce until someone is unfaithful and lies about it or tries to keep it secret. The fact that there are attractions or even infidelities does not mean the marriage is invalid or over. Infidelity is a constant danger in even the best marriage; it is the lying about it that will destroy the union.

In *The Future of Marriage,* Jessie Bernard points out the quandary: "There is an intrinsic and inescapable conflict in marriage. Human beings . . . want to eat their cake and have it too. They want excitement and adventure. They also want safety and security. . . . In the past, the desire for security, though present in both marital partners, has tended to be stronger among women than among men, and the desire for outside—especially sexual—adventure greater among men than among women."

Fidelity is not always automatic and natural, but it is really quite easy. Most people remain faithful most of the time without ill effects. Monogamy is not practiced because you love your mate, because you fear your mate, or even because you made a deal with your mate; monogamy is practiced because it is the commitment that makes your life coherent, because it frees up time and energy for yourself and your loved ones, and because it is the best insurance you can get for your marriage. It offers a life of dignity, honor, and discipline. Sometimes it is a life without ecstasy—but also without agony.

Secrets of Marriage

1. Marry someone who likes you, who has nonsexual friends of your gender, and who is friends with his or her own parents, particularly with the parent of your gender.

193

2. Before you marry anyone, make sure you fully understand the history of your prospective spouse's previous marriages and his or her parents' marriages. History is habit. You can't make a marriage with someone who didn't learn marriage growing up and doesn't get it now.

3. Friendship is an infinitely more stabilizing basis for marriage than romance. Get good at friendship before you even think about falling in love.

4. Forget everything you ever thought you knew about the opposite sex. People who are trying to base the rules and roles of marriage on old-fashioned ideas of gender are just avoiding getting to know one another. The marriage begins when the gender dance ends, so don't marry someone who is flatfootedly literal about gender.

5. If you are not afraid of marriage or at least in awe of it, you are not paying attention.

6. If you didn't know marriages that worked when you were growing up, ask people who are happy and married how they do it. You'll probably find that they don't know how they do it, but they take joy and pride in the effort.

7. Marriage, like a submarine, is only safe if you get all the way inside it.

8. Marital partnership presents manifold rights and privileges, but bad manners are not among them. Intimacy need not be rude.

9. Never consider divorce. Don't talk about it, don't scream about it, don't even think about it. For the

marriage to work, divorce is not an option. Separation definitely, murder perhaps, but not divorce.

10. You're not going to be in love all the time. If you want to recapture that magic from when you were in love, be loving. One of my favorite James Thurber cartoons shows a battling couple kicking over the furniture and shouting: "Well, who made the magic go out of the relationship, you or me?!"

11. Marriage isn't supposed to make you happy; it is supposed to make you married.

12. Do more than your share of the working and loving. What you get from your marriage is in proportion to your investment in it. You don't have to be perfect, your partner doesn't have to be perfect, but you have to be fully there.

13. Sex is good for you and good for marriage. For your sake I hope it is the one thing you do only with your marriage partner. Couples should do it regularly whether they want to or not. If there is conflict about sex, they should do it as often as the more sexually eager partner wants it, but in the manner that the less excited one finds most agreeable. Foreplay should start the day before.

14. Always keep your pants zipped in public.

15. Never sacrifice your marriage for your career. If you are determined to be vocationally successful, recognize that as an imposition on your family and remember to apologize daily.

16. Get gender out of parenting as soon after birth as possible. Men can be just as nurturing as women, but only if they practice. If men as well as women can nurture, it will set everything right for all the relationships in the family. Nurturing must not be only women's work.

17. Stepparents must realize they have no authority but they do have awesome responsibilities to make up for the missing parent they are trying to replace. They must realize that stepchildren, by virtue of having lost a parent somewhere, are walking wounded and need loving friendship.

18. You never know your beloved until the two of you work together during a crisis with an adolescent child. In fact, you never know yourself until then.

19. There is no point in battling age in yourself or in your partner. You'll lose. That's a battle no one has ever won.

20. Fighting has no place in marriage. If your mate hurts you, talk about your hurt rather than acting out your anger. Discuss your anger calmly, as your problem, not as something your mate has done wrong. Stay kind.

21. The purpose of marital conflict should be to understand the issues and the emotions rather than determine who is the winner. The true winner of a marital conflict might be the one who understands the other's point of view first. Either both win or both lose. You can't be right and married at the same time.

7

Love, Lies, and Divorce

Divorce means never having to say you're sorry.

—Said by somebody divorced

I swear, if you existed, I'd divorce you!

—Elizabeth Taylor to Richard Burton in
Who's Afraid of Virginia Woolf?
by Edward Albee

Who Gets Divorced?

YOU WOULD THINK THAT EVERY DIVORCING FAMILY IS UN-
happy in its own way, yet divorcing families have much in
common in addition to one member's frantic need to destroy
the family in order to feel free to pursue happiness. The urge
to divorce is akin to the suicidal impulses of depression, and
plotting the suicide or divorce will actually settle the mind
and bring a sense of peace or purpose for a while. Of course
either impulse is likely to pass if you get busy doing something else instead.

The urge to divorce requires two things: a feeling of unhappiness and a belief that marriage is supposed to bring
happiness.

Acting on the divorce urge usually requires a few more

things: a family history of divorce or a societal culture of divorce that makes it seem like a reasonable thing to do; a relationship or set of relationships that encourages you to divorce, perhaps an affair partner, a friend, or a therapist who would get more of you if you were giving less to your marriage; and a defect in the intimacy of the marriage whereby you are not talking effectively to your partner about what you think you need to make yourself happy.

Several things can damage the intimacy of marriage: romantic narcissism or gender literalism that lead people to expect marital adjustments to occur automatically; the failure to see marriage work in your own family growing up; shame that leads you to hide yourself from your partner or your partner to hide from you; secrets and lies.

It is not necessarily the "unhappily married" who end up divorced. It is not generally the women who are being beaten and insulted. It is not usually the men who are cut off sexually and treated with disregard and contempt. Instead it is those who long for intimacy but are held back, often by secrets and lies, from pursuing it within the marriage.

In my thirty-seven years of working with marriage and divorce, I have seen only a handful of established first marriages that ended in divorce without someone's being unfaithful.

I've seen more women than men who have gotten divorces without infidelity. And while it does not happen much in my practice, divorce does happen often after therapy with a therapist who sees divorce as a healthy form of self-expression for women. Sadly, the problems that drive women to seek "expressive" divorce and escape from patriarchal patterns of relationships are often easy to solve in couples therapy with a therapist who believes that men are capable of changing.

Still, in my upper-middle-class practice of successful, educated people, most of the women who were determined to get out of their marriages were either already in affairs of their own or were working up to them. Of course some women scream and threaten divorce routinely, as the only way to get a wayward or distracted husband's attention. They usually don't mean it, but some emotionally retarded men don't know that.

In my practice the reason men seek divorce or push their wives into it is consistently and almost without exception related to infidelity. Often the infidelity was kept secret through the entire divorce process. A few men have told me convincingly that they wanted a divorce or got a divorce because they were lusting after a woman or a man or a fantasy that they had not yet consummated. Yet no matter how unhappy men may be in their lives or in their marriages—and men don't do a very good job of knowing which is which— they are unlikely to leave unless there is someone else either in their bed or in their head.

Fidelity is the promise at the heart of marriage. With it, all else can be tolerated; without it, the slightest stress or unkindness can blow the marriage apart. Marriages in which one partner has secretly betrayed the other do not feel safe. The couple feels unexplained tension and is not likely to be happy. The first step in saving a marriage that seems headed for divorce is to stop the current affair and reveal the affairs that have gone on before. This scares some guilty people so much that they would rather be divorced than be known.

Infidelity—more because of lying about the illicit sex than because of the sex itself—destroys the intimacy of the marriage. People who screw around regularly and feel entitled to do so come to hide from marriage as if it were an enemy out to catch, expose, and punish them. People who feel guilt about infractions of their principles and boundaries may feel unworthy of their marriage and pull back into themselves, revealing little of their past guilt and inner torment. People who have fallen in love with someone outside the marriage are off in la-la land with a fantasy and are unavailable in the marriage.

People who think they can't endure life unless they are "in love" are dangerous. After thirty-seven years in the trenches of family therapy and thirty-seven years in a totally committed, totally realistic marriage, I have come to see "romantic love" as an absurd, albeit delicious, crisis-induced escape from sanity, a narcissistic intoxication with no relationship to loving.

Fairy tales for children tell us that the prince and princess meet, engage in some sort of adventure, fall in love, and live happily ever after. The literature for grown-ups is different. While the culture holds out romance as an ultimate emotional goal, it also warns of its danger. Romantic love often requires the sacrifice of lives (Romeo and Juliet, Anna Karenina, Tristan and Isolde, Hero and Leander) and body parts (Wotan gave up an eye for Fricka in *The Ring Cycle,* Holly Hunter gave up a finger for Harvey Keitel in *The Piano,* Abelard gave up even more for Heloise).

Despite it all, if one is unpartnered and alone, romantic love can be a resolution to loneliness as magically ecstatic and lifesaving as Robinson Crusoe's spotting of the footsteps in the sand. While it will not last, the fact that it was once there and that memories of it can be conjured up from time to time makes a resultant marriage feel special and right. Of course misery (and/or an extensive sexual and romantic supporting cast) can result if the partners are so foolish as to require continuation of their romantic high for a lifetime.

Romantic love may be a good thing when it hits people who are lonely and unattached, but it is a disaster for those who are committed elsewhere. A parking space may seem a good thing in a crowded lot, but not if it is already occupied. Parades, firework displays, and a spring rain are good things unless they take place in your living room.

If romantic love intrudes into an ongoing life and set of

relationships, and requires human sacrifice to bring it to consummation, it is a disaster for the two people so afflicted, for their partners, and above all for their children. This may occur at a time of depression, which may or may not arise from some dissatisfaction with the marriage. But once people are in affairs, they can come to feel so alienated from their marriage partner that they reverse historical sequence and blame the marriage for the affair! Therapists who see their function as guilt reducers add to the delusion; they can always find some marital imperfection on which to hang the infidelity.

All marriages have problems, but affairs are rarely efforts to solve marital problems. Affairs can occur accidentally in good marriages, but if they are kept secret, they destroy marital intimacy and eat away at the marriage's resiliency, making subsequent problems harder to solve.

People proud of their love shout it from the rooftops and, through it, connect with the whole world. Illicit love requires dishonesty, betrayal of loved ones and honor and integrity, and a withdrawal from the rest of the world. As people in illicit love lead their secret lives, the intrigue produces an intense bond but makes the betrayed marriage and other aboveground alliances adversarial. When the deceit comes out into the open and the seemingly magical relationship is exposed to cruel daylight, it may well shrivel. And once the barriers of shame and dishonesty are removed from the marriage, the affair may look sordid and shallow. But if the romance goes on into a new marriage, the in-loveness will in time relax (at best) into comfortable mundanity and perhaps the realization that too high a price was paid. It is hard to convince people of this while they are disoriented by their in-loveness.

The manic high of the "in-love" state is not likely to strike the same relationship twice, but the "in-love" state has little to do with loving, and the absence of it is surely not grounds for either divorce or suicide. Yet while the in-love state has proven to be an unreliable basis for an enduring marriage, the expectation of it—or the requirement of it—can nevertheless bring about a high level of domestic misery. A societal glorification of romance and distrust of marriage can lead naive people, even therapists, to believe that marriage is about being in love and the institution cannot survive without a dose of passion.

John Gottman finds in *What Predicts Divorce* that long-term marital satisfaction comes from factors such as companionship and friendship, and the ability to provide support, validation, and understanding, rather than passion and in-loveness. It seems to me dangerous for people to stake their happiness in life on romantic love. They are ecstatic when they experience that most engulfing flight from reality, but miserable when they don't. Romance can pull you out of a funk, but it has far more side effects than Prozac.

People who keep their marital unhappiness secret, while enjoying their misery or seeking partners with whom to escape, merely confuse all in their wake. Only people who are overtly miserable in their marriage are in a position to deal with the problems; therefore, the worst marriages have the greatest hope of a favorable outcome and the lowest likelihood of divorce!

Gottman's research sidesteps the matter of infidelity altogether and finds that the marriages that fail are those with a partner who shows contempt, criticizes, complains, and/or withdraws. The first three are often efforts to pursue a withdrawing, distancing partner, perhaps one who is screwing around and hiding. Withdrawers must be reeled in as smoothly, firmly, and gently as a big fish. Hostile efforts to pursue a partner who is hiding just make the distancer dig in deeper. I can't imagine where people learned to get love by rendering themselves as noxiously unpleasant as possible, but angry, guilt-producing pursuit is guaranteed to drive anyone who is a bit loosely connected at the moment to run even farther away.

Divorce apologists often seem to assume that the marriages ending in divorce are the violent and highly conflictual ones, and it is merciful to end them. Indeed, some marriages are horrifying war zones, posing a threat to life and limb. Still, while the couple's pattern of fighting may well determine whether the marriage will succeed or fail, Gottman found that high levels of marital conflict did not predict divorce. It was predicted by the couple's pattern of fighting.

It is not clear how bad marital conflict has to get before it is worse than divorce. Some people seem to divorce because they are especially touchy or squeamish about normal, ordinary, everyday marital conflict, perhaps because they've read too many self-help books blaming divorce on conflict rather than betrayal, secrets, and lies.

Marital conflict is necessary for marriage and for training children about conflict resolution. Marriage at its best is warfare. It takes guts. Married people tend to do what they saw their parents do, which may be noisy, insulting, and mean. And when they are shamed and feeling particularly childish, they fall back on the techniques they used in their competitions with their brothers and sisters. Some women, believing their husbands are acting like children, fall back on the techniques their mothers used with unruly kids. Some men, feeling assaulted by their wives, fall back on techniques they learned in military training or football practice.

People don't usually divorce because they fight, but they do fight during the divorce: One is fighting for the family, and one is fighting against it. The level of conflict and every sort of physical and emotional violence increases enormously during the time preceding a divorce, and certainly during the divorce process itself.

Violence in marriage or in divorce should not be tolerated. I encourage both wives and husbands to call the police when the other spouse gets physically violent. If the violence continues on any level, I urge the couple to separate while therapy intensifies. Continuing violence is a very good reason to get a divorce. Neither adults nor children should have to live with people who run around with guns or knives or fists trying to terrorize and brutalize their loved ones.

Unfortunately, divorce doesn't stop domestic violence—Nicole Simpson is an example—but treatment and intolerance can. Most couples can learn, with the combination of societal intolerance and therapy, to interact without violence. Men who have been socialized to believe that violence is appropriate in marriage can be taught otherwise. Women who believe it is okay for women to be violent toward men but not for men to strike back can be taught otherwise as well. Stopping alcohol and certain drugs may be part of the program. These patterns can often be changed if it is clear that they will not be tolerated by the mate or the society.

Most domestic violence is episodic and situational, and while it destroys the spirit, unbalances the relationship, and makes life hell, it does not maim or kill. But there are a few men who are truly dangerous—violent, alcoholic, paranoid, terroristic. My nephew-in-law Neil Jacobson, along with John Gottman, identified in *When Men Batter Women* a group of these brutal men who actually use torture to calm themselves and seem happy with the pain and abuse they inflict on their loved ones. These men terrify therapists, yet their bruised and bloody wives protect them and say they "love" their husbands. In *Turning Points,* I called these men "Brutes"; Jacobson and Gottman call them "Cobras." We don't think they are fit for marriage, but in the sample of them that Jacobson and Gottman studied and followed, very few of them divorced.

The wrong people are getting divorced and for the wrong reasons. People make these life-shaking decisions on the basis of how they feel—unhappy, wronged, or simply out of love—rather than how they are treated, and whether their lives or their sanity are in danger.

But in our culture of divorce, marriage is supposed to make people happy, so if marriage fails to do so, surely divorce will bring about the expected bliss.

The Culture of Divorce

> PATIENT MERYL STREEP: Marriage doesn't work. You know what works? Divorce!
> THERAPIST MAUREEN STAPLETON: Divorce is only a temporary solution.
>
> —Nora Ephron's *Heartburn*

Child psychiatrist Robert Coles writes in his introduction to Edward W. Beal and Gloria Hochman's *Adult Children of Divorce:*

> Best, then, to regard divorce . . . not as simply a common occurrence, hence a readily available alternative to the pain of a troubled marriage, but rather as a potential tragedy all its own—hence a decision to be confronted with great and earnest and persistent seriousness. . . . Divorce *is* a moral matter as well as a psychological one—because when one prepares to do something that has potentially lasting implications for the way one will live one's life, and the way one's children will live their lives, then one is sorting out rights and wrongs as well as questions of psychology, of "mental health," or of one's "personal welfare."

The narcissistic greed for personal happiness, and the anger when it does not arrive as ordered, may be the root of most human pain. In our pursuit of the stuff we hope will make us happy, we rape, pillage, and plunder. In our pursuit of the person we hope will make us happy, we betray our fellows and even our loved ones. We lash out at those who seem happier than we. But there are few things ordinary people can do in their frantic pursuit of happiness that will cause as much pain to as many people as divorce.

The recent popularity of divorce, and the casualness with which people go about it, is startling and contagious. Living in a world one perceives as noxious or untrustworthy, in a family one sees as treacherous and impermanent, causes a hardening of the individual, a callous determination not to be distracted from survival issues or from the pursuit of self-fulfillment by the concerns of others.

Divorce has always been a necessary remedy for dangerous and disastrous marriages. When a marriage could not be consummated, when it proved infertile, when it was physically abusive, when it had been irreparably betrayed, divorce might have been the remedy. But it was always an unusual method of dealing with an unusual situation, and while the circumstances might have been horrific enough to engender understanding and sympathy, the behavior of one party was sure to have met with disapproval.

Growing up in the 1940s and '50s, I had two friends whose parents were divorced; in both cases the fathers had tried to kill the children, one because he was alcoholic, the other because he was psychotic. There were other couples who were living apart because they hated one another, drove one another crazy, or had taken up with other people, but they did not divorce. Divorce was reserved for matters of life or death.

But as the principles of self-expression and pursuit of self-fulfillment took hold in the postpatriarchal world and women had more options, divorce rates gradually rose—in part because men felt less responsible for women and in part because women felt less dependent on men.

There was a spike in divorces after World War II, when quickie wartime marriages, entered by those who expected to die, were reconsidered by people who now expected to live. But once everyone settled down to a peaceful world and a brief patriarchal revival, men returned to family life, women returned to domestic life, and the divorce rate returned to its low normal rate—from which it slowly rose as ideas about personal freedom supplanted notions of duty.

Early marriage counselors, such as Ernest Groves, called for acceptance of the fact of divorce but saw the failure to adapt to marriage as proof of personal immaturity. Groves viewed "unhappiness" as insufficient justification for divorce since unhappiness is far too global a feeling to attach to the marital institution itself. In *Conserving Marriage and the Family,* he said, "If you are willing to turn away from yourself and look at others, it will be easier to see that happiness as a rule is something that one has in every part of one's life or not at all. We are happy all over or everywhere life seems disappointing. This shows how unconvincing a reason for divorce being unhappy generally is."

But the imperfectly happy were increasingly eager to blame their marriages rather than themselves, and divorce became ever more popular. In the post–World War II years, according to Barbara Whitehead in *The Divorce Culture,*

> Americans began to change their ideas about the individual's obligations to family and society. . . . At least as important as the moral obligation to look after others, the new thinking suggested, was the moral obligation to look after oneself. . . . Divorce was not only an individual right but also a psychological resource. The dissolution of marriage offered the chance to make oneself over from the inside out, to refurbish and express the inner self, and to acquire certain valuable psychological assets and competencies, such as

initiative, assertiveness, and a stronger and better self-image.

By the 1960s, divorce had become a form of self-expression, endorsed by the burgeoning ranks of psychotherapists who assured people that whatever they felt was okay and could be acted upon without regard to its effects on others. There was a literature in praise of disconnection, and it had its own pious poetry and slogans, which were ubiquitous on the posters of the time.

By 1960, at the dawn of the sexual revolution, the divorce rate had slowly risen to nine per one thousand per year. About 20 percent of marriages from that era were fated to end in divorce. The worst was yet to come.

Between 1960 and 1980, the divorce rate almost tripled. There were soon about half as many divorces as marriages. The divorce rate approached 50 percent, not actually because half the people were getting divorced but because those people who divorced in their search for happiness were likely to marry again and divorce again, over and over until they either found the marriage of their dreams or collapsed from the rigors of the search.

Marriage was under siege, and no one could go to sleep secure that the family would be together by morning.

Divorce His, Divorce Hers

The most dramatic change in the lives of young women—although many have no wish to recognize it—is that marriage is not a viable career. Under favorable circumstances it remains a rewarding personal relationship, but it no longer serves as a surrogate career. Today, no law, no father, no brother can force a man

*to support a woman, and the law is not
successfully forcing him to support even their
children properly.*

—Elizabeth Fox-Genovese, *Feminism
Without Illusion*

The first phase of the divorce orgy centered on men who had gone around the world to fight a war, risk their lives, and conquer the world. Once back home, they tried to find their heroism in domestic roles, and they were often demanding workaholics, but they were subject to a delayed effect from the war: the midlife crisis. Some of those who sacrificed their youth for duty left home at middle age, usually to rescue a damsel in distress and get a final taste of macho heroism. Others did not actually cut and run but had that faraway look in their eye, and their sons saw it.

It was the princely sons of the world warriors who rejected the self-sacrificial images of masculinity for which their fathers had been willing to die. The sons of the 1960s refused to go to war, refused to honor the obligations for which their fathers had fought and died, and rebelled. The sexual revolution centered mostly on boys and men demanding the joys of sex without the responsibilities that went with it. Men and boys read Hugh Hefner's *Playboy* and bought its philosophy, deciding that happiness was elsewhere; they joined the revolution, often just dipping a toe into it but sometimes diving in for a total immersion. Men, liberated from duty, intoxicated with narcissism, demanding a level of happiness they were not finding in things as mundane as love and work, ran wild. They not only screwed around, they ran from family and parenthood, leaving wives and mothers as the in-house grown-ups while they sank back into childishly recycling puberty rituals while dreaming of macho glory.

In the movie *Lovers and Other Strangers* in 1970, sideburned, polyester-clad Bob Dishy tells his blind date, "You know, I'm not sure if I dig the whole marriage scene. I mean, yeah, it's all right for some people, I guess, but I don't know if it's today—I mean, you know what I mean 'today'? Today! Today is—is—is—to live. Free. Man. Woman. Love. Oh, you don't need a diploma, do you? Ha-ha-ha!"

Women, understandably, got fed up with these men. Between the 1960s and the 1980s, after sexually rebelling males had stopped being reliable family members, there was a gender revolution and a mythos of "expressive" divorce, as Whitehead terms it—a kind of therapeutic odyssey of self-discovery for the angry, beleaguered, taken-for-granted, ever-adult, ever-dutiful, ever-sacrificial women at home.

Expressive divorce occurred not just in troubled marriages, but in an atmosphere of increasing concern by women that they were getting too comfortable in an unreliable institution. It was assumed the pain would be temporary since it was popularly believed that "almost all growth takes place in the imperative of unhappiness."

Whitehead describes a whole body of popular literature, novels, autobiography, and self-help books, that held out divorce, with or without definable problems in the marriage, as the salvation of women and the route to liberation from the defining roles of wife and mother. In this literature, according to Whitehead, "it is divorce, not marriage, that defines a sense of self and leads to greater maturity and self-knowledge. It is divorce, not marriage, that is stimulating and energizing and growth-enhancing. Thus divorce becomes the defining achievement of women's lives, the great article of their freedom." Therapists, schooled to believe that leaving home was the secret of mental health, often encouraged these blows for personal freedom.

The problem with marriage was not necessarily that it was unpleasant or abusive. Rather, it was comfortable and cozy, and therefore did not motivate women to go forth and find a self independent of relationships and family caretaking. If the sexual revolution had freed men from family life, the subsequent reactive era of expressive divorce set women free from family responsibility.

The Cost of Divorce

"The character traits that keep families together are associated in all other arenas of life with immaturity or nonrationality; family interdependence is now the only thing that stands in the way of 'self-actualization,' " said Stephanie Coontz in *The Way We Never Were*. The divorce culture might make sense if there were no children involved, and some of the divorce apologists act as if the kids are irrevelant to these decisions. Coontz debunks our myths that children were once raised in families:

> Of course children benefit from the involvement of a caring father, but they're obviously better off for the absence of an abusive one, and let's not forget that paternal absence has been the norm in many "traditional" two-parent families. Some therapists argue that emotional absence, more ambiguous than physical loss, may be harder to grieve, causing difficulties that show up much later in life than the disruptions caused by divorce.

Social critics were seeing marriage as a patriarchal institution, inherently exploitative to women, enslaving them with a male-serving, child-centered ideal of duty to which they were expected to sacrifice their freedom and happiness. Divorce was the direct solution to the problem.

Maternal chauvinists insisted that women could do it all, that all a child needed was a liberated mother, however overworked and overextended, who did not feel any need for a man. Men were painted as generally, routinely, and naturally abusive, physically or sexually, or both. There was a movement assuring women that any unhappiness they were feeling was surely the result of a man's abuse of her. If she remembered her father lovingly and pleasantly, then the abuse must have been so horrendous and traumatizing that she forgot it, and therapy would be aimed at "recovering" the "repressed" memory. (The "memories" brought forth in such therapy had no more validity than dreams or snatches of old TV shows, though there may have been people who remembered the abuse all along and used the trappings of memory recovery to justify having kept it hidden. The repressed and recovered memory hoax was cruel, and it undercut the credibility of those who were actually abused, never forgot it, and couldn't stop thinking about it. Such things were bound to happen once it was decreed that men must be blamed for everything in a woman's life.)

Some divorce apologists knew that men were important as fathers if not as husbands. Such divorce apologists insisted that any seemingly destructive impact of divorce was actually due to the resultant poverty of mothers and children brought about by the loss of fathers, about 50 percent of whom disappear economically as well as emotionally from the lives of their children after the divorce. Some divorce apologists have admitted that the loss of fathers was emotionally damaging to children; others only acknowledged the financial loss. Either way, they decreed it was only the irresponsibility of fathers and the economic incompetence of mothers that made divorce look like a bad deal for children.

This divorce chauvinist literature believed that what would make the mother happy would surely be in the best interests of the child. (Doherty calls this the "psychological trickledown" theory.) As the old song goes, "If Mama ain't happy, then ain't nobody happy."

Susan Gettleman and Janet Markowitz in *The Courage to Divorce* tell us children of divorce have "greater insight and freedom as adults in deciding whether and when to marry." An array of postdivorce stepfamilies help them "break away from excessive dependency on their biological parents." In other words, in the typical fashion of its era, divorce was declared good for children because it protected them from getting married and becoming parents. It was only the selfishness of children and their fairy tale notions of intact families, the shortsightedness and emotional greed of the abandoned spouse, and the prejudice of society that kept some foolish people from seeing what a wonderful thing a divorce was for a family.

Before divorce researchers such as E. Mavis Hetherington, Judith S. Wallerstein, Lenore Weitzman, Sara McLanahan, and Gary Sandefur began to give us the actual data on the aftermath of breaking up families, divorce continued to be touted as a safe treatment for depression, as a resolution to life's ennui, as a way of regaining youth and trying again for heroism, as a celebration of gender liberation, and maybe even as a way for getting men back into fathering.

By the 1980s, society stopped to hold its breath and count the casualties of casual divorce. Sociologists such as Andrew J. Cherlin, Barbara Whitehead, David Blankenhorn, David Popenoe, Edward W. Beal, and Gloria Hochman had a full-time job tracking the divorce epidemic.

When the data came in, they showed that divorce was not good for everybody. There were winners and losers in divorce; the partner who didn't want the divorce was likely to end up suffering more and longer, and the one who did want the divorce might be in for some disappointments.

Women got along better in time, even if they were more overburdened, stressed, and deprived at first. Most women, even those who were left, came to accept the divorce and to decide that they were better off without that particular hus-

213

band. Women sought the divorces most of the time. Sixty percent of them were happier after a year or two; 80 percent were happier ten years later. They had more self-respect as they became more self-reliant. Younger women, especially the childless ones, recovered quickly, remarried quickly, usually redivorced, and blamed both men. Older women had more trouble with divorce and took a decade or more to recover. The most wrenching crises were for those women who had been full-time housewives and/or mothers and who had no career they could fall back on. Even they recovered from the divorce as they gained more control over money and more freedom, and as they spent more time with supportive female friends. Most of the older divorced women did not remarry. In time, most of them didn't miss it.

Men, on the other hand, were usually more devastated at the time of the divorce and were far less likely to recover—even if they were the ones who sought the divorce or were the ones betraying the marriage and precipitating the divorce. In fact, all the research indicates that men suffer more from marital disruption than women. Divorced men have more depression, nervous breakdowns, suicide attempts, psychiatric hospitalizations, ill health, and death.

Women jumped into expressive divorce as their response to the instability of marriage brought about by the sexual revolution and the oppressiveness of anachronistic patriarchal attitudes. And many benefited from it. But they might well have gained the same benefits by going to work or getting their husbands to a therapist with a more liberated model of masculinity. However, we must assume the women who felt the need to resort to something as drastic and wrenching as divorce didn't feel enough freedom and power to rearrange their marriage until they had already left it.

Robert J. Samuelson in *The Good Life and Its Discontents* says that "expert opinion, which once decreed that divorce and sexual freedom were healthy ways to achieve self-fulfillment, has shifted. Family breakdown is now seen as having bad effects." Samuelson, a dry and restrained observer of our national misery, looks at the data on happiness and finds little correlation between money and happiness. (There is more misery among the very poor, and there are more "very happy" people among the rich but no fewer unhappy people.) The big measurable difference is that married people, male and female, are happier than those who are single, separated, divorced, or widowed. Family breakdown is the source of most of our society's misery. Samuelson concludes that "the only solution is to reconstruct, somehow, families that provide the love, sense of self-worth, and discipline that children require to develop into responsible, self-sufficient adults. But no one really knows how to do this."

The human family is dissolving throughout the industrialized and narcissistic world, yet those of us who struggle daily with the casualties of this divorce orgy can expect to be looked at askance by the large number of divorce apologists who see marriage as irreparably patriarchal and divorce as the only solution.

The adversarial divorce process is a horror, but at least it makes both partners hate one another so much they are glad to get the divorce by the time it comes. From time to time I see divorce attorneys who are divorcing, and they all would do just about anything to get out of their marriage without having to go through the sort of divorces they sell to others.

The much-divorced Norman Mailer is famous for saying "A man never knows a woman until he meets her in court." He went further: "There are four stages in a marriage. First there's the affair, then the marriage, then children, and finally the fourth stage, without which you cannot know a woman, the divorce."

A divorcing divorce attorney was asked, "Why do divorces cost so much?" He replied, "Because they're worth it."

Once you have betrayed and destroyed a partner, a marriage, and a life, the need to escape is desperate. It is most often the infidel, the resister of adulthood, who wants out most intensely, but the one who has been betrayed must resist an urge to kill. The intensity of the hatred in divorces seems almost parallel to the intensity of the love affair that preceded it. (And, strangely, a large and uncounted number of couples who manage to get through the divorce process without killing each other, end up getting back together.) I've heard all the arguments and still believe the divorce process should be slowed down. Anybody who has fallen in love, who has a secret, or who has just discovered a mate's betrayal is too unstable for divorce right then.

The casualty rate in divorce is high, but the most likely victims of divorce are the children.

The Impact of Divorce on Children

Divorce is the psychological equivalent of a triple coronary bypass.

—Mary Kay Blakely, *American Mom*

Only one in ten children in our study experienced relief when their parents divorced. Divorce is a different experience for children and adults because the children lose something that is fundamental to their development—the family structure.

—Judith S. Wallerstein and Sandra Blakeslee, *Second Chances*

New data on children of divorce began to come out in the late 1980s. The most influential has been the Wallerstein and Blakeslee study which showed that children usually survive divorce but often do not recover from it and show scars for a lifetime. There was a protest among the divorce apologists, who insisted that the research was flawed. It is, but that does not make it invalid. I believe it because it fits what I see hourly in my practice: Nothing that happens in anyone's life has as permanent and profound an impact as the breakup of his or her childhood family.

Wallerstein's families and mine have been mostly upper middle class. Divorce is a financial catastrophe for the less privileged, and it causes poor children to drop out of school, get pregnant, get married, and get arrested as they lose their financial and emotional support and their hopes for their future. No one disputes that. Divorce may hit the more privileged less in the wallet but more in the psyche when pampered, protected children, being groomed not for survival but for success, suddenly discover they are not valued and will no longer be the family's primary investment. They are rudely deprived of their sense of entitlement and security, their dreams of success, their trust in the adult world, and their anticipation of stepping smoothly into the perfect life. Middle-class kids have farther to fall when the family collapses beneath them.

How much conflict does it take for the marriage to be worse for kids than divorce? Sara McLanahan and Gary Sandefur in *Growing Up with a Single Parent* argue that unless marital conflict is high-level, persistent, and marked by physical violence or severe abuse, "the child would probably be better off if the parents resolved their differences and the family remained together, even if the long-term relationship between the parents was less than perfect."

Some divorce apologists have tried to insist that children are better off *after* the divorce. Of course they are! Nobody is better off *during* the divorce or during the craziness that precedes it. The process through which a divorce-minded mate tears down a marriage and destroys a family may begin years before the divorce takes place.

Research shows that the initial impact and the aftershocks over the two to five years following divorce are devastating for children, but they differ on what the toxic factor is that makes divorce so devastating.

Another consistent finding is the loss of live-in fathering. Fifty percent of fathers disappear economically as well as emotionally from their children's lives. Ronald J. Angel and Jacqueline L. Angel in *Painful Inheritance: Health and the New Generation of Fatherless Children* concluded:

> The preponderance of evidence suggests that father absence results in fairly serious emotional and behavioral problems in children. Children in single-parent families suffer more psychiatric illness and are at a developmental disadvantage in comparison to children in two-parent families. These children have more problems at school, have less self-control, and engage in more delinquent acts than children who live with both parents. The evidence also indicates that fathers are important for a girl's sexual development and her ability to form relationships with men.

Whether the children of divorce are suffering from the loss of their family, the conflict that preceded the breakup, the loss of live-in fathering, the chaos of the postdivorce family, the unhappiness of one parent, or the resultant loss of income, the impact is bad and can trigger any form of emergency behavior, such as psychiatric symptoms, antisocial behavior, self-destructiveness, and cries of helplessness. Half the children function at lower levels with less optimism and ambition and show symptoms a decade later.

One of the cruelest effects of divorce is the comforting belief that the parents had no choice but to divorce. Such a belief leads to distrust of the institution of marriage, while the emotional loss for the child leads to a desperate need for a relationship that can be permanent. Anyone who goes into marriage both desperate and distrustful is going to be exhausting for even the most loyal partner. Children of divorce have a far higher divorce rate in their own marriages than people who grew up in a stable family.

The trauma of divorce is not something kids grow out of. The loss of family does not heal with time and cannot be replaced by a new marriage, a new father, a new form of communal pseudo-family living, or a new government program.

Emulsified Families

> *Divorce presents to children a series of never ending changes which they must struggle to integrate into their already chaotic lives.*

—Edward W. Beal and Gloria Hochman,
Adult Children of Divorce

Most of the people who break up their marriages with dewy-eyed optimism are in for a rude shock. While both divorced men and divorced women used to remarry quickly after the divorce, and men still do, the rate of remarriage for divorced women with children continues to drop. Andrew J. Cherlin in *Marriage, Divorce, Remarriage* in 1981 estimated three-fourths of men and two-thirds of women would remarry. Most men still do remarry, but most without success. Most of the older divorced women will not remarry, though those who do are more likely to make it work. Most of the younger ones will remarry, but most will redivorce quickly. Those who stake their happiness on creating a new, more ideal family are likely to be disappointed.

Creating an ideal family out of spare parts is not that easy. Even the most mature and responsible of us—and the ranks of the divorced include many who are not mature and responsible—are likely to have a hard time blending two or more families. Blended families are not very stable; they are more like an emulsion than a blend, and they can curdle and separate easily.

All logic would lead us to expect second marriages to work better because they are entered into by people who are older, wiser, more experienced, and, one would hope, more realistic. Alas, it is not so. Those who marry for the second time not only divorce more often but more quickly.

Many factors doom second marriages. One is conflict over child raising and the unhappiness of the children who are being put through the new family blender. Blending families is confusing, but there are other factors as well. As Cherlin puts it: "The remarried population contains a higher proportion of people who, for one reason or another, are more likely to resort to divorce if their marriage falters. . . . The experience of divorce makes people more averse to remaining in a second unhappy marriage."

Also, the divorced population contains many people of a romantic temperament who expect their happiness to be brought to them by someone else. They are sure to be disappointed. Those who blame the failure of their first marriage on their partner, and only blame themselves for marrying the wrong person, learn nothing from the experience except how to blame others. Neither the romantic nor the blamer has learned anything from his or her mistakes.

Remarriage, at least if there are children involved, is not the utopia it seemed when the initial divorce was instituted. Second marriages involving children bring a lower level of tolerance for the normal rowdiness of kids and a far higher level of physical abuse. Second marriages are likely to show intolerance for the kids who don't leave home on cue at eighteen or thereabouts. Stepfamilies seem to encourage premature emancipations, with more kids dropping out of school and going into early marriages. Stepfamilies are always more complex and more likely to involve crosscurrents of resentment and distrust. And they bring a higher level of sexual abuse.

A lot of research (David Blankenhorn, *Fatherless America;* David Popenoe, *Life Without Father*) shows that younger boys show more behavior problems when living with a single mother and act better when their mother remarries—or at least they act better at first. Teenage boys have increasing conflict with stepfathers. Boys seem to prefer a tight relationship between husband and wife in the new marriage, and thus more distance from both of them.

But younger girls who have bonded tightly with their single mothers tend to get depressed and withdrawn when she remarries, viewing the new man as an intruder. Girls in stepfamilies seem happier if there is less cohesion between their mother and stepfather, and thus more room for her relationship with her mother. Both boys and girls do best when they live with their same-sex parent. Stepmothers have a hell of a time getting a working relationship going with kids who have a lot of contact with their real mothers. Raising a depressed kid who is still angry over the divorce cannot be easy for the stepparent who has replaced the real parent and is a constant reminder of the child's loss.

Still, the second marriages that survive are among the happiest being reported. Several of the enduring marriages we have societally envied have been second marriages: Paul Newman and Joanne Woodward, Jessica Tandy and Hume Cronyn, Ronald and Nancy Reagan, Evita and Juan Perón, Leona and Harry Helmsley. And the Duke of Windsor was his duchess's third try at marriage.

Conclusions About Children and Divorce

There are a few things about which nobody who looks at divorce would seriously disagree.

It is preferable for children to grow up in intact two-parent families even if the parents are not in love.

High levels of marital conflict are bad for children. Moderate levels of marital conflict, without violence or threat of family disruption, can be useful learning experiences about conflict resolution. An absence of parental conflict is not the most desirable atmosphere for the children.

It is not clear whether children are better off living with a high level of conflict or living with divorce, but the threat of divorce is an extremely serious assault on a child's sense of security.

Parental divorce produces a crisis period lasting for at least two years of disordered adjustment and often far longer. During this period, families of divorce tend to have a "chaotic lifestyle" in which adolescents run wild.

Younger children of divorce tend to regress to a stage of greater dependency and obvious symptomatic behavior during this period of postdivorce chaos. Older ones tend to assume an air of hypermaturity and either leave or take over an inappropriately adult role in the disrupted family.

Boys growing up in the midst of high conflict and threat of family disruption, even before the separation, show a far higher level of aggressive and antisocial behavior. Girls are more likely to quietly overfunction. They become more depressive and have lower self-esteem.

Most daughters of divorce continue to be unhappy, lonely, and afraid to make commitments to men. Those who marry have a far higher divorce rate. The boys have even more serious problems in almost every area, as children and after they grow up. Many just stop functioning altogether.

Up to half the children of divorce are still traumatized long after the mothers have recovered. They go into adulthood with diminished chances for successful adult functioning. The older they are at the time of the divorce, the less chance they have to recover and the more adult problems they are likely to have. On the other hand, at least half the children of divorce, especially the ones who were youngest at the time it happened, survive with little or no lasting impairment in their instrumental functioning, though even they are likely to have serious difficulty in their own relationships and marriages.

The greatest and most devastating result of divorce is that fathers tend to drop out of their children's lives. Fathers are indispensable. Most fathers of divorce have been less than ideal husbands and fathers, but a father has to be rather awful to be worse than no father at all. Father hunger in children of divorce is prevalent, with idealization of the missing father and fantasies, often acted out, of going to live with him as soon as they are old enough. During adolescence as many as one-third of the children of divorce try living with their fathers. Most of them are soon disenchanted and return to their mother. This idealization of the missing father can cause severe tension between the child and the custodial mother, which is inevitably worsened by the mother's effort to keep the father out of the child's life. The effort to find the lost father is necessary.

I assume the loss of a mother would be at least as devastating. But losing a parent to death is far less traumatic for the child than losing a parent to divorce. When parents die, the children don't really lose them. Children lose parents only when they leave voluntarily.

Stepfathers may be rescuing heroes, but research in the matter is frightening. Stepfathers are more likely to be unhelpful and may well make things worse. Stepfathers are more likely to be violent, to be abusive, and to push the stepchildren out prematurely. Children living with biological fathers exhibit the least delinquency, and children with stepfathers have the most. Stepfather-stepson relations get worse as the boy moves toward adolescence and beyond. Stepfathering must begin when the child is young if it is to hold together through adolescence. The economic advantage of a stepfather is typically not enough to offset the many social and psychological disadvantages.

Children do best when they have the most continuing relationship with the noncustodial parent. Some fathers of divorce are unreliable and frustrating for the child, intrusive and challenging for the mother, and a general all-around pain in the ass. And some just use visitation to disrupt life for the ex-wife and then dump the child on a hostile stepmother. But the children need enough contact with both parents to learn that on their own.

The trauma of the divorce is never over for the children. Whatever other crises happen in their lives, their parents' divorce remains the most important, the most determinant, and the one they are most likely to think about and reexperience regularly. Children of divorce go through life with a degree of posttraumatic stress disorder from it. One particularly sanguine divorce apologist insisted to me that only about 20 percent of children of divorce become serious psychiatric casualties. But they all bear the scars.

Divorce rates are higher among children of divorce. Experts differ on whether the rate is five times higher or merely three times higher.

Criminal behavior is higher among children of divorce, particularly among men who were raised without a father. Fatherless boys are many times more likely to be imprisoned for violent crimes. There is serious debate about whether poverty or fatherlessness is the major cause of criminality. Most children of divorce suffer both.

Depression, suicide, low self-esteem, and distrust of relationships are far higher among children of divorce. Researchers disagree only on the degree of the difference.

Sometimes parents must sacrifice their pursuit of happiness and instead look for it within themselves for the sake of the children. In the long run they may be better off and even happier doing what would be in the best interests of their loved ones, their honor, and their integrity rather than stake their hopes for happiness on falling in love.

If You Feel You Must Divorce

As awful as the impact of divorce can be for everyone concerned, when the choices boil down to suicide, homicide, and divorce, I usually recommend divorce—with full awareness of the price to be paid and who will pay it. In addition, the rates of suicide and homicide are particularly high for those who are dumped out of the marriage to which they entrusted their life. It is a nasty business, and the people who have been all the way into their marriages, who have played the adult role the most competently, may be the ones most likely to be left behind by a partner who is escaping back into childhood. Every divorce hurts somebody.

The ones hurt the most may be the father who loses his wife and children to a richer man, and the childless older wife who dedicated her life to a marriage from which she is suddenly kicked upstairs for a younger trophy model. The casualty rate is high among those who sacrificed themselves to the ego of narcissists and those who hoped that their love and loyalty would counterbalance the self-indulgences of a partner who sidestepped adulthood in the pursuit of an egocentric model of happiness. It may be tempting to distrust marriage, to hold part of yourself back in the hope of losing less when it ends, but that only coarsens the character and speeds up the marital collapse. Whatever the ultimate outcome, the winner is whoever played the game fairly. Life is long, and people spend many decades living with the decisions made during their lustier, more impatient years. Honor and integrity ultimately prevail, but there may be some bad innings before the game is over.

So if your urge to divorce is so strong that you don't think you can resist it, don't rush off to the divorce attorney. Slow down and try a few other things first. Divorce is extremely serious and should not be contemplated because you're angry, embarrassed, depressed, or your pride requires it. It will seriously damage your children and thus your grandchildren, and it will be a hell of a thing for you to go through as well, even as you gloatingly hope it will hurt your partner even more.

Here's the best advice I can offer for dealing with this messy business of divorce.

1. Define the problems that make your marriage unsatisfactory and consider how you think a divorce will make it better. Remember that a divorce is not going to get the parent of your children out of their life or out of yours. You may find that you can make the necessary changes in you and your life without putting yourself and everyone through a divorce to get it. Most of the men who just had to have a taste of someone new could have simply tried a different approach at home. Most of the women who make themselves competent and self-reliant after a divorce could have done so simply by getting a career.

2. Identify the things your spouse is doing that you don't like and make it known that you can't live with the behavior anymore. Don't talk about your feelings, as one usually does in civilized domestic negotiations; talk about the behavior. It's not "I don't love you anymore";

it's "I'm unwilling to live with your affairs, lies, drinking, filth, screaming, violence, laziness, TV watching, spending, talking on the telephone, cutting your toenails in bed, and so forth."

3. If you are in an affair, stop it, reveal it, and apologize for it. Affairs are so emotionally and instinctually disorienting, consider yourself temporarily insane. Of course your marriage feels wrong right now, but you are what is wrong with your marriage. Work on what is wrong with you rather than what is wrong with your mate.

4. If your mate is in an affair (and if your marriage hasn't been hell but your mate wants out before Saturday night, assume an affair is going on), accept the reality of it, express your hurt, avoid blowing the fragile relationship apart with your anger, apologize for your many shortcomings, and state your intentions to hang in there while your straying partner gets out of it, gets over it, and gets sane. Be patient, which is one of the most adult things I ever ask anyone to do.

5. If you have been secretly unfaithful in the past and still remember it, then it may still be an important barrier to the intimacy of your marriage. Reveal it now with appropriate explanations and apologies.

6. If there really is no past or present infidelity, the divorce impulse may be a symptom of depression. Rather than blaming your depression on your marriage, blame it correctly on your disordered brain chemistry.

7. Get a life. Get a job. Get a career. Get some exercise. Stop expecting your marriage to make you happy.

8. Explore your parents' marriage to find out how you learned about marriage and divorce.

9. Hang out with happy and married people, and find out how they do it differently.

10. Get into therapy, but only with a therapist who believes in marriage. Make clear your goal is to save your marriage whether it makes you happy or not; then learn to be happy rather than expecting it to be brought to you.

11. Take Prozac. It has far fewer side effects than divorce, it works more quickly, and it is more reliable in relieving unhappiness.

12. If you are determined the only thing that will keep you from killing your partner or yourself is a divorce, separate with a clear message that you're fed up, you aren't going to take it anymore, and you want things to change. Then wait and watch while you work on changing yourself.

13. Once separated, slow down. Resist the temptation to get on with it. If finances require it, get a postnuptial agreement while you try living apart. Stick with therapy. If your mate won't go, go alone. Make sure your therapist wants you to grow up rather than wanting to protect you from the pain of life. Treat you, not your mate, as the problem.

14. If neither you nor your mate is willing to make the necessary changes, divorce may be inevitable. But remember that one of the things you give up in a divorce is the right to criticize or complain about your

children's other parent. Ex-mates must be treated as politely, correctly, and cautiously as any other in-law.

15. Working out problems with an ex-partner or soon-to-be ex-partner requires a lot of talking, but it does not require any fighting at all. You have a legal right to fight with your marriage partner but not your divorce partner. Divorce is far too serious, delicate, and fragile to use as a psychodrama exercise in anger expression. Cool it.

16. Keep things as stable as possible for the children. Keep the changes minimal for them. Resist the temptation and pressure from your affair partner or your anger to move away, start over, and create a new life without their other parent (unless he or she is a homicidal maniac).

17. Your ex-mate is now your partner in the business of child raising. You must communicate a lot. Make it friendly. Be more than cooperative. Don't lecture, don't disapprove, don't compete. Marriage to an impossible person may be easier than divorce from him or her. You get a chance now to learn the skills you didn't develop during the marriage.

18. Make sure the kids understand the full history of what *you* did wrong so they can learn from it. We assume your ex-partner will reveal what he or she did wrong as soon as he or she is sufficiently grown up. But don't detail your partner's deficiencies to the kids.

19. Don't remarry as long as you are naive enough to think you "married the wrong person." You aren't fit for remarriage until you know what you did wrong.

20. Don't try to normalize what is happening. Never forget for a moment that this is not so much your loss or your victory as it is your children's tragedy. One day it may be over for you. It will never be over for them.

21. Grown-ups may have to stay married for the children's sake, but that is not sufficient. It only works if you stay happily married for the children's sake. If you are starved for love, the way to bring more love into your life is to be more loving.

8

The Magic of Raising Children

*Children are life renewing itself, Captain
Butler. And when life does that, danger seems
very unimportant.*

—Melanie Wilkes in Margaret Mitchell's
Gone with the Wind

*Babies, war, and taxes! There's never a
convenient time for any of them.*

—Scarlett O'Hara in Margaret Mitchell's
Gone with the Wind

WHEN JUSTIN WESLEY WAGERS, THE OLDEST OF OUR THREE
grandsons and thus the first of what we hope will be many,
was born, Betsy and I went out to Boulder, Colorado, to
bond with him. I spent a week snuggling with him and getting my breath and heart rate in rhythm with his, understanding that people have children in order to get
grandchildren. In due time we turned Justin over to the alternate shift of grandparents and came back to earth. We
had been transformed. We glowed in the dark. We had been
declared gods and turned into constellations. We were now
immortal—maybe, a little.

When people have children, there is this hope for some

little piece of immortality. Parents and grandparents don't actually become immortal, but if they are paying attention, they do become part of *everything* that has gone on before or that will go on after them. That is wonderful, but it is even more wonderful if they fully realize that their children and grandchildren (even those as perfect as Justin) are no different or more special than everyone else's children and grandchildren, and that every other parent and grandparent is going through the same thing with them.

Having children has limited benefits at best, of course, and can even be an expression of greediness and narcissism, an imposition on one's neighbors and even on the planet itself; the magical experience is *raising* them. Those people who want the pride, the potential glory, and the self-expansion of parenthood without the humbling, enlightening turmoil of hands-on parenting are not just missing the magic but are cheating.

There are naive scientists who try to make sense out of human sexuality by assuming the human animal has an overriding instinctive investment in the survival of its sperm and egg cells, and is drawn to behaviors that will spawn the largest numbers of fertilized eggs. The human animal could not have survived, no matter how many of our ignorant, immobile, dependent offspring were deposited on the ground, if there were not parents who stuck around to raise them. Human babies require *parents*; not just a parent but *parents*—more than one, preferably more than two. And human babies require parents not just for their physical survival but for their humanity. Feral children raised in the woods by wolves or on the streets by peers are not likely to be fully human in large part because they lack the experience of their parents investing love in a being who is not yet able to give anything back.

The human species survived against all probability in a hostile environment because there were people who valued us enough to join forces and take care of us, not just feed and shelter us but teach us the increasingly complex things that we soft, slow, unarmed beings need to know to survive and to serve our biological function of creating others, taking care of them, teaching them what they need to know, and loving them enough to make them yearn to love others and to pass it on.

Child raising has always been the most important activity of the human animal, male or female. But since the industrial revolution some imbeciles claiming to speak for sociology and psychology have come forth with the outrageous idea that child raising is "women's work," that men have something more important to do than the care and feeding and education and emotional training of the next generation. (I can't imagine what would be more important. War? Business? Government? Sports on TV? Reassuring themselves of their masculinity by seducing other women? Get serious!) The man who cannot be servant to a child, who expects his children or those of other people to exist for his own glory or comfort, is the center of his own universe and is unlikely to be capable of loving anything outside himself. He may have slipped back into the wrong generation by mistake.

The end product of child raising is not the child, who still must go forth to raise himself or herself, but the parent. For the parent, raising children is magic. Football, military schools, prison, and war have been touted as the experience that can turn a boy into a man. Nonsense! The experience that makes a man is fathering—not sperm donation or absentee patriarchism but hands-on fathering. I have no desire to shake the hand that has never changed a diaper.

People who don't raise children, their own or someone else's, as an important and even central part of their identity are in danger of remaining members of the self-indulgent child generation. They may have trouble moving on to the parent generation in which there is joy and pride from investing in something outside themselves. Non-parents are certainly more to be pitied than censured, but they definitely develop differently from the rest of us. By bypassing their biological function in life, they may miss their biological connection with life and may even feel above and beyond the basic nature of the human animal.

Raising Postpatriarchal Children

The old gender arrangements just won't do. When boys or girls grow up with the experience of love and nurturing coming only from women, the boys don't learn how to give love, only how to demand and receive it, and the girls don't learn how to get loved by men, only how to overvalue and underutilize them. Boys can't afford to grow up expecting too much from women, and girls can't afford to grow up expecting too little from men. Children of both genders need to be loved by parents of both genders. Ideally, fathers and mothers should be interchangeable in their children's lives, both demonstrating play and work, both showing love and nurturance, both overflowing with adult care and generativity.

Most important, status in the home and in the world should not be determined by gender. I encourage parents to set up a gender-neutral and gender-egalitarian atmosphere and then avoid teaching their children anything about gender. The kids will get quite enough of that from the world. Parents should be available to help them get a perspective on the state of change in the world.

Ideally, the tasks the grown-ups do should not be divided by gender. Children's lives should not be dominated by gender, either. Toys should not be distributed by gender. Boys need dolls and girls need trucks; both need balls and neither needs guns. Emotions should not be divided by gender; both boys and girls should see both men and women experience and express the full range of human emotions. Boys must learn to cry at times; girls must learn not to cry at times.

As the parents deal with the messages from the world about gender, they have to examine themselves, their own parents, and their world. There is nothing quite like raising a daughter to cure a man of patriarchy, and there is nothing quite like raising a son to get a woman past any lingering thoughts of male supremacy. Simply, the way to raise postpatriarchal children is to raise them in a postpatriarchal family.

Raising Responsible Children

The best way to raise responsible kids is to surround them with responsible adults who delight in doing what they do for one another and for the world. They can inspire the child to emulate the joys of responsible living and engage in the give-and-take of relationships that make both people feel good. Parents of responsible children talk regularly about the manifold ways in which people affect one another and react to one another, making the child constantly aware of the responsibilities people have in others' lives. Responsible parents teach their children to think systemically, to think familially, and to think intergenerationally. Responsible parents are constantly concerned and make their children constantly concerned with values and conflicting values; how to do the right thing, how to figure out what is the right thing to do, what to do when you do the wrong thing, and what to do when other people do the wrong thing. Religion offers opportunities for parents and children to think about their relationships to the universe and to one another, but so do books and movies and the manifold traumas and crises of daily living. Learning to feel powerful and responsible is a full-time, lifelong process and a fascinating and generally joyful one.

Irresponsible parents occasionally produce a responsible

child by default when the child steps in to be the surrogate grown-up and takes care of the infantile parents. But hypermature children who become adults before they have had a chance to be children don't seem to be a happy bunch, and unless they have some corrective emotional experiences along the way, they don't give of themselves willingly to the next generation. Parentless parents, parents without models, are permanent amateurs. There is no substitute for responsible grown-ups. Interestingly, those resilient people who turned out well despite growing up in horrifying circumstances all seem to have had some responsible adult—a relative, a teacher, a coach, a minister, the parent of a friend—who treated them as special and saw hope and opportunity rather than just deprivation and victimhood.

But it is not enough to care for a child or treat a child as special. For the child to grow up responsible, he or she must also be useful. Families used to breed children for labor, to work in the mines or the mills, and the children were rewarded with a little pay and a lot of honor. Growing up in the country, I had farmwork to do and animals to feed and tend, and I loved it because it made me feel useful. In parts of the world, families have seeing-eye children for the blind adults. Children are natural, eager apprentices, excited to learn whatever the parents know how to do, delighted to follow the parents around to learn their skills. There should be no thought of having someone around the house who does not share in the work that needs to be done. Children, if they are to become adults, should be functional and proud of it.

One- and two-year-olds can fetch and carry. My grandson Justin, at two and a half, can do many things for his baby brother, Christopher, and values himself and Christopher all the more because of it. But if a child is introduced to the concepts of work and duty and responsibility after a free ride that has lasted too long, His Majesty the Child may be outraged at the idea that anything should be expected in return. It may take more effort to get a previously useless child to clean his room or take out the garbage than it does to do it yourself, but getting the garbage out is only half the point: Teaching a child to work is creating an adult.

In those families in which a father is a useful, functioning member of the household, children may eagerly join him in doing whatever work he dignifies by doing it himself. In those families in which he drops by to rest and supervise while his wife waits on him, children will see laziness as power and demand it for themselves. Kids are eager to work *with* parents and loathe to work *for* them.

If parents are needy enough, appreciative enough, and respectful enough, they may have no trouble at all teaching a child to be useful and proud of it.

Angry children may resist parents, but a child who would declare global nuclear war rather than pick up his underwear may eagerly slave away for minimum wage at McDonald's. Working for someone other than parents can seem like empowerment and a step toward usefulness in the world, while working for an irritable and impatient parent just seems too much like punishment and discipline and displays of parental power. Responsibility on any level, for people of any age, must be a victory rather than a defeat.

Raising Someone Else's Children

Raising your own children (wherever the genes come from) must be life's most magical experience. Raising someone else's children—children who have parents of their own but you do the dirty work—can be just as magical, or it can be hell. There are reasons that fairy tales picture stepmothers as witches and stepfathers as giants and ogres—a lot of stepparents botch the job badly. They may enter into it impatiently after it has already gotten under way; they may want to hurry up and get it over with; they may assume more authority then they have, undercutting or disdaining the parents they are replacing; they may resent the lack of appreciation that ensues. But if you understand the job description of a stepparent, it can be just as enlightening and gratifying as being an aunt or uncle, and sometimes as glorious and transformational as being a hands-on, live-in mother or father.

If you have a child who is growing up in someone else's family, you must show as much respect for that family as you expect in return—not as much as you get but as much you'd like to get. You must treat that family—even if you used to be married to one of them and hate the guts of all of them—as if they are doing you the enormous favor of taking care of your child for you. You must make friends with them, however they act. But you must realize that you cannot criticize them or supervise them. It takes a real grown-up to be a good noncustodial parent.

If you have stepchildren under the same roof with you, they may be in deep depression and simmering rage over the loss of their family and may despise you because you have replaced one of their parents. You have absolutely no authority over stepchildren, yet you must love them and become their friend without in any way undermining the authority of their parent, your mate. This calls for skills at aunting or uncling, offering children a connection to the adult world that is different from parenting and its unrelenting efforts to improve, protect, and perfect children who, at least some of the time, just want to be kids.

Stepparents have to give a lot more love and a lot more approval and do a lot more for the child, but it is well worth it, especially if the "real" parents appreciate the difficult nature of the job and show it.

AUNTING AND UNCLING

There are children all around us who could use an extra parent or two. An old African proverb declares that "it takes a whole village to raise a child." As the institutions of marriage and fathering collapse, we may have to become a society of uncles and aunts. The avuncular relationship can be an especially compatible one.

I have certainly felt vitally, joyously connected with my own nieces and nephews. I was almost as connected with some of them as I was with my own kids, and I had the same sense of wonder and excitement as I watched them grow up. But I had less sense of personal responsibility for the outcome, so I wasn't as anxious, and I could feel the magic more freely and could pass on my feelings more spontaneously. With my nieces and nephews I could be myself rather than try to be whatever I thought a parent should be. At times I have liked them better than I have my own children; I've often felt I was a better friend to them. I certainly think I was a better uncle than a father because I didn't catch on quickly enough that raising your kids involves sharing the experience with them but does not require perfecting them or fixing them. Aunts and uncles are called on to offer alternate realities to children. They don't have to know the true secrets of life; instead, they can explore them together. Anyone unlucky enough to lack nieces and nephews, or aunts and uncles, can find likely candidates and adopt them into those relationships. We all need people who are not our parents and not our children but who belong to other generations and will let us be part of their life cycle.

Never forget that the end product of child raising is not the child but the parent.

The Uses of Children

What is it that people get from raising children? What are the uses of children? Why would anyone want to share life with such creatures? Babies leak. Toddlers spill things. Children make noises. Adolescents keep parents awake and worried at night. When they graduate from sucking you dry, they start to bleed you dry. The financial investment is astounding, but the emotional investment is even more extravagant. And it will take two or three decades before they have their own children and suddenly appreciate what you put into them. Why would sane people put themselves through such an ordeal when they could be taking cruises or spicing up their sex lives or polishing their toys instead?

If men or women will let themselves learn from child raising rather than just trying to control or perfect children, the children can lead the parents through all the stages of human development from the other side and help make them aware of how men and women develop, how masculinity and femininity are taught and learned, and how to become complete human beings.

Babies can carry our genes and, more important, our stories into the world and into the future. Babies connect us with our inescapable biology. Babies connect us with all other parents and all other generations. Babies are hope.

Children teach us how to learn and how to see, hear, feel, taste, and smell everything in our world we've come to take for granted. Children teach us again how to play and how not to be afraid. The things children fear, such as the dark or being left alone, no longer scare us, while the things we fear, such as humiliation or loss of status or having our secret shames revealed, have no meaning for children until we infect them with our own anxieties. When we see our fears acted out by our children, we know that the fear itself is more destructive than any danger could be.

Little children are the audience grown-ups need. They are the repositories and guardians of our stories, thereby giving meaning to our lives. Older children make great companions. It is much easier for middle-aged children to satisfy our longings for childlike pleasures if a real child is willing to go along. Children are joy.

But then when they become adolescents, they toughen us, stretch our limits, and make us aware of just how much panic and disorder we can survive. Adolescent children are not, admittedly, an unadulterated joy. They are more exciting and more fascinating than at any other time in their lives, although they cause more anxiety, more expense, and more trouble. It is not surprising that so many parents want to turn them over to others to raise at this point, sending them to boarding schools, psychiatric hospitals, or out to sea until the hormonal storms pass and they rejoin the human race.

I've been kidnapped, I've been shot at, I've been psychoanalyzed; I've been through earthquakes, tornadoes, medical school, an alcoholic mother, and thirty-seven years of marriage; and I was pretty well in charge of the mental health of Atlanta from 1968 to 1972 (of all times). But I got more therapy and emotional exercise from my children's adolescence than any adventure I have ever been through.

Adolescents are indeed therapy. They threaten our equanimity; they challenge our sense of ourselves. Why would they rebel against us when we are still adolescents ourselves, still rebelling against our own parents? Why would they see us as the enemy? We avoided all the errors of our own parents. We are not trying to turn them into model adults; we just want to keep them alive and out of jail. Yet, at the stroke of puberty, we become the outsiders. They are suddenly citizens of a whole different nationality. They see us not at all the way we are, but the way other kids of their generation see their parents. After getting over our shock and sense of betrayal, we begin to realize that our parents are not as we had seen them, that we, too, had seen them through the eyes of a generational craziness that was not at all personal.

Adolescence is something else, but in time the tragedies on

both sides of adolescence become just the scherzo of the human comedy.

When children grow up, they still need us and we still need them. They must stand ready to take care of us when we can no longer take care of ourselves. Meanwhile, they need to check with us to find out Uncle Dave's formula for wood finish or Grandmother Boyd's recipe for congealed broccoli salad. We have become the repository of family lore; they have replaced us as the scouts who go ahead to find new adventures to enrich our lives.

And when they are fully grown and no longer have to show us that they don't need us any more than we need them, they can be our best friends and we can be theirs.

What Parents Cannot Expect

With all the emotional exercise and the character building that go into parenting, there are still things children cannot do for their parents, things parents cannot expect from their children.

You *can't expect* to get the benefits of parenthood from sperm donation or other forms of surrogate parenthood.

Nor can you expect to run out on your family or destroy it or ignore it without your children suffering terrible repercussions. I don't know who came up with the notion of "quality time," the idea that parenting could be done efficiently. Parenting is what happens when people of different generations hang out together and compare their experience of the world. It affects one about as much as it affects the other. So even if you get your picture taken with the child on ceremonial occasions or come home at night to a house filled with the child's artefacts or hear the child's bloodcurdling music coming from a locked bedroom or see the child perform at athletic or artistic displays, the experience will have little impact on you if you are not totally involved in the experience of the child's life, along with the corresponding revelations of your own life, your relationship to the world, and the human condition you both share. If what you are doing with your child is not changing your life, then don't expect it to change the child's.

I also don't know who came up with the idea that parents "*shouldn't* stay together for the children's sake." That's absurd, though I would certainly agree that staying together while turning family life into a war zone and blaming it on the kids is not good for anybody's mental health, even the neighbors'. Children do not require perfect love or brilliant innovative parenting techniques or a life that is free of germs or disappointments or traumas, but they do require the security of knowing that their parents will put up with each other's mild to moderate obnoxiousness and repulsiveness for the sake of the family.

It is not sufficient for parents to stay married for the children's sake; they must stay *happily* married for the children's sake. Happy marriage is a decision that comes when people decide this is their real life, this is their real world, this is their real marriage—and stomping their foot and holding their breath because it is not the life, the world, and the marriage of their dreams is not going to get them a better deal, so they might as well grin and bear it. When they measure the pros and cons of such drastic action as divorce, they must include the costs to their children. Parents may learn the hard way that running out on parenting for a while to recapture some piece of their own lost youth breaks the bond, and it may never be reforged.

The crippling trauma of a divorce, and the child's resulting lifelong insecurity about life and relationships, may be worse than the vague or even fairly certain hope that the next stepparent will be the magical one who will make everything rosy for you and your child. Every child needs a secure family, not a perfect one.

You *can't expect* to raise perfect children even if you are perfect parents. We like to think—and our therapists and the writers of our favorite self-help books like to reassure us—that everything which isn't ideal in our life is surely our parents' fault. You may be right in thinking that therapists are likely to blame you for your kid's hang-up, that your child's teachers are going to think your child's failures are because you are not sufficiently involved (even though the therapist is probably telling you the kid is a screwup because you are too involved). Your parents and in-laws overflow with critical wisdom, which may or may not be applicable, and the neighbors have another set of ideas about how you are making a mess of things. Everybody will blame you except the child. But if you are too willing to blame yourself, the child will take the cue from you and blame you for his or her failures, and that's a lot worse.

You can't have a perfect child merely because you are in some contest with other parents or because you are afraid the inspection committee will come along and tell you what you have suspected all along: that you are a terrible parent and a terrible person. Anyway, children learn from their mistakes, not from their parents' anxiety that they will make mistakes. You can require your children to face life and even to develop competence in the basic skills, but excellence can only come from their own hunger for it, and that can come only when their initial efforts are praised.

In some ways, damaged children are actually more gratifying to raise, especially if the disability shows. If a kid is blind or deaf or missing a body part or two, the world does what the world should do for all kids: assesses the child's performance on the basis of his or her own merits and the child's own development rather than as part of some contest with other kids.

Just stop trying to fix your normal children, show the joy you take in them, talk to them about their experience of the world, and tell them about yours, and they will become just like you. You have no way of making them turn out better than you; they have to do that on their own. And if you are really perfect in some way, they will have to find their own way to distinguish themselves.

You *can't expect* children to repay your investment in them. Some parents believe that if they put enough time and money into it, the child will reward them with a comparable amount of parental pride. But children, however dutiful, can only dedicate their lives to their own dreams of glory, not the fulfillment of their parents' dreams. If a father's fantasies overwhelm a son and the boy loses his sense of self by buckling under and merging with his father's ego, he cannot go on.

All three of my children had their areas of excellence, mostly in the two activities at which I most miserably and visibly failed—singing and running. Only after claiming their own areas of excellence, thereby defeating me and making me proud by doing so, could they go on to achieve success in the things I had excelled in before them. Having worked with many families in which fathers coach their children, becoming good coaches and bad fathers, I have learned that children must first feel safe in an activity; next they must become competent at it; then they must pull back and differentiate. Only then can they excel and remain their own persons, capable of pride in their skills and respect for their parents.

It works so much better for me to have pride in what my children are as people, without counting trophies or even noticing the contests they enter. Their successes are theirs, not mine; their comfort in life and their ability to love are the sources of my pride.

You *can't expect* children to show appreciation for your

efforts. If a child takes the parent for granted—not giving or taking offense, and not keeping score on who owes whom what—that should be appreciation enough. It shows the child feels the parent's steady love and knows the parent has gotten as much as has been given from the parenting process.

The child may adore and cherish the parent and may still take the parent for granted and forget to send a card on Mother's Day. When Cordelia refused to cheapen her love for her father by reciting high-blown tributes, as her sisters had done, and when King Lear failed to recognize her plain-spoken acceptance as real love, he brought about the tragedy that engulfed them all.

Lear is not the only parent who ever brought tragedy on the family by failing to honor and cherish the imperfect but honest gift of a child's love. God's rejection of Cain's offering led to the tragedy of Cain and Abel, a tragedy echoed in John Steinbeck's retelling of the story in *East of Eden*. Likewise, the crusty old man in *I Never Sang for My Father* could give to his children and take pride in doing so, but he could not be on the receiving end of the relationship and thus let his son become a grown-up, too. It's not enough for parents to bestow emotional and physical bounty on their children; the parent must also let the child give something back and honor and value that gift.

In fact, children can't really grow up until the parent finds them helpful and useful and appreciates what they do. Tributes of appreciation should go both ways. I know I got as much from my children as they did from me, and my parents got as much from me and my sister.

You *can't expect* your children to give you the exclusive loyalty and dedication that you might reasonably expect from marriage. A parent might naively assume that the kids owe allegiance because "I was always there for them while their father worked or played golf or screwed around" or "I was always cheerful and upbeat and never lost my temper" or "I stayed with them after he left" or "I supported them while she lay around watching TV and drinking." It may feel like betrayal in a divorce or a marriage at war when the kids take the "good" parent for granted and throw themselves at the "bad" parent who escapes parenthood for another go at childhood, but it is necessary for the child who doesn't know a parent to find out personally what is missing, what is wrong.

There are parents who destroy their children by getting between them and the other parent or their grandparents or the child's friends or even mates or their in-laws or their own children.

The child-raising process is not supposed to turn a baby into the parent's parent or mate. When a parent tries to get his or her life from the grown child, it can destroy the child or the relationship. Recycling an adult through childhood so that the parents can feel loved without having to risk a relationship with another adult is cumbersome at best. If parents want unquestioning loyalty from a creature who will never desert them, they should get a dog. Dogs are a lot cheaper at every stage of development, and you don't have to worry about their growing up, leaving you, and telling a therapist what a miserable parent you were.

You *can't expect* children to save a relationship. Some women foolishly have babies to save a bad marriage or get pregnant in order to get some guy to marry them, or they may even give the guy a baby hoping he'll drop by from time to time and be nice to her. It is not a good idea. Having a baby with a guy who is afraid of commitment and family life, afraid of husbandhood and fatherhood, will not reliably bring him closer to you. And if he doesn't like you very much to start with, he's not likely to like you better when you wake him up in the middle of the night to throw a wet, hungry, feces-smeared, squishy noisemaker at him.

Men, who didn't get much fathering in recent generations,

may not know what a father is for, and women, who usually got even less fathering than men did, are likely to be even more misinformed about what men are capable of doing. If the father feels left out or if the mother leaves him out, it bodes badly for the relationship. A man can't easily intrude on a fresh mother-child bond and compete with the mother. If he's not invited in, he is likely to distance himself from the whole symbiotic unit. A fresh baby is not likely to be appealing as the arena in which a man can demonstrate his masculine mastery. He generally does it initially because of his commitment to the mother, not to the child, and if that relationship is not a loving one, he may have trouble bonding with his son or daughter—unless of course, he has bonded well with his own father.

You *can't expect* the benefits of child raising to come immediately. Child raising, like farming, requires patience. There is no way to speed it up; in fact, any effort to speed it up will just screw it up. Child raising forces busy people to slow down and live their lives in real time, moving no faster than the earth does, blocked from taking any shortcuts. Once you are operating on earth time with your child, you begin to see and hear and smell and feel things you had forgotten all about. You may not get as much done, but you will get far more from everything you do. Don't worry, you won't miss a thing.

And, finally, you *must expect* to make one crucial concession to child raising. As you raise your children, you will have to forgive your parents for either loving you too much or not loving you enough. The act of becoming a parent involves the willingness to expose yourself to having your child feel toward you the way you feel toward your parents. Those who try to go through life as their own pampered child or as an indignant victim, without making these concessions to intergenerational forgiveness and acceptance, cannot anticipate forgiveness and acceptance from their children when the time comes.

Secrets of Savoring the Joys of Parenthood

1. Don't consider your child to be any different in kind or quality or rights or privileges than any other child. Let your child connect you with all the world's parents who are feeling just what you are feeling.

2. Don't let your desire to go back into your own childhood compete with your child's need to be the child while you are the adult. Don't destroy your child's childhood so you can relive yours. Stick it out for the long haul. Don't worry: If you can stick it out and maintain your sanity through the readjustments of adolescence, you will ultimately be much rewarded. You'll become a grown-up and may be rewarded with a grandchild and get to start the process all over again.

3. Don't teach children to be violent by being violent with them. Learn not to be violent yourself, especially if you were raised violently.

4. Don't teach children to be unpleasant and abusive by being unpleasant and abusive with them. Be polite to children. You are teaching them (and yourself) how to behave properly, so treat conflicts as exercises in manners rather than revelations of basic inner rottenness.

5. Teach your children to delight in learning. You can't teach a child too much. The child will eagerly and joyously learn everything you eagerly and joyously teach. You and your child will learn together.

6. Toss out or shoot out the television set. If you read, the child will read. If you exercise, the child will exercise. If you work, the child will work. If you watch TV, the child will become a couch potato like you.

7. Don't teach a child to fear unfamiliar things, such as strangers, danger, novelty, or nature, or unpleasant things, such as failure, conflict, or sadness. Instead, let the child teach you to stop fearing the things you fear now.

8. Provide structure, like specific mealtimes and regular family outings, and expect the child to fit into the family schedule. Give the child something valuable to do, not as discipline or punishment or evidence of parental control but because the family needs it done. The child must be a valuable, functioning member of the family.

9. Express constant pride in your kids, not just for their successes but for the workings of their mind, body, and emotions. Adore them just for letting you be part of it, and then feel the pride you are expressing.

10. Punish children rarely and minimally. Instead, talk to them about the complexities of knowing the right thing to do in a confusing world. Always express your optimism about the child's basic goodness. Children will become whatever you tell them they are. You must never insult or ridicule a child. You'll love yourself for it.

11. Whatever age your kids are, try to hold them every day. You'll get your hugs at the same time.

12. Don't pull back from loving your children during adolescence just because they pull back from you and your efforts to control, protect, or fix them. It is just

when they hate you most that they most need your steady, reliable love. Consider it an investment.

13. Stay connected with your adolescent kids. Get them out in the woods or up on a mountain, anyplace you are not in control and where you are dependent on one another. Celebrate their puberty. If they take their sexuality underground because it embarrasses you, they will quickly follow it and may not emerge for a few years. Don't let your teenage kids shock you. Insist on hearing it all, and honestly compare your own adolescence. Adolescents aren't alienated; their parents are. Reconnect.

14. Keep adolescents moving. They are only a problem when they stop. Sports and work save lives. Yours, too.

15. Don't try to protect older kids from natural consequences and substitute your punishment. They learn about reality from natural consequences. They only learn about you from your punishment of them.

16. Don't turn matters of style into matters of substance. Let them get themselves up in weird ways without making it a moral issue. Your adolescent styles would look pretty dumb today.

17. Never let your kids embarrass you or let the reactions of shocked friends, gawking strangers, or indignant teachers be more important than the feelings of your beloved child who just made a humiliating mess. Don't shame a child for not excelling and leaving you feeling ashamed around the parents of more successful kids.

18. In raising adolescents, cultivate a bad recent memory. Refuse to recall what they did wrong the day before. Start off each day as if it were a whole new relationship. They change so rapidly and self-consciously, it probably is.

19. Don't respect your children's privacy. If you can't tolerate the mess in their room, close the door, but don't let them hide in there keeping their lives secret from you. You must know where your children are and what they are doing, especially if you know you have no control over it.

20. If older teenagers don't value and respect the privileges and comforts of family life, and won't let you into their lives, let them leave. If they get along okay without you, then you'll have to realize they were right: They didn't need you after all. But if you're not too unpleasant, pretty soon they will see that they want you, and that's better for both them and you.

21. Remember that adolescence is a time of normal psychosis, certainly the most painful time in anyone's life. You've been there, so you can see it from the adolescent's perspective, but the adolescent can't yet see it from yours.

Keep thinking about how wonderful it will be when adolescence is over and your kids are free to become just like you. Remember: Your kids will come to love you just as much as you love your parents because they'll learn this, as they'll ultimately learn everything else—not from what you tell them is right but from your example.

Hodding Carter gave me my favorite quote about parents and children when he said, "There are only two lasting bequests we can hope to give our children. One of these is roots; the other, wings." I would add to that. Roots and wings are exactly the two lasting bequests that children give parents, connecting you with your familial, biological, and personal origins, and enabling you to live many lives other than your own.

9

The Secrets of Happiness

Happiness Is a Warm Puppy.

> —Book title by Charles Schulz

Happiness Is Just a Thing Called Joe.

> —Song by E. Y. "Yip" Harburg and
> Harold Arlen

*This lovely car has not brought us happiness.
You agree, Morris? That is why I am now
thinking in terms of having the entire house
recarpeted.*

> —*New Yorker* cartoon caption by
> J. B. Handelsman

ALL OF US WANT TO BE HAPPY, AND MOST OF US DEDICATE our lives to its pursuit. Those of us who seem to be wandering aimlessly in unlikely places may seem lost but are just looking for happiness without a map or a compass. Just about all of human behavior makes sense if we realize that all of us are trying to make ourselves happy or get others to make us happy, but most of the people in the world are doing it with a faulty instruction book.

Even those who seem to be going out of their way to be

unhappy, who dedicate themselves to suffering and sacrificing unnecessarily and making a mess of their lives (and we all do that some of the time), are doing what they do because they believe that is the only way they can get loved or get taken care of and thus have some hope for happiness. They're like beggars with self-inflicted disabilities, disabling themselves for security. If you have ever been married to one of these people, or have been raised by one or even been one of them yourself, you know that they torture their loved ones because it is the only way they know to get love.

There are only two ways to get happy: One is by not thinking about it and just letting it come upon us while we are busy living a life, and the other is by understanding it thoroughly and coming to realize that we can create a happy life for ourselves and our loved ones if we take responsibility for what we do with the life we've been given, wherever we find ourselves now and however we got there; responsibility for how we treat ourselves and others and the world we live in; and responsibility for the reactions we have and the choices we make. Without responsibility there can be no happiness.

Even the least responsible of us, like Hamlet's mother, who left her "self to heaven," and Blanche DuBois, who "relied upon the kindness of strangers," still have our moments of pleasures. We can be irresponsible and can still feel good when we're lucky, when things work out just right, and when others care enough to do their very best for us. But there cannot be the gratification, the pride, the honor and integrity that come from doing the right things and having it work out well not only for ourselves but for others we care about. Happiness involves not just comfort and joy but also a sense of responsibility to others.

Happiness has nothing to do with good fortune, good luck, or prosperity. Whatever we get by luck is not really ours. Happiness cannot fall on us from out of the heavens; it cannot be bestowed on us. It must grow from the inside out.

Happiness has more to do with our relationship with our self than it does with our relationship with the world. It involves contentment and honor, satisfaction with who we are and what we have done and will do. Happiness involves the feeling, especially on our part and perhaps on the part of our loved ones, that we are a good-enough person. It is hard but far from impossible to achieve happiness when we live with people who don't like us very much. It just requires that we understand them and why they feel as they do and act as they do, and we usually find that those who treat us the worst are doing so either because they want to help us be better or because they want us to love them more. By contrast, it is impossible for us to achieve happiness, no matter how much we are loved by others, if we don't like the sort of person we are and the sorts of things we do, and if we are not doing anything to make ourselves better.

Those who don't develop happiness within themselves but demand it from outside clearly don't know how to bring it about and are likely to be angry about it. And since one can't be happy and angry at the same time, they will end up unhappy.

Those who confuse happiness with highs of either pleasure or pain will be so busy bouncing up and down that they won't be able to achieve the steady state of happiness. They don't know what happiness is and wouldn't recognize it if it overtook them.

Happiness is not a state of peace. It emerges from the struggle of life, the danger and opportunity of life's inevitable crises. William James, in a letter to Wanda Lutoslawski in 1906, explained: "Most people live, whether physically, intellectually, or morally, in a very restricted circle of their potential being. They *make use* of a very small portion of their possible consciousness, and of their soul's resources in general, much like a man who, out of his whole bodily organism, should get into a habit of using and moving only his little finger. Great emergencies and crises show us how much greater our vital resources are than we had supposed."

Carl Jung applied the same principle to marriage: "Seldom, or perhaps never, does a marriage develop into an individual relationship smoothly and without crises; there is no coming to consciouness without pain."

Happiness is not the absence of pain and certainly not the absence of crisis. If anything, it is the comforting belief that pain and crisis can be faced, endured, and even put to use in achieving more strength and maturity.

Happiness cannot be obtained by jumping at it or grasping for it. In *Lovers and Other Strangers,* an exceptionally wise comedy from Joseph Bologna and Renee Taylor in 1970, Joseph Hindy announces that he wants to divorce Diane Keaton because he isn't happy. (We later learn that she is much disenchanted and has withdrawn from her marriage because "his hair no longer smells like raisins" to her.) His father, Richard Castellano, bewails, "These kids today! All they're looking for is happiness." His mother, Beatrice Arthur, echoes her husband and wisely intones, "Don't look for happiness, Richie. It'll only make you miserable."

Or, as the old Japanese proverb goes, "Looking for happiness is like clutching the shadow or chasing the wind."

Or, according to Nathaniel Hawthorne in *American Notebooks,* "Happiness in this world, when it comes, comes incidentally. Make it the object of pursuit, and it leads us a wild-goose chase, and is never attained. Follow some other object, and very possibly we may find that we have caught happiness without dreaming of it."

Happiness is a Grown-up Thing

Age is a very high price to pay for maturity.

—Tom Stoppard, *Rosenkrantz and Guildenstern Are Dead*

Actually, age is not too high a price to pay for maturity. It is worth it. Adulthood means getting far enough outside oneself to do as Margaret Mead urged: "to cherish the life of the world," that is, to connect with life itself rather than just with oneself, to overcome the narcissism of our youth and make give-and-take connections from which we can feel the pain and the pleasure of others rather than crouching selfishly and alone in our own protective skins.

To me, the maturing function of psychotherapy is to get people past a narcissistic state where they notice only what other people do and how it makes them feel, and move them to a mature state where they notice what they do and how it makes other people feel.

Adulthood is empowering. Grown-ups know we have the ability to do things, to make things happen, to impact other people. And if we feel powerful, we can get the necessary attention from other people by doing things and saying things that will make them feel good rather than doing what infants do most of the time and adolescents do some of the time: make themselves heard and felt by jarring and disturbing others with noisiness, nastiness, and shock effects.

Adulthood is liberating. Grown-ups can define themselves rather than just pleasing or displeasing those who would define them. Once we are free to do the right thing of our own choosing, we are most likely to do so. And if we know we are doing it, it will have far more power to make us happy.

Adulthood is mellow. Grown-ups have become what they are going to be. The frantic struggle of rapid changes in body and soul is over. The fear and desperation are gone. We have arrived. We are at home in the world. We can relax and go to bed before our bedtime without the fear of missing anything.

Happiness is a grown-up thing. It is connectedness—not just connectedness with our loved ones but connectedness with life. It is sharing the experiences that all humans share. It is joining the life cycle and thereby moving away from the loneliness of living a life all alone. Once we know that our life is not really much different from everyone else's and the outcome is the same, we have nothing more to fear.

In *Life and How to Survive It,* Robin Skynner insists that his "life has got steadily better from the age of eighteen months. . . . In fact, life should get altogether more rich and enjoyable, not least because you should have become a lot wiser and gained more control of your life and of yourself."

It takes more than maturity to produce happiness, of course, but maturity is at the root of it.

I've made much here of a few central tasks of adults, tasks that will ultimately enable us to be happy:

First, to be a full-scale grown-up, we must connect with the other generations. We must come to understand our parents well enough to forgive them, not just so we won't go through life as innocent victims or adult children but so we can forgive ourselves when we don't do parenting just right. Parenting is so central to maturing, creating happiness, and connecting with the past and future that we need to do whatever we can to free ourselves to risk it. Forgiving our parents means coming to understand how they got to be the way they were, what they grew up with both at home and in their culture, and what they felt as they led their lives and as they made the decisions they made that affected our lives. This may be the major hurdle in moving from the child generation to the parental one.

Second, we find the meaning to our lives as grown-ups when we realize that we ourselves are not the culmination of Western civilization, of human evolution, or of God's creations. Our function in this life is to raise children, not necessarily and certainly not exclusively our own children but the subsequent generations of humankind. Our work and our very being exist for that aim. Growing up and raising children is in no way the sacrifice of our lives; it is the fulfillment and application of our own childhood. It is the process by which we become our own person and by which we join the succession of generations that keeps us connected with all of life and all of human history. The impact of this endeavor, although it is a full-time job and takes a lifetime, is wonderously liberating. Some cannot or do not have children of their own and must therefore find other children or other adults who are raising children, and make connections over time with them, in the hope of getting some of the meaning of life outside themselves. But unless we invest our life in children, wherever we can find them, we run the risk of becoming our own pampered child.

Third, to be a full-scale grown-up we need to create a family in which we can be humbled, disappointed, disillusioned, and stripped of our romantic expectations and still survive, a family in which we can learn to give love even when we're not getting it, a family in which we discover that we can be happy even if our dreams don't come true, a family in which we can reveal ourselves in all our shame and guilt and still be accepted—because we accept the others who share our family. Family is where they have to take us in, where we can take our girdles off, and where we don't need to tell lies to get ourselves accepted because we already belong and we live there. We need that sort of family a lot more than we need ideal love. Permanent marriage, made to last, built out of concrete blocks rather than romantic plywood curlicues, is at the center of it.

Fourth, to be a full-scale grown-up we must get over the restrictions of our gender training. We can either retain or discard the trappings of gender, but we will never get over the gender identity with which we have been raised, and that's quite okay. The important thing is to fill out the functional and emotional range that was narrowed as we were molded by our parents and the world in stereotypical maleness or femaleness. Finding, developing, and reconnecting the parts that were lost will take us at least a lifetime, but—

and here is the wonderful part—we don't have to do it just right, even if the bullying thought police of gender concretism or the bullying thought police of political correctness are breathing down our necks. One of the most liberating freedoms of adulthood is to take gender so casually that we have the freedom to do it wrong.

All four of these tasks happen almost automatically as we raise our children, as we nurse our aging parents through to the end of their lives, and as we survive the unending crises, disappointments, and revelations of holding on to a marriage for a lifetime.

There are other aspects of happy adulthood as well:

CHEMISTRY

Happiness does not take place in the world when everything aligns itself just as we had hoped and dreamed. Happiness takes place inside our brain. It really is, even if the idea seems both unfair and deplorable, simply a chemical state. It requires a high level of serotonin and at least a moderate supply of norepinephrine in the brain cells so the brain can do its work of projecting into the future and anticipating a favorable and pleasurable outcome. Some people have brains that register happiness more readily than others do. William James said, "In many persons, happiness is congenital and irreclaimable." It is tempting to envy people who are made happy so easily, but it is impossible to be happy and envious at the same time. (And I'm sure that people who are made happy entirely too easily end up being undiscriminating, unadventurous, uninspiring, and dull.)

People who are trying too desperately to make themselves happy may do so by assaulting their brains with stimulants and sedatives, and their schedules with jarring and life-threatening adventures. Such things can really give us a kick but can't make us happy. We can't be happy unless our brain can register happiness, and it can't register something as sublime and subtle as happiness if it is being bludgeoned with crude drugs like alcohol or cocaine and crude emotions like anger or fear.

If your brain is chemically unable to slip into happiness even after you have stopped drinking, started exercising daily, conquered your anger, revealed all your secret shames, stopped the behavior that made you feel guilty, became more loving to everyone than they were to you, taken up a full complement of work and play, and learned how to be a grown-up and practiced it, then you may benefit from antidepressants. But do all the other things first, before you start blaming your genes.

LOVE

Most people think of love as the thing that is most likely to make them happy. The people who believe that love is one of the secrets of happiness are right as long as they aren't confusing "falling in love" with "loving." *Marvin's Room* is a play and a movie about two sisters. One of the sisters (Meryl Streep) neglected and abused her children as she ran through many men in her futile search for lasting romantic love. The other (Diane Keaton) never married, never had children, and stayed home all her life caring for their stroked-out father and dotty old aunt. When Keaton finds that she is dying, she tells her sister:

> KEATON (beaming radiantly): Oh, Lee. I've been so lucky. I've been so lucky to have Dad and Ruth, to have such love in my life. You know, I look back and I've had such love.
> STREEP (uncomprehendingly): They love you very much.
> KEATON: No, that's not what I mean. No, no. I mean that I love them. I've been so lucky to be able to love someone so much.

Streep fails to understand that Keaton is happy because of the love she has given, not the love she has gotten. Her sister understands that the greatest happiness comes from the giving of love, and she's missed it.

People who want to be happy are loving. They go around doing nice things for other people. Sometimes it is reciprocated. Sometimes it is not. Loving makes us feel good about ourselves, and we may get responses that reaffirm those good feelings about our ability to give and receive love. It protects us from the ups and downs of an inevitably more volatile, desperate, and sensitive romantic relationship. People who love only the one they are in love with are in a vulnerable, precarious situation. One relationship is not enough (though it sure beats hell out of two romantic ones going on at the same time).

Loving is not that difficult. It isn't absolutely necessary that we like our loved ones very much in order for us to be happy with them; it is a lot more important that we like ourselves as we love them. Admittedly, some people are easier to love than others, but our happiness depends on how well we love, not how lovable they are.

WORK

I don't like work—no man does—but I like what is in work—the chance to find yourself. Your own reality—for yourself, not for others—what no other man can ever know.

—Joseph Conrad, *Heart of Darkness*

In *Spellbound,* a mourning Ingrid Bergman was told by her psychiatrist boss, "It is very sad. To love—and lose somebody. But in a while, you will forget. And you will take up the threads of your life where you left off—not so long ago. And you will work hard. There is lots of happiness in working hard. Maybe the most."

Our work defines who we are in relationship to everyone else. Certainly it defines our status in the world, but more important it defines our usefulness. It is what we do to give back to the rest of the world what they give to us. It is impossible for any of us to be happy without paying our own way with whatever goods or services we have to offer, especially including all the care we give to others.

Of course, one of the pleasures of any job is the right to complain about it. Some jobs are not much fun and some working conditions are far from pleasant, but few people are asked to do such arduous and hazardous duty as the sort of thing they do for fun. Few people are called upon by their jobs to go out in the cold and tackle or block one another in mud or stay up long after our bedtime, drinking toxic fluids and breathing smoky air, listening to blaring and thumping sounds and intermittently getting up and dancing around in a crowded space with others who are as sweaty as we are.

We don't have to like our job in order to be happy; we have to like ourselves as we do it. People don't get happy by doing what they like but by liking whatever it is they have to do. Happy people ennoble the work they do.

It is nice if we can come to like doing the jobs we can do since most of us have to work anyway. And it isn't just that we can't be a functioning part of the world unless we do it, we can't be happy unless we do. Happiness, like sweat, is a by-product of activity. It can't be bought, borrowed, or begged. We can't get it from someone else. We have to work for it ourselves.

The truly miserable people are the ones who have no work to do and thus have lost their sense of themselves, their pride, and their right to expect sustenance and tolerance, much less happiness. Those lazy, worthless, childlike people who think they can achieve happiness by getting out of work and investing as little energy into the world as possible, and making sure they get more than they put in, are going to be unhappy and aren't going to understand why. They haven't earned happiness, so it cannot be theirs.

PLAY

We do things for fun, and unless we are pretty severely depressed, we have fun doing them. But the pursuit of pleasure is not the same as the pursuit of happiness. Happiness is, almost by chemical definition, the ability to get pleasure from the anticipation or the memory of it, rather than just from the stimulation of pleasure itself. Happy people can enjoy thinking of other people having pleasure. Happy people don't have to be actively playing to feel pleasure. In fact, the pleasures that happy people experience are particularly satisfying because the good feeling is not just part of the isolated pleasurable experience but is part of life. The happiness lasts long after the pleasure passes. Happy people don't need much playtime. Living life is enough play for them.

Circumscribed, contrived play is never as much fun for anyone as the playfulness with which happy people go about their business and their interplay with others. Thoreau warned us that we should "beware of all enterprises that require new clothes." I would add that any form of play that requires much new equipment can't possibly be much fun.

Play shouldn't be so much trouble. I worry a bit about the happiness level of people who need to jump out of planes to risk their lives, go to Las Vegas to risk their money, or take up with dangerous strangers to risk their marriage or their sanity in the hope of feeling pleasure.

There is so much to enjoy that is easily accessible, and the happiest people are those whose pleasures are the cheapest and most available. Maria in *The Sound of Music* said a few of her "favorite things" were raindrops on roses and whiskers on kittens.

Woody Allen still stayed under budget and came somewhat closer to my sense of things in *Manhattan* when he spelled out his reasons for believing that life is worth living: "For me, umh, Groucho Marx, Willie Mays, the second movement of the Jupiter Symphony, Louis Armstrong's recording of 'Potato Head Blues,' Swedish movies naturally, *Sentimental Education* by Flaubert, Marlon Brando, Frank Sinatra, those incredible apples and pears by Cézanne, the crabs at Sam Wo's, Tracey's face . . ."

There are those whose idea of play involves killing endangered species, making sights and sounds that will offend others, and breaking rules or other people's property. They need to start over with the whiskery kittens and the wet roses. Play cannot be mean and hateful if it is to be part of human happiness. In adolescence one's happiness may come from feeling the power to make others unhappy. Adults don't do that because they don't need to.

Adults learn to experience joy gently. In learning to sense the pleasures in us and around us, it helps to avoid overwhelming sensory experiences of the sort that keep our ears ringing, our nose running, our gut burning, and our knees knocking for days afterward. We need to train the body and soul to respond to soft pleasures: the smell of familiar bodies without perfume, the sound of unamplified music, perhaps Mozart with no cannons shooting off in the background, the taste of pears without syrup or ice cream without cookies crumbled in it, the feel of dancing without throwing anyone over our head.

HONOR

Exercise, sex, joy, and triumph can produce the hormones necessary to permit happiness, but happiness won't happen even then unless you do things that make you feel proud of yourself. Angry or competitive exercise, guilty or selfish sex, dangerous or destructive joy, and dishonorable or cruel triumph will not produce happiness. There can be no enduring happiness without honor and integrity. Happiness is akin to honor.

Happiness requires victory over shame—not *guilt*, which is necessary to monitor our relationship with the world and to remind us of our power to do better, but *shame*. Shame is perhaps the greatest psychological barrier to happiness. Shame is this nagging sense that we aren't good enough, that we are in some way inferior. Shame comes when the gap is too great between our self concept and our ego ideal, our sense of what we are and our sense of what we should be.

Nobody's perfect. You may be a jerk some of the time. We all are. That's no cause for shame, just guilt. If you don't like yourself when you do something, then don't do it. We need to nurture our guilt and lose our shame.

We can't overcome our shame by blaming our parents or the world or our first marriage partner for setting the bar too high and insulting us when we failed to clear it. We overcome shame by taking responsibility for the models to which we so brutally compare ourself. We may have to find more compatible models and make them our own.

We overcome shame by becoming a better person, and we become a better person by practicing doing better things, such as what we should do rather than what we want to do. We might even consider letting other people's feelings be as important to us as our own. It seems as if I heard all of this somewhere before.

If we want to feel more honorable and virtuous, we can do something nice for someone else every day. And then we can do something nice for ourself every other day.

HONESTY

The best way we have for getting over our shame is to expose ourselves to others. If we keep significant secrets from those we want to love us, we won't receive love or we won't trust the love we receive. People who go through life hiding their vulnerabilities are lonely and stand little chance of happiness.

Honesty by itself cannot produce happiness, and radical honesty will not further magnify happiness. I'm not suggesting that we show our hemorrhoids on national television, come out on *Hard Copy* from whatever closet we hide in, or even hang out our dirty laundry in front of the neighbors. But there can be no real happiness without sufficient honesty for our loved ones to know us and have the opportunity to love us anyway.

I Love Lucy and most other TV sitcoms involve the complexities that occur when well-meaning but shamed people try to keep from being known and understood. Lucy and Ethel each week used to do something silly, ranging from denting a fender to inviting the president over for dinner, and tried to keep it from their husbands, who would get increasingly exasperated until they finally found out the truth and all would be resolved. This was the plot of essentially all Shakespearean comedies as well.

Lies are childish, generally based on shame, and intended to keep us from being known. In the process they keep us from being happy. There is great tragedy for those who must, for some reason, sit on significant secrets. They can never achieve intimacy. In fact, the power of sexual affairs comes from the human reality that we bond with whoever shares our secrets and we feel adversarial toward those we fear would not tolerate us or love us if they knew our shameful secrets, if they really knew us.

MANNERS

Honesty, and for that matter essentially all other human interaction, must always be tempered by manners. Manners work. I notice that happy people thank other people a lot and apologize a lot. In both cases we are letting other people know they are important to us. It makes the other people feel important, makes them like us, and makes them treat us better.

Manners used to be considered more important than they are now, which is why they are more important now than they ever were. There is a lot of rudeness going on lately, as if it is necessary for self-expression and the pursuit of individual happiness.

The mental health industry has contributed to this rudeness in the past by encouraging people to go around telling everyone everything they felt, especially venting their anger and other unpleasantnesses. It quickly became clear that the world needed manners far more than it needed mental health.

Rudeness is not the path to happiness, despite Erich Segal's absurd but popular line in *Love Story,* "Love means never having to say you're sorry"—as if the proof of love and intimacy was the lack of need for politeness and consideration. If we go around offending others without thinking about it, it will make it harder for us to get the love we need. Manners is simply an awareness of and respect for the sensibilities of others.

Manners do not interfere with speaking the truth but certainly soften the blow. Anything that ever needs to be said can be said with good manners. My great-grandmother used to tell me that a gentleman or a lady never offends anyone *un*intentionally. Sometimes—albeit rarely, I hope—we may want to hurt someone else, but we should know we are doing it and why.

We can only be happy if we clearly respect the feelings of others, and only then can we reasonably expect that our feelings will be respected in return.

HEALTH AND EXERCISE

Joseph Addison in *The Spectator* in 1711 explained: "Exercise ferments the humors, casts them into their proper channels, throws off redundancies, and helps nature in those secret distributions, without which the body cannot subsist in its vigor, nor the soul act with cheerfulness."

It is hard for a brain to be happy in a body that is toxic. A happy brain requires a well-exercised body. Exercise is not only the first-line treatment for depression, and even a necessary accompaniment of antidepressant medication, but it is also the most overlooked secret of happiness. Exercise produces the neurotransmitters, such as serotonin and norepinephrine, that enable us to be happy.

Exercise also makes us proud of our bodies, proud of how we look and feel, proud of what we can do. It makes our muscles want to move; toned-up muscles want to take us places and do things for us.

Some people, perhaps unaccustomed to exercise, perhaps recalling childhood failures to achieve athletic glory, or perhaps associating it with burdensome labor rather than with active play, resist exercise as if their lives depended on it. They have associated happiness with leisure, and they find it hard to start the positive addiction of regular exercise.

William James recommended exercise for the very reason that it feels burdensome at the beginning (once an exercise routine has been begun, it becomes compelling and the muscles themselves pull you forward into it). James said in *The Principles of Psychology* in 1890, "Keep the faculty of effort alive in you by a little gratuitous exercise every day. That is, be systematically ascetic or heroic in little unnecessary points, do every day or two something for no other reason than that you would rather not do it, so that when the hour of dire need draws nigh, it may find you not unnerved and untrained to stand the test."

Serious athletes may be intellectually boring, verbally dumb, and often in pain, or they may not be. But either way, they tend to be happy people, far less disgruntled and competitive than academics, for instance. Athletes are well trained for following rules, for ignoring irrelevant nonsense, and for figuring out what is important to happiness. I've rarely known a dedicated athlete (whether obscenely rich or obscenely poor—there is no in-between) who was not a basically happy person, eager to let others share the happiness. I think it is the exercise that does it.

When I leave my office after a day of angry people screaming at their loved ones and trying to intimidate one another, I may go to the mellow gym where hulking behemoths, with layer upon layer of bulging muscles and hundreds of pounds of steel held over their heads, treat one another with the most delicate politeness and consideration. People who exercise their bodies enough don't need to exercise their emotions much at all.

NATURE

Nearness to nature keeps the spirit sensitive to impressions not commonly felt, and in touch with the unseen powers.

—Ohiyesa, *The Soul of the Indian*

Happy people love life, and love, value, and honor the world; they do not shrink from it. They don't protect themselves from the natural world but embrace it and let it embrace them. This may or may not lead to a concept of God that will give people some affirmation of their basic nature and some meaning to their relationships to the universe. But anything that gets people outside their own heads, to see something of value beyond their own feelings and needs, is bound to be good for their happiness.

As Michael J. Dee said in his *Conclusions* in 1917, "Nature aborts all her works to make room for more. She never finishes anything nor permits anything to become perfect." People who expect their own natures to be perfected are placing the job in the wrong hands. Our nature is what it is, and we might as well assume that is what it is supposed to be. And while it is mostly universal, there are individual variations that make life a bit easier or a bit harder in some situations than in others. Since our nature will not change to suit our needs and wants or the needs and wants of others, we must transcend our nature, act better than we are inclined to be, and overcome some of the natural impulses that would abort us or our loved ones. It is only ourselves, not our nature, over which we have and must have dominion.

People who try to control the natural world will create a host of problems and unhappinesses. People who are at home in nature, who are capable of breathing real rather than artificially cooled and pasteurized air, who don't mind getting wet or dirty, are far happier than those who must shield themselves from natural forces in an attempt to keep themselves artificially above and apart from the messiness of life in the real world.

I remember sitting next to a very rich old woman who was hosting her granddaughter's wedding reception that night. She had not just redecorated and repainted her house for the occasion but had had the grounds replanted as well so that everything in sight would be blooming all at the same time. She had indeed gained the appearance of victory over time, decay, and the seasons. But she spent the evening relating her enormously frustrating and necessarily failing efforts to hold back the waves from the shore in front of her beach house, to keep the sand from washing out to sea. Her face showed the undeniable signs of trying to hold back time as well.

Our lives, and the lives we invest our lives in to carry parts of us into the future, depend on keeping the world alive. Adult happiness involves many things, but one of them is the faith that the world will go on after us.

THE LIFE CYCLE

The unexamined life is not worth living.

—Plato

Life can only be understood backwards; but it must be lived forwards.

—Kierkegaard, *Stages on Life's Way*

As the man said, "If you are not beautiful by the age of thirty, strong by the age of forty, rich by fifty, and wise by sixty, you're never going to be beautiful, strong, rich, or wise." The rest of us, not just having given up on being beautiful, strong, rich, and wise but having gotten over the need for it, are never complete; we are always in the process of becoming. It may be tempting to hold the moment, even to turn back the clock, but the meaning of life is always yet to come, around the next bend in the road. If life consists of practicing for our time at bat, taking our swings to whatever effect, and then retiring to the dugout, it really doesn't amount to much. It is merely an experience and not a process, and it is isolating and unfulfilling because it is merely autobiographical, disconnected from the life that goes on around us, the life that has gone before, and the life that is to follow us. If we are only concerned with our own life and our own moment of glory, we are missing the point. We must be connected with all life if we are to feel fully and permanently alive.

Happy grown-ups join the life cycle rather than fight it. They enjoy and wonder at each age of life and find the joys in it rather than making themselves miserable over not being older or younger.

Obviously, the most natural way to connect with the life cycle is by raising kids. At the far end of the spectrum, taking care of old people or just taking note of them can dispel the horrors of aging. As Bette Davis said, "Old age is not for sissies," but courage comes from knowing it can be done with joy and curiosity rather than just with carefully measured dignity.

Understanding the life cycle keeps people from fearing it and trying to defeat it. Accepting it is necessary and ultimately unavoidable. Trying to stay forever young is absurd because it prevents you from continuing to learn and experience each new age and condition of life. Life is not just for the young.

I see people who considered themselves fully formed and stopped learning at twenty-one or even at eighteen because they demanded of themselves, and felt required by the world, that they be beyond criticism at that point. No one is ever fully adult, and life would be over for them if they achieved it. Adulthood and happiness both require openness to change—change inside and outside. And they require awareness that the rest of the people out there are going through the same sorts of things, the same emotions, even the same experiences. Drama and literature and country music exist to remind us of that, and so does therapy.

Our daughter, Ginger Pittman Pistilli, was an actress in New York for a few years, and when she came back to get her doctorate in psychology and become a therapist, she was fascinated with the realization that both professions are trying to connect people with the universality of emotional experience and thus get them past their shame, fear, and sense of isolation. Whichever job she's doing, Ginger is connecting other people to life going on and empowering them to join the human comedy and accept the human life cycle. We can only be happy in the world when we know it's filled with people who share with us the realities and inevitabilities of life.

SIMPLICITY

Happiness doesn't require great worldly success or any special equipment. I have worked with many people who were rich and famous and miserable. The most reliable harbinger of happiness is low expectations. People who can feel good about cleaning out their sock drawer are going to be a lot happier than those who can't relax until they change or conquer the world.

Happiness may be a direct outgrowth of the simple life, though I recall a patient who was a member of the League for Plain Living and became obsessed with making everything simple. Finding ever more complex ways for simplifying his life kept him up late, interfered with his exercise, and drove his wife nuts.

My favorite essay on the simple life comes from André Gregory and Wallace Shawn in *My Dinner with André*. Wally is regaled at dinner with André's adventures in the pursuit of happiness and the meaning of life. André rattles on, deadpan, about being rebaptized with forty unemployed Jewish actresses and a suckling teddy bear in Poland, of being buried alive on Halloween in Long Island, of eating sand and throwing up all night with a Buddhist monk in the Sahara, of roofless buildings in Scotland that would go up and meet flying saucers, of an altar behind which appears a six-foot-eight-inch blue-skinned half-bull with poppies in his toes.

André assures Wally that events in a cigar store on Seventh Avenue can be just as significant as events at the top of Mount Everest, but he still wants to increase the impact of a production of Euripides' *Bacchae* by passing a human head through the audience. As André imagines a life in which each day could become an incredibly monumental task and ponders whether he has squandered his own life, I joined an increasingly incredulous Wally in thinking that the search for meaning in life can be carried too far.

I soon found myself awed by André but unable to imagine leading a life of such intellectual, emotional, aesthetic, and spiritual adventure—or needing to. I preferred Wally's safe world in which he keeps a little list of his tasks for the day and checks off each task as he does it, and shows the woman he lives with his list with the tasks checked off. He puts a cup of coffee beside his bed, and if he wakes up and there is no dead roach in his cold cup of coffee, he expects it to be a good day. Wally's life is made more comfortable by an electric blanket or by reading Charlton Heston's autobiography. Wally wonders why it should be necessary to have more than that, how it could be possible to have more than that.

Keeping it simple may be the most difficult of these components of happiness, especially in a postmodern world in which the choices and distractions are mind-boggling. Almost all the secrets of happiness center on just going ahead, taking responsibility, and growing up.

Secrets of a Happy Adulthood

1. **Happy grown-ups forgive their parents.** They learn how their parents learned the well-intentioned nonsense they passed on to them. They correct the instruction book of life they were given.

2. **Happy grown-ups mate for life and work at making it equal.** They don't expect their marriage to make them happy; instead, they insist that it make them married. Then they will be free to pursue happiness.

3. **Happy grown-ups transcend the limitations of gender.** They don't bother with the trappings of gender

or the show of it, but absorb the skills and the wisdom of the other gender as well as those of their own.

4. **Happy grown-ups raise children.** They throw themselves into it. They know it's the most important thing any of us do in life. If they have no children to parent, they find some they can aunt or uncle.

5. **Happy grown-ups have healthy brain chemistry.** They take care of their brains as they would their other vital organs. They don't assault it with toxic chemicals or toxic emotions.

6. **Happy grown-ups love.** They work at loving people more than people love them, no matter how they feel about the people they love. Those who like the way it makes them feel to love others will love others.

7. **Happy grown-ups work.** They do the work they have to do and like it because it rewards them with belonging to the functioning fellowship of human beings. People probably won't get to do what they like, so it makes them happy to like what they do.

8. **Happy grown-ups play.** They learn to turn whatever they do into play. They adopt gentle pleasures and bypass the harsh ones.

9. **Happy grown-ups do what is mentally and physically good for them, especially if they don't want to.** They get over the idea that they must do what they feel like doing.

10. **Happy grown-ups do the right thing.** And they take pride in it. If they're proud of the choices they make

and the things they do, they'll like themselves, and so will we.

11. **Happy grown-ups turn their shame into guilt.** It is empowering to know they can do the right thing, and they do. They kick themselves when they don't.

12. **Happy grown-ups exercise.** They make sure they exercise almost every day, but without anger or competition.

13. **Happy grown-ups enjoy sex, alone or with someone else.** But they don't do sexual things that cause guilt or shame, or should cause guilt or shame. They would feel guilty if they were sexually selfish or dishonest.

14. **Happy grown-ups make sure their pleasures don't hurt them or anyone else.**

15. **Happy grown-ups savor success and experience triumph, but only if it is honorable.**

16. **Happy grown-ups tell the truth, but only to those who care.**

17. **Happy grown-ups have good manners.** They learn how to say what needs to be said in a polite manner. The world nowadays needs manners a lot more than it needs mental health.

18. **Happy grown-ups don't fight against any nature but their own.** They join the world and cherish it.

19. **Happy grown-ups accept the life cycle.** It does no good to fight against it.

20. **Happy grown-ups keep it simple.**

21. **Above all, happy grown-ups take responsibility.** They take responsibility for their bodies, their characters, and their relationships. They own their lives and they own up to the choices they make. Finding the responsible thing to do is the lifelong quest for grown-ups. And it leads to real, grown-up happiness, since once you find your responsibility—not just what you feel like doing, but the right thing for you to do, the thing that gives you your sense of honor and integrity—and then you just do it, you can feel not only your own happiness but also that of everyone else in your life.

Reinhold Niebuhr realized that "life has no meaning except in terms of responsibility." If we are merely acted upon by people and nature and fate, then what is the point of life? So what if we complain loud and long about it? If there is no one to act, then there is no one to care and nothing to be done. What we go through in life takes on meaning only if we are sharing the experience with others and if we have the power to take action that will change things.

We aren't inert objects at the mercy of forces outside ourselves, such as the natural world, the culture, and the other people in our lives, and of forces inside ourselves, such as emotions, memories, and the messages of our bodies.

In the final scene of *East of Eden,* as the prodigal son, James Dean, is reconciled with his father, Raymond Massey, on the old man's deathbed, the boy apologizes for his wrongdoing and tells his father, "I tried to believe it was born in me and that I couldn't help it, but that's not so. Man has a choice. You used to say that was where we differed from an animal. See, I remember. 'Man has a choice, and it's the choice that makes him a man.'" The father asks his son, whom he has always rejected, to dismiss the nurse and stay with him, take care of him. The father smiles. The boy, empowered and anointed, tenderly kisses the girlfriend who has brought about the reconciliation, and pulls his chair up to his father's bed, ready to take his place as a member of the adult world, accept his responsibility, and bask in his happiness.

We have a choice. We have the power to make things different. In *Roving Commission: My Early Life*, Winston Churchill exhorted us: "Don't be content with things as they are. 'The earth is yours and the fullness thereof.' Enter upon your inheritance; accept your responsibilities."

If we accept our responsibilities, if we act to make things better for ourselves and others, if each of us increases the level of love and consideration and cheerfulness in the world ever so slightly, even by just one smile, by one tender gesture, then we can make the world a little bit better for all of us. Knowing that we have the power to increase the level of happiness in the world may be the ultimate secret of happiness.

> **TODAY'S THOUGHT:** Happiness isn't a matter of finding the secret. It's a matter of following the rules. We don't discover happiness. We create it.

Bibliography

BOOKS AND ARTICLES

Addison, Joseph. *The Spectator*, 1711.

Angel, Ronald J., and Jacqueline L. Angel. *Painful Inheritance: Health and the New Generation of Fatherless Children*. Madison: University of Wisconsin, 1993.

Arndt, Bettina. *Private Lives*. Australia: Penguin, 1986.

Bach, George R., and Peter Wyden. *The Intimate Enemy*. New York: William Morrow, 1969.

Beal, Edward W., and Gloria Hochman. *Adult Children of Divorce*. New York: Delacorte, 1991.

Beavers, Robert. *Successful Marriage*. New York: Norton, 1985.

de Beauvoir, Simone. *The Second Sex*. New York: Knopf, 1953.

Bernard, Jessie. *The Future of Marriage*. New Haven, CT: Yale University Press, 1982.

Blankenhorn, David. *Fatherless America*. New York: Basic Books, 1995.

Bly, Robert. *The Sibling Society*. Reading, MA: Addison-Wesley, 1996.

Bombeck, Erma. *Motherhood, the Second Oldest Profession*. New York: McGraw-Hill, 1983.

Bowen, Murray. "A Family Concept of Schizophrenia." In *The Etiology of Schizophrenia*, D. D. Jackson, ed. New York: Basic Books, 1960.

Bradburn, Norman. *In Pursuit of Happiness: A Pilot Study of Behavior Related to Mental Health*. Washington, D.C.: National Opinion Research Center, 1963.

Brown, Lyn Mikel, and Carol Gilligan. *Meeting at the Crossroads*. Cambridge: Harvard University Press, 1992.

Brownmiller, Susan. *Femininity*. New York: Fawcett-Columbine, 1984.

Carter, Hodding. Quoted in *Peter's Quotations*, Laurence J. Peter, ed. New York: Morrow, 1977.

Cherlin, Andrew J. *Marriage, Divorce, Remarriage*. Cambridge, MA: Harvard University Press, 1981 and 1992.

Churchill, Winston. *Roving Commission: My Early Life*, 1930.

Coontz, Stephanie. *The Way We Never Were*. New York: Basic Books, 1992.

"Declaration," Women's Rights Convention, Seneca Falls, New York, 1848. Quoted by Betty Friedan in *The Feminine Mystique*. New York: Dell, 1963.

D'Emilio, John, and Estelle B. Freedman. *Intimate Matters*. New York: Harper & Row, 1988.

Diagnostic and Statistical Manual for Mental Disorders, 4th ed. Washington, D.C.: American Psychiatric Association, 1994.

Dinnerstein, Dorothy. *The Mermaid and the Minotaur*. New York: Harper & Row, 1976.

Doherty, William J. *Soul Searching*. New York: Basic Books, 1995.

Eisler, Riane. *The Chalice and the Blade*. San Francisco: HarperCollins, 1987.

Erikson, Erik. *Insight and Responsibility*. New York: Norton, 1964.

———. *Identity: Youth and Crisis*. New York: Norton, 1968.

———. *The Life Cycle Completed*. New York: Norton, 1986.

Faludi, Susan. *Backlash*. New York: Anchor, 1991.

Fox-Genovese, Elizabeth. *Feminism Without Illusions*. Chapel Hill: University of North Carolina, 1991.

Freud, Sigmund. *Mourning and Melancholia*, 1917, in James Strachey (ed.). *The Standard Edition of the Complete Psychological Works of Sigmund Freud, Volume XIV*. London: Hogarth Press and the Institute of Psycho-Analysis, 1953.

Friedan, Betty. *The Feminine Mystique*. New York: Dell, 1963.

Gardner, John W. *Self-Renewal: The Individual and the Innovative Society*. New York: Harper & Row, 1963.

Gettleman, Susan, and Janet Markowitz. *The Courage to Divorce*. New York: Simon & Schuster, 1974.

Gilligan, Carol. *In a Difference Voice*. Cambridge: Harvard University Press, 1982.

Gilmore, David D. *Manhood in the Making*. New Haven, CT: Yale University Press, 1990.

Ginsberg, Susan. *Family Wisdom: The 2000 Most Important Things Ever Said About Parenting, Children, and Family Life*. New York: Columbia University Press, 1996.

Gottman, John. *Why Marriages Succeed or Fail*. New York: Simon & Schuster, 1994.

———. *What Predicts Divorce*. Hillsdale, NJ: Erlbaum, 1993.

Goulter, Barbara, and Joan Minninger. *The Father-Daughter Dance*. New York: Putnam, 1993.

Groves, Ernest. *Conserving Marriage and the Family*. New York: Macmillan, 1945.

Haley, Jay. *Leaving Home*. New York: McGraw-Hill, 1980.

Hetherington, E. Mavis. "Coping with Family Transitions: Winners, Losers, and Survivors," *Child Development* 60 (1989): 1–14.

Hetherington, E. Mavis, Martha Cox, and Roger Cox. "The Aftermath of Divorce." In *Mother-Child, Father-Child Relations*, J. H. Stevens, Jr., and M. Matthews, eds., Washington, D.C.: National Association for the Education of Young Children, 1978.

Ibsen, Henrik. *A Doll's House*, 1879.

Jacobson, Neil, and John Gottman. *When Men Batter Women: New Insights into Ending Abusive Relationships*. New York: Simon & Schuster, 1998.

James, William. "Letter to Wanda Lutoslawski, 1906," in *The Letters of William James*, 1920.

———. *The Varieties of Religious Experience*, 1902.

———. *Principles of Psychology*, 1890.

Kipling, Rudyard. "If," in *Rewards and Fairies*, 1910.

Knef, Hildegard. *The Gift Horse*. New York: McGraw-Hill, 1971.

Kramer, Peter. *Listening to Prozac*. New York: Viking, 1993.

Lasch, Christopher. *The Culture of Narcissism*. New York: Norton, 1978.

Lerner, Gerda. *The Creation of Patriarchy.* New York: Oxford, 1986.

Leupnitz, Deborah. *The Family Interpreted.* New York: Basic Books, 1988.

Levant, Ronald F. "The New Psychology of Men," *Professional Psychology: Research and Practice* 27:3 (1996): 259–65.

Levant, Ronald F., and G. Kopecky. *Masculinity Reconstructed.* New York: Dutton, 1995.

Lindbergh, Anne Morrow. *War Within and Without.* New York: Harcourt Brace Jovanovich, 1980.

Lombardi, Vince. Quoted in *Simpson's Contemporary Quotations,* James B. Simpson, ed. Boston: Houghton-Mifflin, 1988.

Mailer, Norman. Quoted in *Simpson's Contemporary Quotations,* James B. Simpson, ed. Boston: Houghton-Mifflin, 1988.

McLanahan, Sara, and Gary Sandefur. *Growing Up with a Single Parent.* Cambridge, MA: Harvard University Press, 1994.

Michael, Robert T., et al. *Sex in America.* Boston: Little, Brown, 1994.

Mill, John Stuart. *Autobiography,* 1873.

Minuchin, Salvador. *Families and Family Therapy.* Cambridge: Harvard University Press, 1974.

Niebuhr, Reinhold. *Faith and History,* 1949.

Pittman, Frank. *Man Enough: Fathers, Sons, and the Search for Masculinity.* New York: Putnam, 1993.

———. *Private Lies: Infidelity and the Betrayal of Intimacy.* New York: Norton, 1989.

Pittman, Frank S., III. *Turning Points: Treating Families in Transition and Crisis.* New York: Norton, 1987.

Popenoe, David. *Life Without Father.* New York: Free Press, 1996.

Samuelson, Robert J. *The Good Life and Its Discontents.* New York: Times Books, 1995.

Schwartz, Pepper. *Peer Marriage* (aka *Love Among Equals*). New York: Free Press, 1994.

Secunda, Victoria. *Women and Their Fathers.* New York: Delacorte, 1992.

Shakespeare, William. *Hamlet,* 1601.

Signoret, Simone. Quoted in *An Uncommon Scold,* Abby Adams, ed. New York: Simon & Schuster, 1989.

Skynner, Robin, and John Cleese. *Life and How to Survive It.* London: Methuen, 1993.

Smiley, Jane. *A Thousand Acres.* New York: Ivy Books, 1991.

Spoto, Donald. *The Decline and Fall of the House of Windsor.* New York: Simon & Schuster, 1995.

Steinem, Gloria. *Outrageous Acts and Everyday Rebellions.* New York: Henry Holt, 1983.

Styron, William. *Lie Down in Darkness.* Indianapolis: Bobbs-Merrill, 1951.

Tavris, Carol. *The Mismeasure of Women.* New York: Simon & Schuster, 1992.

Thoreau, Henry David. *Journal,* March 11, 1856.

——. *Walden, or, Life in the Woods,* 1854.

Tolstoy, Leo. *Anna Karenina,* 1873.

——. *War and Peace,* 1869.

Tournier, Paul. *The Meaning of Persons.* New York: Harper & Row, 1957.

Viorst, Judith. *Necessary Losses.* New York: Ballantine, 1986.

Walker, Barbara. *The Crone.* New York: Harper & Row, 1985.

Wallerstein, Judith S., and Joan Berlin Kelly. *Surviving the Breakup.* New York: Basic Books, 1980.

Wallerstein, Judith S., and Sandra Blakeslee. *Second Chances.* Boston: Houghton-Mifflin, 1989.

Watzlawick, John, John Weakland, and Richard Fisch. *Change: Principles of Problem Formation and Problem Resolution.* New York: Norton, 1974.

Weitzman, Lenore. *The Divorce Revolution.* New York: Free Press, 1985.

Whitaker, James. *Royal Blood Feud.* New York: Dutton, 1993.

Whitehead, Barbara Dafoe. *The Divorce Culture.* New York: Knopf, 1997.

Wolfe, Tom. *Bonfire of the Vanities*. New York: Farrar, Straus & Giroux, 1987.

———. "The 'Me' Decade," 1976.

Wollstonecraft, Mary. *A Vindication of the Rights of Men*, 1790.

———. *A Vindication of the Rights of Woman*, 1792.

FILMS, MUSICALS, AND OPERAS

All About Eve by Joseph L. Mankiewicz, 1950, from "The Wisdom of Eve," a story by Mary Orr.

Annie Hall by Woody Allen and Marshall Brickman, 1977.

Babe by George Miller and Chris Noonan, 1995, from *The Sheep-Pig*, a novel by Dick King-Smith.

Bambi by Larry Morey, 1942, from the book by Felix Salten.

Barefoot in the Park by Neil Simon, 1967.

Basic Instinct by Joe Eszterhas, 1992.

Boyz N the Hood by John Singleton, 1991.

The Bridges of Madison County by Richard LeGravenese, 1995, from the novel by Robert James Waller.

Bull Durham by Ron Shelton, 1988.

Bye Bye, Love by Gary David Goldberg and Brad Hall, 1995.

Citizen Kane by Herman J. Mankiewicz and Orson Welles, 1941.

City Slickers by Lowell Ganz and Babaloo Mandel, 1991.

Dad by William Wharton, 1989.

Dangerous Liaisons by Christopher Hampton, 1988, from the novel by Pierre Choderlos de Laclos.

Dead Man Walking by Tim Robbins, 1995, from the book by Helen Prejean.

A Delicate Balance by Edward Albee, 1973.

The Diary of Anne Frank by Frances Goodrich and Albert Hackett, 1959, from *The Diary of a Young Girl* by Anne Frank.

Diner by Barry Levinson, 1982.

The Dirty Dozen by Nunnally Johnson and Lukas Heller, 1967, from the novel by E. M. Nathanson.

East of Eden by Paul Osborn, 1955, from the novel by John Steinbeck.

Emma by Douglas McGrath, 1996, from the novel by Jane Austen.

The English Patient by Anthony Minghella, 1996, from the novel by Michael Ondaatje.

The Fantasticks (musical play) by Tom Jones, 1960.

Fatal Attraction by James Dearden, 1987.

Field of Dreams by Phil Alden Robinson, 1989, from *Shoeless Joe,* the novel by W. P. Kinsella.

Four Seasons by Alan Alda, 1981.

Four Weddings and a Funeral by Richard Curtis, 1994.

The Full Monty by Simon Beaufoy, 1997.

Gallipoli by Peter Weir and David Williamson, 1981.

Gaslight by John Van Druten, Walter Reisch, and John L. Balderston, 1944, from the play by Patrick Hamilton.

Giant by Fred Guiol and Ivan Moffat, 1956, from the novel by Edna Ferber.

Gigi by Alan Jay Lerner, 1958, from the novel by Colette.

The Godfather trilogy by Mario Puzo and Francis Ford Coppola, 1972, 1974, and 1990.

Gone with the Wind by Sidney Howard, 1939, from the novel by Margaret Mitchell.

The Graduate by Calder Willingham and Buck Henry, 1967, from the novel by Charles Webb.

The Grapes of Wrath by Nunnally Johnson, 1940, from the novel by John Steinbeck.

Hamlet by Kenneth Branagh, 1996, from the play by William Shakespeare.

The Heartbreak Kid by Neil Simon, 1972, from the story by Bruce Jay Friedman.

Heartburn by Nora Ephron, 1986.

Howards End by Ruth Prawer Jhabvala, 1992, from the novel by E. M. Forster.

I Never Sang for My Father by Robert Anderson, 1970.

Jerry Maguire by Cameron Crowe, 1996.

Kramer vs. Kramer by Robert Benton, 1979, from the novel by Avery Corman.

Lohengrin (opera), music and libretto by Richard Wagner, 1850.

Lovers and Other Strangers by Renee Taylor, Joseph Bologna, and David Zelag Goodman, 1970.

Love Story by Erich Segal, 1970.

The Madwoman of Chaillot by Edward Anhalt, 1969, from the play by Jean Giraudoux.

The Man Who Would Be King by John Huston and Gladys Hall, 1975, from the story by Rudyard Kipling.

Manhattan by Woody Allen and Marshall Brickman, 1979.

Marvin's Room by Scott MacPherson, 1996.

The Miracle of Morgan's Creek by Preston Sturges, 1944.

Mommie Dearest by Frank Yablans, Frank Perry, Tracy Hotchner, and Robert Getchell, 1981, from the memoir by Christina Crawford.

Moonstruck by John Patrick Shanley, 1987.

Murder, She Said by David Pursall and Jack Seddon, 1961, from *The 4:50 from Paddington*, the novel by Agatha Christie.

My Dinner with André by Wallace Shawn and André Gregory, 1981.

My Fair Lady by Alan Jay Lerner, 1964, from *Pygmalion*, the play by George Bernard Shaw.

My Left Foot by Shane Connaughton and Jim Sheridan, 1989, from the book by Christy Brown.

Nobody's Fool by Robert Benton, 1994, from the novel by Richard Russo.

Nothing in Common by Rick Podell and Michael Preminger, 1986.

Of Mice and Men by Horton Foote, 1992, from the novel by John Steinbeck.

Ordinary People by Alvin Sargent, 1980, from the novel by Judith Guest.

Out of Africa by Kurt Luedtke, 1985, from the memoir by Isak Dinesen.

The Piano by Jane Campion, 1993.

Pillow Talk by Stanley Shapiro & Maurice Richlin, 1959, from a story by Clarence Greene & Russell Rouse.

Planet of the Apes by Michael Wilson and Rod Serling, 1968, from the novel by Pierre Boulle.

The Prince of Tides by Pat Conroy and Becky Johnson, 1991, from the novel by Pat Conroy.

Psycho by Joseph Stefano, 1960, from the novel by Robert Bloch.

The Rack by Rod Serling and Stewart Stern, 1956.

Raising Arizona by Ethan and Joel Coen, 1987.

Rebel Without a Cause by Stewart Stern and Irving Schulman, 1955, from the story by Nicholas Ray.

Resurrection by Lewis John Carlino, 1980.

Der Ring des Nibelungen (opera cycle), music and libretto by Richard Wagner, 1869–76.

A River Runs Through It by Richard Friedenberg, 1992, from the story by Norman Maclean.

Rosenkrantz and Guildenstern Are Dead by Tom Stoppard, 1990.

Schindler's List by Steven Zaillian, 1993, from the book by Thomas Keneally.

The Searchers by Frank S. Nugent, 1956, from the novel by Alan LeMay.

Secrets and Lies by Mike Leigh, 1997.

Sense and Sensibility by Emma Thompson, 1995, from the novel by Jane Austen.

She's Having a Baby by John Hughes, 1988.

Silence of the Lambs by Ted Tally, 1991, from the novel by Thomas Harris.

Sophie's Choice by Alan J. Pakula, 1982, from the novel by William Styron.

The Sound of Music by Richard Rodgers and Oscar Hammerstein II, 1965.

Spellbound by Ben Hecht and Angus MacPhail, 1945, from the novel by Francis Breeding.

Stand by Me by Raynold Gideon and Bruce A. Evans, 1986, from *The Body*, the story by Stephen King.

Steel Magnolias by Robert Harling, 1989.

A Streetcar Named Desire by Tennessee Williams, 1951.

Sunset Boulevard by Charles Brackett, Billy Wilder, and D. M. Marchman, Jr., 1950.

Taxi Driver by Paul Schrader, 1976.

Terms of Endearment by James L. Brooks, 1983, from the novel by Larry McMurtry.

Thelma and Louise by Callie Khouri, 1991.

The Thin Man by Albert Hackett and Frances Goodrich, 1934, from the novel by Dashiell Hammett.

A Thousand Acres by Laura Jones, 1997, from the novel by Jane Smiley.

Three Musketeers by George MacDonald Fraser, 1974, from the novel by Alexandre Dumas.

Turandot (opera), music by Giacomo Puccini, libretto by Giuseppe Adami and Franco Simone, 1926, from the play by Carlo Gozzi.

Ulee's Gold by Victor Nuñez, 1997.

Waiting to Exhale by Terry McMillan and Ronald Bass, 1995, from the novel by Terry McMillan.

Who's Afraid of Virginia Woolf? by Ernest Lehman, 1966, from the play by Edward Albee.

The Wizard of Oz by Noel Langley, 1939, from *The Wonderful Wizard of Oz*, the novel by L. Frank Baum.

Women in Love by Larry Kramer, 1970, from the novel by D.H. Lawrence.

Wuthering Heights by Ben Hecht and Charles MacArthur, 1939, from the novel by Emily Brontë.

Yentl by Jack Rosenthal and Barbra Streisand, 1983, from *Yentl, the Yeshiva Boy*, the book by Isaac Bashevis Singer.

About the Author

Dr. Frank Pittman is a psychiatrist and family therapist in private practice, specializing in men's issues, marriage, and infidelity. In addition to his three books, *Man Enough, Private Lies,* and *Turning Points,* he has written a column entitled "Not for Men Only" in *New Woman* and an advice column in *Psychology Today.* For fourteen years he has regularly contributed articles and reviewed movies for *Family Therapy Networker,* and he has served on the board of a number of professional journals, including *Family Process* and *Journal of Marriage and Family Therapy.*

Dr. Pittman served on the board of directors of the American Family Therapy Academy for many years and was the recipient of the Academy's first award for Distinguished Achievement in Family Therapy Research. He is currently a fellow and an approved supervisor of the American Association for Marriage and Family Therapy, and has served on its foundation board as well. He volunteers as a clinical assistant professor of psychiatry at Emory University School of Medicine and is an adjunct professor of psychology at Georgia State University.

A noted authority on marital and family issues, Dr. Pittman lectures around the world. In his spare time he works as a movie script consultant to the actor/writer/producer John Cleese. He lives in Atlanta with his wife, Betsy, and has three married children and three grandchildren.